SAFETY SYMBOLS

	HAZARD	EXAMPLES	PRECAUTION	REMEDY
DISPOSAL	Special disposal procedures need to be followed.	certain chemicals, living organisms	Do not dispose of these materials in the sink or trash can.	Dispose of wastes as directed by your teacher.
BIOLOGICAL	Organisms or other biological materials that might be harmful to humans	bacteria, fungi, blood, unpreserved tissues, plant materials	Avoid skin contact with these materials. Wear mask or gloves.	Notify your teacher if you suspect contact with material. Wash hands thoroughly.
EXTREME TEMPERATURE	Objects that can burn skin by being too cold or too hot	boiling liquids, hot plates, dry ice, liquid nitrogen	Use proper protection when handling.	Go to your teacher for first aid.
SHARP OBJECT	Use of tools or glassware that can easily puncture or slice skin	razor blades, pins, scalpels, pointed tools, dissecting probes, broken glass	Practice common-sense behavior and follow guidelines for use of the tool.	Go to your teacher for first aid.
FUME	Possible danger to respiratory tract from fumes	ammonia, acetone, nail polish remover, heated sulfur, moth balls	Make sure there is good ventilation. Never smell fumes directly. Wear a mask.	Leave foul area and notify your teacher immediately.
ELECTRICAL	Possible danger from electrical shock or burn	improper grounding, liquid spills, short circuits, exposed wires	Double-check setup with teacher. Check condition of wires and apparatus.	Do not attempt to fix electrical problems. Notify your teacher immediately.
IRRITANT	Substances that can irritate the skin or mucous membranes of the respiratory tract	pollen, moth balls, steel wool, fiberglass, potassium permanganate	Wear dust mask and gloves. Practice extra care when handling these materials.	Go to your teacher for first aid.
CHEMICAL	Chemicals that can react with and destroy tissue and other materials	bleaches such as hydrogen peroxide; acids such as sulfuric acid, hydrochloric acid; bases such as ammonia, sodium hydroxide	Wear goggles, gloves, and an apron.	Immediately flush the affected area with water and notify your teacher.
TOXIC	Substance may be poisonous if touched, inhaled, or swallowed	mercury, many metal compounds, iodine, poinsettia plant parts	Follow your teacher's instructions.	Always wash hands thoroughly after use. Go to your teacher for first aid.
OPEN FLAME	Open flame may ignite flammable chemicals, loose clothing, or hair	alcohol, kerosene, potassium permanganate, hair, clothing	Tie back hair. Avoid wearing loose clothing. Avoid open flames when using flammable chemicals. Be aware of locations of fire safety equipment.	Notify your teacher immediately. Use fire safety equipment if applicable.

 Eye Safety Proper eye protection should be worn at all times by anyone performing or observing science activities.

 Clothing Protection This symbol appears when substances could stain or burn clothing.

 Animal Safety This symbol appears when safety of animals and students must be ensured.

 Radioactivity This symbol appears when radioactive materials are used.

Glencoe Science

Astronomy

NATIONAL GEOGRAPHIC SOCIETY

 **Glencoe McGraw-Hill**

New York, New York   Columbus, Ohio   Woodland Hills, California   Peoria, Illinois

Glencoe Science

ASTRONOMY

Student Edition
Teacher Wraparound Edition
Interactive Teacher Edition CD-ROM
Interactive Lesson Planner CD-ROM
Lesson Plans
Dinah Zike's Teaching Science with Foldables
Directed Reading for Content Mastery
Foldables: Reading and Study Skills
Assessment
    Chapter Review
    Chapter Tests
    ExamView Pro Test Bank Software
    Assessment Transparencies
    Performance Assessment in the Science Classroom
    The Princeton Review Test Practice Booklet
Directed Reading for Content Mastery in Spanish
Spanish Resources
English/Spanish Guided Reading Audio Program
Reinforcement

Enrichment
Activity Worksheets
Section Focus Transparencies
Teaching Transparencies
Laboratory Activities
Science Inquiry Labs
Critical Thinking/Problem Solving
Reading and Writing Skill Activities
Mathematics Skill Activities
Cultural Diversity
Laboratory Management and Safety in the Science Classroom
MindJogger Videoquizzes and Teacher Guide
Interactive CD-ROM with Presentation Builder
Vocabulary PuzzleMaker Software
Cooperative Learning in the Science Classroom
Environmental Issues in the Science Classroom
Home and Community Involvement
Using the Internet in the Science Classroom

"Study Tip," "Test-Taking Tip," and the "Test Practice" features in this book were written by The Princeton Review, the nation's leader in test preparation. Through its association with McGraw-Hill, The Princeton Review offers the best way to help students excel on standardized assessments.

The Princeton Review is not affiliated with Princeton University or Educational Testing Services.

Glencoe/McGraw-Hill

A Division of The McGraw-Hill Companies

The cover is a montage of images of Jupiter, Io, Mars, and the Andromeda Galaxy. Their size and orbits are not to scale.

Send all inquiries to:
Glencoe/McGraw-Hill
8787 Orion Place
Columbus, OH 43240

ISBN 0-07-825581-3
Printed in the United States of America.
    7 8 9 10 027/043 06 05

Author

National Geographic Society
Education Division
Washington, D.C.

Ralph Feather, Jr., PhD
Science Department Chair
Derry Area School District
Derry, Pennsylvania

Dinah Zike
Educational Consultant
Dinah-Might Activities, Inc.
San Antonia, Texas

Consultants

Content

William C. Keel, PhD
Department of Physics/Astronomy
University of Alabama
Tuscaloosa, Alabama

Safety

Sandra West, PhD
Associate Professor of Biology
Southwest Texas State University
San Marcos, Texas

Aileen Duc, PhD
Science II Teacher
Hendrick Middle School
Plano, Texas

Math

Teri Willard, EdD
Department of Mathematics
Montana State University
Belgrade, Montana

Reading

Carol A. Senf, PhD
Associate Professor of English
Georgia Institute of Technology
Atlanta, Georgia

Nancy Woodson, PhD
Professor of English
Otterbein College
Westerville, Ohio

Activity Testers

Mary Helen Mariscal–Cholka
William D. Slider Middle School
El Paso, Texas

Science Kit and Boreal Laboratories
Tonawanda, New York

Reviewers

Mary Helen Mariscal–Cholka
William D. Slider Middle School
El Paso, Texas

Nerma Coats Henderson
Pickerington Jr. High School
Pickerington, Ohio

Mary Ferneau
Westview Middle School
Goose Creek, South Carolina

Annette Garcia
Kearney Middle School
Commerce City, Colorado

Sharon Mitchell
William D. Slider Middle School
El Paso, Texas

Michael Mansour
John Page Middle School
Madison Heights, Michigan

CONTENTS

CHAPTER
4

Stars and Galaxies — 102

Field Guide

Skill Handbooks

Reference Handbook

English Glossary — 174

Spanish Glossary — 178

Index — 182

Interdisciplinary Connections/Activities

Feature Contents

Activities/Science Connections

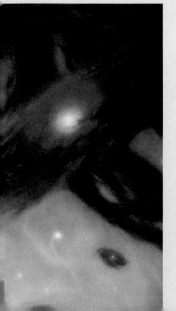

THE
PRINCETON
REVIEW

Feature Contents

Life on Mars

I s there life on Mars? Ever since the 1600s, when scientists first looked at the sky with telescopes and determined that Mars is the most Earthlike planet in the solar system, they have asked this question.

In 1877, Italian scientist Giovanni Schiaparelli saw a network of lines on the surface of Mars and believed they were channels. Later, the American scientist Percival Lowell saw the same lines and claimed they were canals dug by martians.

Today scientists know that flowing water created many of the martian surface features. But scientists still wonder whether simple life-forms existed on Mars or might even exist today. To answer this question, they began undertaking space missions. One objective of the missions is to gather information on whether Mars has or ever had the conditions necessary for life, such as the presence of flowing water.

In 1964, scientists sent a space probe to take photographs of Mars. Examining the photos, they decided the planet is too cold and dry for life. Later probes showed that Mars might have been warm and wet billions of years ago. However, scientists still thought it had been cold and dry since those times.

Figure 1
This martian rock fell to Earth (Antarctica) as a meteorite.

Figure 2
Scientists now know that the lines on Mars's surface were created by flowing water.

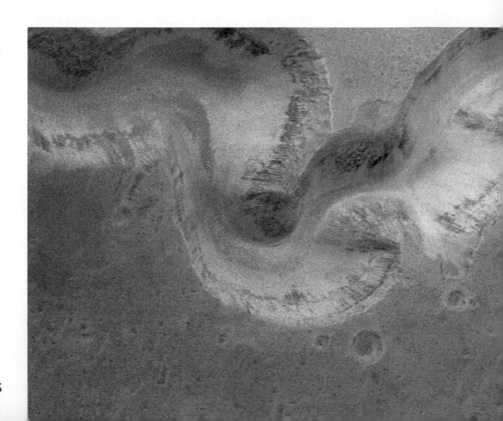

Then, in June 2000, scientists made an astounding discovery. Photographs taken by a new space probe showed evidence of recent erosion by running water. But if Mars is so cold, how could liquid water exist?

Further study of the new photographs convinced scientists that lava had flowed on Mars in the recent past. This means that Mars's interior must be warmer than previously thought. This heat could melt underground ice and allow it to flow to the surface as liquid water. Liquid water could help support life.

In 1984, scientists in Antarctica found a martian meteorite—a small piece of rock that was blasted into space when Mars was hit by a much larger meteorite. When scientists examined the meteorite with microscopes, they discovered strange shapes inside.

Similar shapes have been found in Earth's rocks and are thought to be the fossilized remains of bacteria that lived billions of years ago. Some scientists thought that the shapes in the martian meteorite were fossils of tiny forms of martian life.

Others thought the shapes were only globules of minerals formed when water changed the rocks on Mars. To test this idea, scientists tried to reproduce the shapes in a laboratory. When their experiment was completed, they saw globules of minerals like those in the martian meteorite. They concluded that the shapes probably were not fossils of martian life-forms.

Figure 3
The darker areas in this photograph are newer lava flows that broke up along their edges.

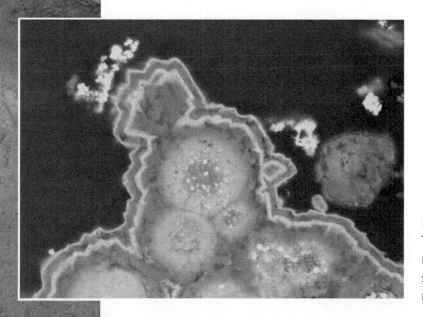

Figure 4
These globules of minerals made in a lab look like the shapes inside the martian meteorite.

Science

Trying to find out whether life ever existed on Mars is just one example of doing science. Science is the process of observing, experimenting, and thinking about the universe to create knowledge. In fact, the word *science* comes from the Latin word *scientia*, which means knowledge. Every time you answer a question by observing the world or testing an idea, you are doing science.

The Earth sciences study Earth—its land, oceans, and atmosphere—as well as other objects in the universe. In this book, you will learn about astronomy, the study of outer space.

Figure 5
Scientists use scientific methods to answer questions about life on Mars.

Scientific Methods

1. **Identify a question.**
   Determine a question to be answered.
2. **Form a hypothesis.**
   Gather information and make an educated guess about the answer to the question.
3. **Test the hypothesis.**
   Perform experiments or make observations to see if the hypothesis is supported.
4. **Analyze results.**
   Look for patterns in the data that have been collected.
5. **Draw a conclusion.**
   Decide what the test results mean. Communicate your results.

Scientific Methods

Many scientists are working to answer the question of whether life ever existed on Mars. These scientists use a variety of methods to try to answer the question. These methods are commonly called scientific methods. **Scientific methods** are procedures used to investigate a question scientifically.

Identifying a Question

The first step in doing science is identifying a question. One such question is *Did life ever exist on Mars?* Answering this question could lead to many others. Scientists might want to know under what kinds of conditions life can survive. They also might want to ask whether the surface of Mars could have met such conditions. If you have ever participated in a science fair, you had to identify a question before you began your project.

Forming a Hypothesis

The next step is to gather information about the question and form a hypothesis. You can gather information by going to the library and reading books or magazines, by using the Internet, or by talking to other people about the question. A **hypothesis** is an educated guess about the answer to a question. One hypothesis about the shapes in the martian meteorite is that *the shapes are fossils of tiny life-forms that lived on Mars long ago.* Another hypothesis is that *the shapes are globules of minerals formed inside martian rocks.*

Testing the Hypothesis

To find out whether a hypothesis is correct, scientists must test it. They do this by performing experiments or making observations. When scientists tried to produce globules of minerals that looked like the shapes in the martian meteorite, they were testing their hypothesis.

Analyzing Results

As scientists perform tests, they collect lots of information, or **data**, that must be analyzed. Data about the martian meteorite include measurements, microscope photographs, and chemical studies of the strange shapes. The test data must be organized and studied. Many times scientists make graphs so they can see patterns in the data. They also use computers to check the data.

Figure 6
Scientists often use microscopes and other equipment to test hypotheses.

Drawing a Conclusion

Often, the last step in a scientific method is to draw a conclusion. In this step, scientists decide what the results of their tests and observations mean. Sometimes the original hypothesis is not supported by the data. When this happens, the scientists begin again with a new hypothesis. Other times, though, the original hypothesis is supported. If a hypothesis is supported by repeatable experiments and many observations over time, it could become a theory. In science, a **theory** is an idea that has been tested and can explain a large set of observations. For instance, the claim that liquid water has, at some time, flowed over the martian surface is a theory. It might be many years before scientists know whether any of the hypotheses about the martian meteorite and life on Mars are correct.

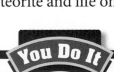

In recent years, scientists have discovered microscopic organisms living kilometers beneath the surface of Earth. Some scientists have hypothesized that simple life-forms might exist deep below the surface of Mars, too. Describe one way that scientists could test this hypothesis.

Exploring Space

Stars and planets have always fascinated humans. We admire their beauty, and our nearest star—the Sun—provides energy that enables life to exist on Earth. For centuries, people have studied space from the ground. But, in the last few decades, space travel has allowed us to get a closer look. In this chapter, you'll learn how space is explored with telescopes, rockets, probes, satellites, and space shuttles. You'll see how astronauts like Shannon Lucid, shown here, now can spend months living and working aboard space stations.

What do you think?

Science Journal Look at the picture below with a classmate. Discuss what you think this might be or what might be happening. Here's a hint: *It's part of a dusty trail that's far, far away.* Write your answer or best guess in your Science Journal.

You might think exploring space with a telescope is easy because the visible light coming from stars is so bright and space is dark. But space contains massive clouds of gases, dust, and other debris called nebulae that block part of the starlight traveling to Earth making it more difficult for astronomers to observe deep space. What does visible light look like when viewed through clouds of dust or gas?

Model visible light seen through nebulae

1. Turn on a lightbulb and darken the room.
2. View the lightbulb through a sheet of dark plastic.
3. View the lightbulb through different-colored plastic sheets.
4. View the light through a variety of different-colored balloons such as yellow, blue, red, and purple. Observe how the light changes when you slowly let the air out of each balloon.

Observe
Write a paragraph in your Science Journal describing how this activity modeled the difficulty astronomers have when viewing stars through thick nebulae?

Before You Read

FOLDABLES
Reading & Study Skills

Making a Sequence Study Fold Identifying a sequence helps you understand what you are experiencing and predict what might occur next. Before you read this chapter, make the following Foldable to prepare you to learn about the sequence of space exploration.

1. Place a sheet of paper in front of you so the short side is at the top. Fold the paper in half from the left side to the right side.
2. Fold the top and bottom in to divide the paper into thirds. Unfold the paper so three sections show.
3. Through the top thickness of paper, cut along each of the fold lines to the left fold, forming three tabs. Label the tabs "Past", "Present", and "Future", as shown.
4. As you read the chapter, write what you learn under the tabs.

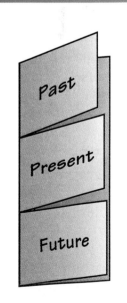

SECTION 1

Radiation from Space

As You Read

What You'll Learn

■ **Explain** the electromagnetic spectrum.
■ **Identify** the differences between refracting and reflecting telescopes.
■ **Recognize** the differences between optical and radio telescopes.

Vocabulary

electromagnetic spectrum
refracting telescope
reflecting telescope
observatory
radio telescope

Why It's Important

You can learn much about space without traveling there.

Electromagnetic Waves

As you just read, living in space now is possible. The same can't be said, though, for space travel to distant galaxies. If you've dreamed about racing toward distant parts of the universe—think again. Even at the speed of light, it would take years and years to reach even the nearest stars.

Light from the Past When you look at a star, the light that you see left the star many years ago. Although light travels fast, distances between objects in space are so great that it sometimes takes millions of years for the light to reach Earth.

The light and other energy leaving a star are forms of radiation. Radiation is energy that is transmitted from one place to another by electromagnetic waves. Because of the electric and magnetic properties of this radiation, it's called electromagnetic radiation. Electromagnetic waves carry energy through empty space and through matter.

Electromagnetic radiation is everywhere around you. When you turn on the radio, peer down a microscope, or have an X ray taken—you're using various forms of electromagnetic radiation.

Figure 1
The electromagnetic spectrum ranges from gamma rays with wavelengths of less than 0.000 000 000 01 m to radio waves more than 100,000 m long. *How does frequency change as wavelength shortens?*

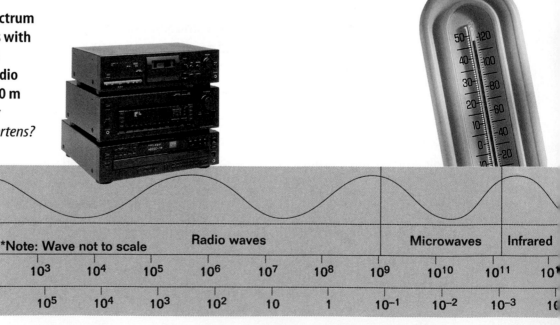

*Note: Wave not to scale	Radio waves							Microwaves		Infrared
10^3	10^4	10^5	10^6	10^7	10^8	10^9	10^{10}	10^{11}	10^{12}	
10^5	10^4	10^3	10^2	10	1	10^{-1}	10^{-2}	10^{-3}	10^{-4}	

Electromagnetic Radiation Sound waves, which are a type of mechanical wave, can't travel through empty space. How, then, do we hear the voices of the astronauts while they're in space? When astronauts speak into a microphone, the sound waves are converted into electromagnetic waves called radio waves. The radio waves travel through space and through Earth's atmosphere. They're then converted back into sound waves by electronic equipment and audio speakers.

Radio waves and visible light from the Sun are just two types of electromagnetic radiation. Other types include gamma rays, X rays, ultraviolet waves, infrared waves, and microwaves. **Figure 1** shows these forms of electromagnetic radiation arranged according to their wavelengths. This arrangement of electromagnetic radiation is called the **electromagnetic spectrum.** Forms of electromagnetic radiation also differ in their frequencies. Frequency is the number of times a wave vibrates per unit of time. The shorter the wavelength is, the more vibrations will occur, as shown in **Figure 1.**

Speed of Light Although the various electromagnetic waves differ in their wavelengths, they all travel at 300,000 km/s in a vacuum. This is called the speed of light. Visible light and other forms of electromagnetic radiation travel at this incredible speed, but the universe is so large that it takes millions of years for the light from some stars to reach Earth.

When electromagnetic radiation from stars and other objects reaches Earth, scientists use it to learn about its source. One tool for studying electromagnetic radiation from distant sources is a telescope.

Health
INTEGRATION

Many newspapers include an ultraviolet (UV) index to urge people to minimize their exposure to the Sun. Compare the wavelengths and frequencies of red and violet light, shown below in **Figure 1.** Infer what properties of UV light cause damage to tissues of organisms.

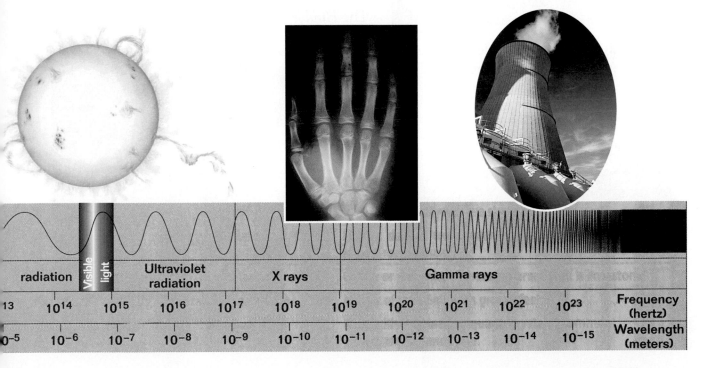

radiation	Visible light	Ultraviolet radiation		X rays		Gamma rays				
10^{13}	10^{14}	10^{15}	10^{16}	10^{17}	10^{18}	10^{19}	10^{20}	10^{21}	10^{22}	10^{23}	**Frequency (hertz)**
10^{-5}	10^{-6}	10^{-7}	10^{-8}	10^{-9}	10^{-10}	10^{-11}	10^{-12}	10^{-13}	10^{-14}	10^{-15}	**Wavelength (meters)**

Optical Telescopes

Optical telescopes use light, which is a form of electromagnetic radiation, to produce magnified images of objects. Light is collected by an objective lens or mirror, which then forms an image at the focal point of the telescope. The focal point is where light that is bent by the lens or reflected by the mirror comes together to form a point. The eyepiece lens then magnifies the image. The two types of optical telescopes are shown in **Figure 2.**

A **refracting telescope** uses convex lenses, which are curved outward like the surface of a ball. Light from an object passes through a convex objective lens and is bent to form an image at the focal point. The eyepiece magnifies the image.

A **reflecting telescope** uses a curved mirror to direct light. Light from the object being viewed passes through the open end of a reflecting telescope. This light strikes a concave mirror, which is curved inward like a bowl and located at the base of the telescope. The light is reflected off the interior surface of the bowl to the focal point where it forms an image. Sometimes, a smaller mirror is used to reflect light into the eyepiece lens, where it is magnified for viewing.

Using Optical Telescopes Most optical telescopes used by professional astronomers are housed in buildings called **observatories.** Observatories often have dome-shaped roofs that can be opened up for viewing. However, not all telescopes are located in observatories. The *Hubble Space Telescope* is an example.

Figure 2
These diagrams show how each type of optical telescope collects light and forms an image.

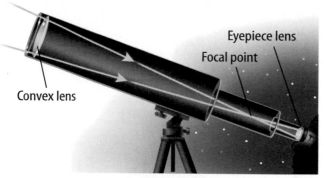

A In a refracting telescope, a double convex lens focuses light to form an image at the focal point.

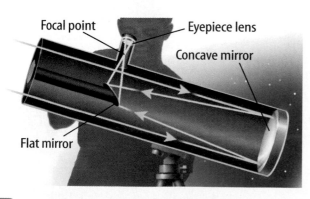

B In a reflecting telescope, a concave mirror focuses light to form an image at the focal point.

C Optical telescopes are widely available for use by individuals.

Hubble Space Telescope The *Hubble Space Telescope* was launched in 1990 by the space shuttle *Discovery*. Because *Hubble* is located outside Earth's atmosphere, which absorbs and distorts some of the energy received from space, it should have produced clear images. However, when the largest mirror of this reflecting telescope was shaped, a mistake was made. As a result, images obtained by the telescope were not as clear as expected. In December 1993, a team of astronauts repaired the *Hubble Space Telescope* by installing a set of small mirrors designed to correct images obtained by the faulty mirror. Two more missions to service *Hubble* were carried out in 1997 and 1999, shown in **Figure 3**. Among the objects viewed by *Hubble* after it was repaired in 1999 was a large cluster of galaxies known as Abell 2218.

Reading Check *Why is* Hubble *located outside Earth's atmosphere?*

Figure 3
The *Hubble Space Telescope* was serviced at the end of 1999. Astronauts replaced devices on *Hubble* that are used to stabilize the telescope.

Observing Effects of Light Pollution

Procedure

1. Obtain a **cardboard tube** from an empty roll of paper towels.
2. Go outside on a clear night about two hours after sunset. Look through the cardboard tube at a specific constellation decided upon ahead of time.
3. Count the number of stars you can see without moving the observing tube. Repeat this three times.
4. Calculate the average number of observable stars at your location.

Analysis

1. Compare and contrast the number of stars visible from other students' homes.
2. Explain the causes and effects of your observations.

Large Reflecting Telescopes Since the early 1600s, when the Italian scientist Galileo Galilei first turned a telescope toward the stars, people have been searching for better ways to study what lies beyond Earth's atmosphere. For example, the twin Keck reflecting telescopes, shown in **Figure 4,** have segmented mirrors 10 m wide. Until 2000, these mirrors were the largest reflectors ever used. To cope with the difficulty of building such huge mirrors, the Keck telescope mirrors are built out of many small mirrors that are pieced together. In 2000, the European Southern Observatory's telescope, in Chile, consisted of four 8.2-m reflectors, making it the largest optical telescope in use.

☑ **Reading Check** *About how long have people been using telescopes?*

Active and Adaptive Optics The most recent innovations in optical telescopes involve active and adaptive optics. With active optics, a computer corrects for changes in temperature, mirror distortions, and bad viewing conditions. Adaptive optics is even more ambitious. Adaptive optics uses a laser to probe the atmosphere and relay information to a computer about air turbulence. The computer then adjusts the telescope's mirror thousands of times per second, which lessens the effects of atmospheric turbulence. Telescope images are clearer when corrections for air turbulence, temperature changes, and mirror-shape changes are made.

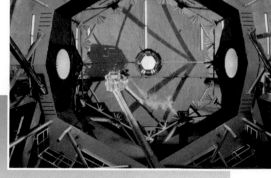

Figure 4

The twin Keck telescopes on Mauna Kea in Hawaii can be used together, more than doubling their ability to distinguish objects. A Keck reflector is shown in the inset photo. Currently, plans include using these telescopes, along with four others to obtain images that will help answer questions about the origin of planetary systems.

Radio Telescopes

As shown in the spectrum illustrated in **Figure 1,** stars and other objects radiate electromagnetic energy of various types. Radio waves are an example of long-wavelength energy in the electromagnetic spectrum. A **radio telescope,** such as the one shown in **Figure 5,** is used to study radio waves traveling through space. Unlike visible light, radio waves pass freely through Earth's atmosphere. Because of this, radio telescopes are useful 24 hours per day under most weather conditions.

Radio waves reaching Earth's surface strike the large, concave dish of a radio telescope. This dish reflects the waves to a focal point where a receiver is located. The information allows scientists to detect objects in space, to map the universe, and to search for signs of intelligent life on other planets.

Later in this chapter, you'll learn about the instruments that travel into space and send back information that telescopes on Earth's surface cannot obtain.

Figure 5
This radio telescope is used to study radio waves traveling through space.

Section Assessment

1. What is the difference between radio telescopes and optical telescopes?

2. If red light has a longer wavelength than blue light, which has a greater frequency?

3. Compare and contrast refracting and reflecting telescopes.

4. How does adaptive optics in a telescope help solve problems caused by atmospheric turbulence?

5. **Think Critically** It takes light from the closest star to Earth (other than the Sun) about four years to reach Earth. If intelligent life were on a planet circling that star, how long would it take for scientists on Earth to send them a radio transmission and for the scientists to receive their reply?

Skill Builder Activities

6. **Sequencing** Sequence these electromagnetic waves from longest wavelength to shortest wavelength: *gamma rays, visible light, X rays, radio waves, infrared waves, ultraviolet waves,* and *microwaves.* **For more help, refer to the Science Skill Handbook.**

7. **Solving One-Step Equations** The magnifying power (Mp) of a telescope is determined by dividing the focal length of the objective lens (FL_{obj}) by the focal length of the eyepiece lens (FL_{eye}) using the following equation:

$$Mp = FL_{obj}/FL_{eye}$$

If $FL_{obj} = 1{,}200$ mm and $FL_{eye} = 6$ mm, what is the telescope's magnifying power? **For more help, refer to the Math Skill Handbook.**

Building a Reflecting Telescope

Nearly four hundred years ago, scientist Galileo Galilei saw what no human had ever seen before. Using the telescope he built, Galileo discovered moons revolving around Jupiter, observed craters on the Moon in detail, and saw sunspots on the surface of the Sun. What was it like to make these discoveries? You will find out as you make your own reflecting telescope.

What You'll Investigate
How do you construct a reflecting telescope?

Materials
flat mirror
shaving or cosmetic mirror (a curved, concave mirror)
magnifying lenses of different magnifications (3–4)

Goals
■ **Construct** a reflecting telescope.
■ **Observe** magnified images using the telescope and different magnifying lenses.

Safety Precautions
WARNING: *Never observe the Sun directly or with mirrors.*

Procedure

1. Position the cosmetic mirror so that you can see the reflection of the object you want to look at. Choose an object such as the Moon, a planet, or an artificial light source.

2. Place the flat mirror so that it is facing the cosmetic mirror.

3. Adjust the position of the flat mirror until you can see the reflection of the object in it.

4. View the image of the object in the flat mirror with one of your magnifying glasses. Observe how the lens magnifies the image.

5. Use your other magnifying lenses to view the image of the object in the flat mirror. Observe how the different lenses change the image of the object.

Conclude and Apply

1. **Describe** how the image of the object changed when you used different magnifying lenses.

2. **Identify** the part or parts of your telescope that reflected the light of the image.

3. **Identify** the part or parts of your telescope that magnified the image of the object.

4. **Explain** how the three parts of your telescope worked to reflect and magnify the light of the object.

5. **Infer** how the materials you used would have differed if you had constructed a refracting telescope instead of a reflecting telescope.

*C*ommunicating
Your Data

Write an instructional pamphlet for amateur astronomers about how to construct a reflecting telescope. **For more help, refer to the** Science Skill Handbook.

2 Early Space Missions

The First Missions into Space

You're offered a choice—front-row-center seats for this weekend's rock concert, or a copy of the video when it's released. Wouldn't you rather be right next to the action? Astronomers feel the same way about space. Even though telescopes have taught them a great deal about the Moon and planets, they want to learn more by going to those places or by sending spacecraft where humans can't go.

Rockets The space program would not have gotten far off the ground using ordinary airplane engines. To break free of gravity and enter Earth's orbit, spacecraft must travel at speeds greater than 11 km/s. The space shuttle and several other space-crafts are equipped with special engines that carry their own fuel. **Rockets,** like the one in **Figure 6,** are engines that have everything they need for the burning of fuel. They don't even require air to carry out the process. Therefore, they can work in space, which has no air. The simplest rocket engine is made of a burning chamber and a nozzle. More complex rockets have more than one burning chamber.

Rocket Types Two types of rockets are distinguished by the type of fuel they use. One type is the liquid-propellant rocket and the other is the solid-propellant rocket. Solid-propellant rockets are generally simpler but they can't be shut down after they are ignited. Liquid-propellant rockets can be shut down after they are ignited and can be restarted. The space shuttle uses liquid-propellant rockets and solid-propellant rockets.

As You Read

What **You'll Learn**

■ **Compare and contrast** natural and artificial satellites.
■ **Identify** the differences between artificial satellites and space probes.
■ **Explain** the history of the race to the Moon.

Vocabulary

rocket	Project Mercury
satellite	Project Gemini
orbit	Project Apollo
space probe	

Why **It's Important**

Early missions that sent objects and people into space began a new era of human exploration.

Figure 6
Rockets differ according to the types of fuel used to launch them. This rocket uses liquid oxygen for fuel.

Figure 7
In this view of the shuttle, a red-colored external liquid fuel tank is behind a white, solid rocket booster.

Rocket Launching Solid-propellant rockets use a powdery or rubberlike fuel and a liquid such as liquid oxygen. The burning chamber of a rocket is a tube that has a nozzle at one end. As the solid propellant burns, hot gases exert pressure on all inner surfaces of the tube. The tube pushes back on the gas except at the nozzle where hot gases escape. Thrust builds up and pushes the rocket forward.

Liquid-propellant rockets use a liquid fuel and, commonly, liquid oxygen, stored in separate tanks. To ignite the rocket, the liquid oxygen is mixed with the liquid fuel in the burning chamber. As the mixture burns, forces are exerted and the rocket is propelled forward. **Figure 7** shows the space shuttle, with both types of rockets, being launched.

Math Skills Activity

Using a Grid to Draw

Points are defined by two coordinates, called an ordered pair. To plot an ordered pair, find the first number on the horizontal *x*-axis and the second on the vertical *y*-axis. The point is placed where these two coordinates intersect. Line segments are drawn to connect points.

Example Problem
Using an *x-y* grid and point coordinates, draw a symmetrical house.

Solution

1 On a piece of graph paper, label and number the x-axis 0 to 6 and the y-axis 0 to 6, as shown here.

2 Plot the following points and connect them with straight line segments, as shown here. (1,1), (5,1), (5,4), (3,6), (1,4)

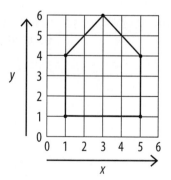

Section	Points
1	(1,−8) (3,−13) (6,−21) (9,−21) (9,−17) (8,−15) (8,−12), (6,−8) (5,−4) (4,−3) (4,−1) (5,1) (6,3) (8,3) (9,4) (9,7) (7,11) (4,14) (4,22) (−9,22) (−9,10) (−10,5) (−11,−1) (−11,−7) (−9,−8) (−8,−7) (−8,−1) (−6,3) (−6,−3) (−6,−9) (−7,−20) (−8,−21) (−4,−21) (−4,−18) (−3,−14) (−1,−8)
2	(0,11) (2,13) (2,17) (0,19) (−4,19) (−6,17) (−6,13) (−4,11)
3	(−4,9) (1,9) (1,5) (−1,5) (−2,6) (−4,6)

Practice Problem

Label and number the *x*-axis −12 to 10 and the *y*-axis −22 to 23. Draw an astronaut by plotting and connecting the points in each section. Do not draw segments to connect points in different sections.

For more help, refer to the Math Skill Handbook.

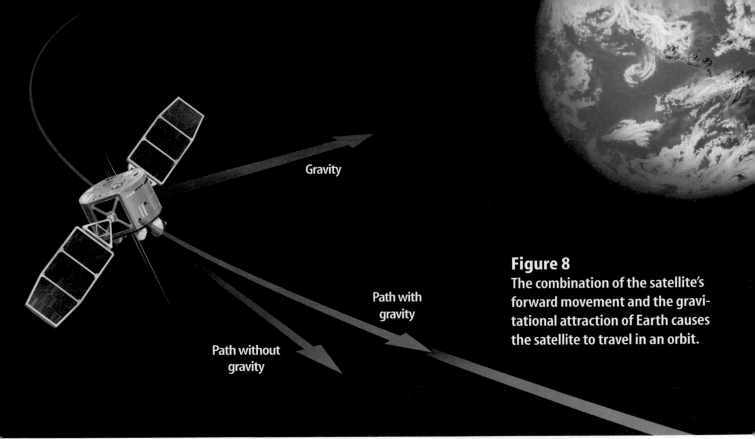

Gravity

Path with
gravity

Path without
gravity

Figure 8
The combination of the satellite's forward movement and the gravitational attraction of Earth causes the satellite to travel in an orbit.

Satellites

The space age began in 1957 when the former Soviet Union used a rocket to send *Sputnik I* into space. *Sputnik I* was the first artificial satellite. A **satellite** is any object that revolves around another object. When an object enters space, it travels in a straight line unless a force, such as gravity, makes it turn. Earth's gravity pulls a satellite toward Earth. The result of the satellite traveling forward while at the same time being pulled toward Earth is a curved path, called an **orbit,** around Earth. This is shown in **Figure 8.** *Sputnik I* orbited Earth for 57 days before gravity pulled it back into the atmosphere, where it burned up.

Figure 9
Data obtained from the satellite *Terra,* launched in 1999, illustrates the use of space technology to study Earth. This false-color image includes data on spring growth, sea-surface temperature, carbon monoxide concentrations, and reflected sunlight, among others.

Satellite Uses

Sputnik I was an experiment to show that artificial satellites could be made and placed into orbit around Earth.

Today, thousands of artificial satellites orbit Earth. Communication satellites transmit radio and television programs to locations around the world. Other satellites gather scientific data, like those shown in **Figure 9,** which can't be obtained from Earth, and weather satellites constantly monitor Earth's global weather patterns.

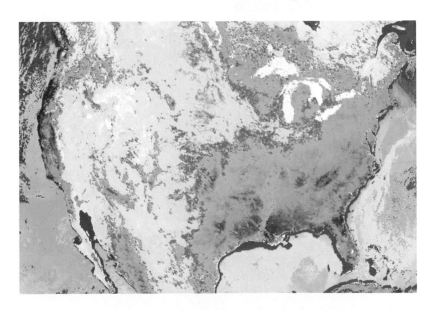

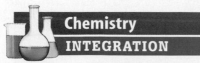

Space Probes

Not all objects carried into space by rockets become satellites. Rockets also can be used to send instruments into space to collect data. A **space probe** is an instrument that gathers information and sends it back to Earth. Unlike satellites that orbit Earth, space probes travel far into the solar system as illustrated in **Figure 10.** Some even have traveled out of the solar system. Space probes, like many satellites, carry cameras and other data-gathering equipment, as well as radio transmitters and receivers that allow them to communicate with scientists on Earth. **Table 1** shows some of the early space probes launched by the National Aeronautics and Space Administration (NASA).

Table 1 Some Early Space Missions

Mission Name		Date Launched	Destination	Data Obtained
Mariner 2		August 1962	Venus	verified high temperatures in Venus's atmosphere
Pioneer 10		March 1972	Jupiter	sent back photos of Jupiter—first probe to encounter an outer planet
Viking 1		August 1975	Mars	orbiter mapped the surface of Mars; lander searched for life on Mars
Magellan		May 1989	Venus	mapped Venus's surface and returned data on the composition of Venus's atmosphere

Figure 10

P robes have taught us much about the solar system. As they travel through space, these car-size craft gather data with their onboard instruments and send results back to Earth via radio waves. Some data collected during these missions are made into pictures, a selection of which is shown here.

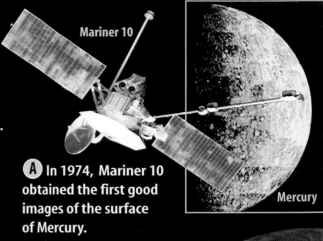

Mariner 10

Mercury

A In 1974, Mariner 10 obtained the first good images of the surface of Mercury.

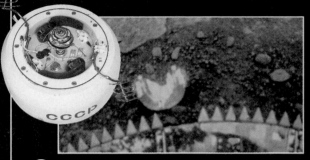

Venera 8

B A Soviet Venera probe took this picture of the surface of Venus on March 1, 1982. Parts of the spacecraft's landing gear are visible at the bottom of the photograph.

Magellan

D In 1990, Magellan imaged craters, lava domes, and great rifts, or cracks, on the surface of Venus.

Venus

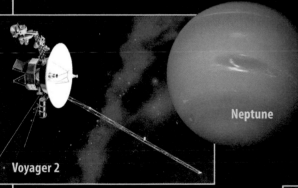

Neptune

Voyager 2

C The Voyager 2 mission included flybys of the outer planets Jupiter, Saturn, Uranus, and Neptune. Voyager took this photograph of Neptune in 1989 as the craft sped toward the edge of the solar system.

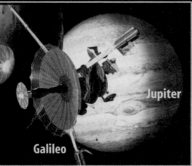

Jupiter

Galileo

E NASA's veteran space traveler Galileo nears Jupiter in this artist's drawing. The craft arrived at Jupiter in 1995 and sent back data, including images of Europa, one of Jupiter's 16 moons, seen below in a color-enhanced view.

Europa

Voyager and Pioneer Probes Space probes *Voyager 1* and *Voyager 2* were launched in 1977 and now are heading toward deep space. *Voyager 1* flew past Jupiter and Saturn. *Voyager 2* flew past Jupiter, Saturn, Uranus, and Neptune. These probes now are exploring beyond the solar system as part of the Voyager Interstellar Mission. Scientists expect these probes to continue to transmit data to Earth for at least 20 more years.

Pioneer 10, launched in 1972, was the first probe to survive a trip through the asteroid belt and encounter an outer planet, Jupiter. As of 2000, *Pioneer 10* is more than 11 billion km from Earth, and will continue beyond the solar system. The probe carries a gold medallion with an engraving of a man, a woman, and Earth's position in the galaxy.

Galileo Launched in 1989, *Galileo* reached Jupiter in 1995. In July 1995, *Galileo* released a smaller probe that began a five-month approach to Jupiter. The small probe took a parachute ride through Jupiter's violent atmosphere in December 1995.

Before being crushed by the atmospheric pressure, it transmitted information about Jupiter's composition, temperature, and pressure to the satellite orbiting above. *Galileo* studied Jupiter's moons, rings, and magnetic fields and then relayed this information to scientists who were waiting eagerly for it on Earth.

Life Science INTEGRATION

Studies of Jupiter's moon Europa by *Galileo* indicate that an ocean of water may exist under the surface of Europa. A cracked outer layer of ice makes up Europa's surface, shown in **Figure 11.** The cracks in the surface may be caused by geologic activity that heats the ocean underneath the surface. Sunlight penetrates these cracks, further heating the ocean and setting the stage for the possible existence of life on Europa. *Galileo* ended its study of Europa in 2000. More advanced probes will be needed to determine whether life exists on this icy moon.

✔ **Reading Check** *What features on Europa suggest the possibility of life existing on this moon?*

In October and November of 1999, *Galileo* approached Io, another one of Jupiter's moons. It came within 300 km and took photographs of a volcanic vent named Loki, which emits more energy than all of Earth's volcanoes combined. *Galileo* also discovered eruption plumes that shoot gas made of sulfur and oxygen.

Figure 11
Future missions will be needed to determine whether life exists on Europa.

Moon Quest

Throughout the world, people were shocked when they turned on their radios and television sets in 1957 and heard the radio transmissions from *Sputnik I* as it orbited Earth. All that *Sputnik I* transmitted was a sort of beeping sound, but people quickly realized that launching a human into space wasn't far off.

In 1961, Soviet cosmonaut Yuri A. Gagarin became the first human in space. He orbited Earth and returned safely. Soon, President John F. Kennedy called for the United States to send humans to the Moon and return them safely to Earth. His goal was to achieve this by the end of the 1960s. The race for space was underway.

The U.S. program to reach the Moon began with **Project Mercury.** The goals of Project Mercury were to orbit a piloted spacecraft around Earth and to bring it back safely. The program provided data and experience in the basics of space flight. On May 5, 1961, Alan B. Shepard became the first U.S. citizen in space. In 1962, *Mercury* astronaut John Glenn became the first U.S. citizen to orbit Earth. **Figure 12** shows Glenn preparing for liftoff.

✔ **Reading Check** *What were the goals of Project Mercury?*

Project Gemini The next step in reaching the Moon was called **Project Gemini.** Teams of two astronauts in the same *Gemini* spacecraft orbited Earth. One *Gemini* team met and connected with another spacecraft in orbit—a skill that would be needed on a voyage to the Moon.

The *Gemini* spacecraft was much like the *Mercury* spacecraft, except it was larger and easier for the astronauts to maintain. It was launched by a rocket known as a *Titan II,* which was a liquid fuel rocket.

In addition to connecting spacecraft in orbit, another goal of Project *Gemini* was to investigate the effects of space travel on the human body.

Along with the Mercury and Gemini programs, a series of robotic probes was sent to the Moon. *Ranger* proved that a spacecraft could be sent to the Moon. In 1966, *Surveyor* landed gently on the Moon's surface, indicating that the Moon's surface could support spacecraft and humans. The mission of *Lunar Orbiter* was to take pictures of the Moon's surface that would help determine the best future lunar landing sites.

Figure 12
An important step in the attempt to reach the Moon was John Glenn's first orbit around Earth.

Modeling a Satellite

WARNING: *Stand a safe distance away from classmates. Use heavy string.*

Procedure
1. Tie one end of a 2-m-long **string** to a **rubber stopper.**
2. Thread the string through a 15-cm piece of **hose.**
3. Tie the other end of the string securely to several large **steel nuts.**
4. Swing the rubber stopper in a circle above your head. Swing the stopper at different speeds.

Analysis
Based upon your observations, explain how a satellite stays in orbit above Earth.

Figure 13
The Lunar Rover vehicle was first used during the *Apollo 15* mission. Riding in the moon buggy, *Apollo 15, 16,* and *17* astronauts explored large areas of the lunar surface.

Project Apollo The final stage of the U.S. program to reach the Moon was **Project Apollo.** On July 20, 1969, *Apollo 11* landed on the Moon's surface. Neil Armstrong was the first human to set foot on the Moon. His first words as he stepped onto its surface were, "That's one small step for man, one giant leap for mankind." Edwin Aldrin, the second of the three *Apollo 11* astronauts, joined Armstrong on the Moon, and they explored its surface for two hours. While they were exploring, Michael Collins remained in the Command Module; Armstrong and Aldrin then returned to the Command Module before beginning the journey home. A total of six lunar landings brought back more than 2,000 samples of moon rock and soil for study before the program ended in 1972. **Figure 13** shows an astronaut exploring the Moon's surface from the Lunar Rover vehicle.

Sharing Knowledge During the past three decades, most missions in space have been carried out by individual countries, often competing to be the first or the best. Today, countries of the world cooperate more and work together, sharing what each has learned. Projects are being planned for cooperative missions to Mars and elsewhere. As you read the next section, you'll see how the U.S. program has progressed since the days of Project Apollo and what may be planned for the future.

Section Assessment

1. Explain why Neptune has eight satellites even though it is not orbited by human-made objects.

2. *Galileo* was considered a space probe as it traveled to Jupiter. Once there, however, it became an artificial satellite. Explain.

3. List several discoveries made by the *Voyager 1* and *Voyager 2* space probes.

4. Draw a time line beginning with *Sputnik* and ending with Project Apollo. Include descriptions of important missions.

5. **Think Critically** Is Earth a satellite of any other body in space? Explain.

Skill Builder Activities

6. **Using an Electronic Spreadsheet** Use a spreadsheet program to generate a table of recent successful satellites and space probes launched by the United States. Include a description of the craft, the date it was launched, and its mission. **For more help, refer to the Technology Skill Handbook.**

7. **Solving One-Step Equations** Suppose a spacecraft were launched at a speed of 40,200 km/h. Express this speed in kilometers per second. **For more help, refer to the Math Skill Handbook.**

Current and Future Space Missions

The Space Shuttle

Imagine spending millions of dollars to build a machine, sending it off into space, and watching its 3,000 metric tons of metal and other materials burn up after only a few minutes of work. That's exactly what NASA did with the rocket portions of spacecraft for many years. The early rockets were used only to launch a small capsule holding astronauts into orbit. Then sections of the rocket separated from the rest and burned when reentering the atmosphere.

A Reusable Spacecraft NASA administrators, like many others, realized that it would be less expensive and less wasteful to reuse resources. The reusable spacecraft that transports astronauts, satellites, and other materials to and from space is called the **space shuttle,** shown in **Figure 14,** as it is landing.

At launch, the space shuttle stands on end and is connected to an external liquid-fuel tank and two solid-fuel booster rockets. When the shuttle reaches an altitude of about 45 km, the emptied, solid-fuel booster rockets drop off and parachute back to Earth. These are recovered and used again. The external liquid-fuel tank separates and falls back to Earth, but it isn't recovered.

Work on the Shuttle After the space shuttle reaches space, it begins to orbit Earth. There, astronauts perform many different tasks. In the cargo bay, astronauts can conduct scientific experiments and determine the effects of spaceflight on the human body. When the cargo bay isn't used as a laboratory, the shuttle can launch, repair, and retrieve satellites. Then the satellites can be returned to Earth or repaired onboard and returned to space. After a mission, the shuttle glides back to Earth and lands like an airplane. A large landing field is needed as the gliding speed of the shuttle is 335 km/h.

Figure 14
The space shuttle is designed to make many trips into space.

Space Stations

Astronauts can spend only a short time living in the space shuttle. Its living area is small, and the crew needs more room to live, exercise, and work. A **space station** has living quarters, work and exercise areas, and all the equipment and support systems needed for humans to live and work in space.

In 1973, the United States launched the space station *Skylab,* shown in **Figure 15.** Crews of astronauts spent up to 84 days there, performing experiments and collecting data on the effects on humans of living in space. In 1979, the abandoned *Skylab* fell out of orbit and burned up as it entered Earth's atmosphere.

Figure 15
Astronauts performed a variety of tasks while living and working in space onboard *Skylab*.

Crews from the former Soviet Union have spent more time in space, onboard the space station *Mir,* than crews from any other country. Cosmonaut Dr. Valery Polyakov returned to Earth after 438 days in space studying the long-term effects of weightlessness.

Cooperation in Space

In 1995, the United States and Russia began an era of cooperation and trust in exploring space. Early in the year, American Dr. Norman Thagard was launched into orbit aboard the Russian *Soyuz* spacecraft, along with two Russian cosmonaut crewmates. Dr. Thagard was the first U.S. astronaut launched into space by a Russian booster and the first American resident of the Russian space station *Mir.*

Figure 16
Russian and American scientists have worked together to further space exploration.

In June 1995, Russian cosmonauts rode into orbit onboard the space shuttle *Atlantis,* America's 100th crewed launch. The mission of *Atlantis* involved, among other studies, a rendezvous and docking with the space station *Mir.* The cooperation that existed on this mission, as shown in **Figure 16,** continued through eight more space shuttle-*Mir* docking missions. Each of the eight missions was an important step toward building and operating the *International Space Station.* In 2001, the abandoned *Mir* space station fell out of orbit and burned up upon reentering the atmosphere. Cooperation continued as the *International Space Station* began to take form.

The International Space Station

The *International Space Station (ISS)* will be a permanent laboratory designed for long-term research projects. Diverse topics will be studied, including research on the growth of protein crystals. This particular project will help scientists determine protein structure and function, which is expected to enhance work on drug design and the treatment of many diseases.

The *ISS* will draw on the resources of 16 nations. These nations will build units for the space station, which then will be transported into space onboard the space shuttle and Russian launch rockets. The station will be constructed in space. **Figure 17** shows what the completed station will look like.

Figure 17
This is a picture of what the proposed *International Space Station* will look like when it is completed in 2006.

 **Reading Check** *What is the purpose of the* International Space Station?

Phases of *ISS* NASA is planning the *ISS* program in phases. Phase One, now concluded, involved the space shuttle-*Mir* docking missions. Phase Two began in 1998 with the launch of the Russian-built *Zarya Module,* also known as the Functional Cargo Block, and will end with the delivery of a U.S. laboratory onboard the space shuttle. The first assembly of *ISS* occurred in December of 1998 when a space shuttle mission attached the Unity module to *Zarya.* During Phase Two, crews of three people were delivered to the space station.

Living in Space The project will continue with Phase Three when the Japanese Experiment Module, the European Columbus Orbiting Facility, and another Russian lab will be delivered.

It is hoped that the *International Space Station* will be completed in 2006. A three- or four-person crew then should be able to work comfortably onboard the station. A total of 47 separate launches will be required to take all the components of the *ISS* into space and prepare it for permanent habitation. NASA plans for crews of astronauts to stay onboard the station for several months at a time. NASA already has conducted numerous tests to prepare crews of astronauts for extended space missions. One day, the station could be a construction site for ships that will travel to the Moon and Mars.

SCIENCE *Online*

Research Visit the Glencoe Science Web site at **science.glencoe.com** for more information on the *International Space Station.* Share your information with the class.

Figure 18
Gulleys, channels, and aprons of sediment imaged by the *Mars Global Surveyor* are similar to features on Earth known to be caused by flowing water. This water is thought to seep out from beneath the surface of Mars.

Exploring Mars

Two of the most successful missions in recent years were the 1996 launchings of the *Mars Global Surveyor* and the *Mars Pathfinder. Surveyor* orbited Mars, taking high-quality photos of the planet's surface as shown in **Figure 18.** *Pathfinder* descended to the Martian surface, using rockets and a parachute system to slow its descent. Large balloons absorbed the shock of landing. *Pathfinder* carried technology to study the surface of the planet, including a remote-controlled robot rover called Sojourner. Using information gathered by studying photographs taken by *Surveyor,* scientists determined that water recently had seeped to the surface of Mars in some areas.

✔ **Reading Check** *What type of data were obtained by the* Mars Global Surveyor?

Although the *Mars Global Surveyor* and the *Mars Pathfinder* missions were successful, not all the missions to Mars have met with the same success. The *Mars Climate Orbiter,* launched in 1998, was lost in September of 1999. An incorrect calculation of the force that the thrusters were to exert caused the spacecraft to be lost. Engineers had used English units instead of metric units. Then, in December of 1999, the *Mars Polar Lander* was lost just as it was making its descent to the planet. This time, it is believed that the spacecraft thought it had landed and shut off its thrusters too soon. NASA tried to make contact with the lander but never had any success.

New Millennium Program

To continue space missions into the future, NASA has created the New Millennium Program (NMP). The goal of the NMP is to develop advanced technology that will let NASA send smart spacecraft into the solar system. This will reduce the amount of ground control needed. They also hope to reduce the size of future spacecraft to keep the cost of launching them under control. NASA's challenge is to prove that certain cutting-edge technologies, as well as mission concepts, work in space.

Exploring the Moon

Does water exist in the craters of the Moon's poles? This is one question NASA intends to explore with data gathered from the *Lunar Prospector* spacecraft shown in **Figure 19.** Launched in 1998, the *Lunar Prospector's* one-year mission was to orbit the Moon, mapping its structure and composition. Early data obtained from the spacecraft indicate that hydrogen might be present in the rocks of the Moon's poles. Hydrogen is one of the elements found in water. Scientists now hypothesize that ice on the floors of the Moon's polar craters may be the source of this hydrogen. Ice might survive indefinitely at the bottom of these craters because it would always be shaded from the Sun.

Other things could account for the presence of hydrogen. It could be from solar wind or certain minerals. The *Lunar Prospector* was directed to crash into a crater at the Moon's south pole when its mission ended in July 1999. Scientists hoped that any water vapor thrown up by the collision could be detected using special telescopes. However, it didn't work. Further studies are needed to determine if water exists on the Moon.

Data Update For an online update on the New Millenium Program, visit the Glencoe Science Web site at **science.glencoe.com**

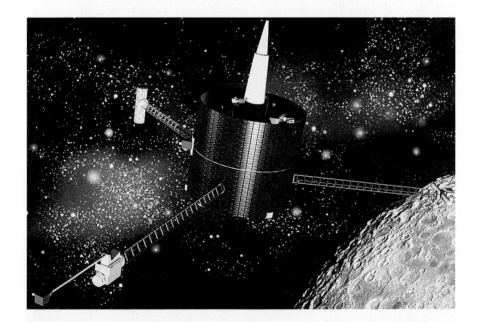

Figure 19
The *Lunar Prospector* analyzed the Moon's composition during its one-year mission.

Cassini

In October 1997, NASA launched the space probe *Cassini*. This probe's destination is Saturn. *Cassini*, shown in **Figure 20,** will not reach its goal until 2004. At that time, the space probe will explore Saturn and surrounding areas for four years. One part of its mission is to deliver the European Space Agency's *Huygens* probe to Saturn's largest moon, Titan. Some scientists theorize that Titan's atmosphere may be similar to the atmosphere of early Earth.

Figure 20
Cassini **is currently on its way to Saturn. After it arrives, it will spend four years studying Saturn and its surrounding area.**

The Next Generation Space Telescope Not all space missions involve sending astronauts or probes into space. Plans are being made to launch a new space telescope that is capable of observing the first stars and galaxies in the universe. The *Next Generation Space Telescope,* shown in **Figure 21,** will be the successor to the *Hubble Space Telescope.* As part of the Origins project, it will provide scientists with the opportunity to study the evolution of galaxies, the production of elements by stars, and the process of star and planet formation. To accomplish these tasks, the telescope will have to be able to see objects 400 times fainter than those currently studied with ground-based telescopes such as the twin Keck telescopes. NASA hopes to launch the *Next Generation Space Telescope* as early as 2009.

Figure 21
The *Next Generation Space Telescope* **will attempt to observe stars and galaxies that formed early in the history of the universe.**

Everyday Space Technology Items developed for space exploration don't always stay in space. In fact, many of today's cutting-edge technologies are modifications of research or technology used in the space program. For example, NASA space suit technology, shown in **Figure 22,** was used to give a child with a skin disorder the opportunity to play outside. Without the suit, the child could have been seriously hurt by the Sun's rays.

Space technology also has been used to understand, diagnose, and treat heart disease. Programmable pacemakers, developed through space technology, have given doctors more programming possibilities and more detailed information about their patients' health.

Other advances include ribbed swimsuits that reduce water resistance. Also, badges have been designed that warn workers of toxic chemicals in the air by turning color when the wearer is exposed to a particular chemical. Jet engines capable of much higher speeds than current jet engines are being developed as well.

A new technology that may prevent many accidents also has been developed. Equipment on emergency vehicles causes traffic lights to turn yellow and then red for other vehicles approaching the same intersections. The equipment activates the traffic lights when fast-moving emergency vehicles come close to such an intersection, preventing crashes.

Figure 22
Space technology has helped children go places and do things that they otherwise wouldn't be able to do.

Section Assessment

1. What is the main advantage of the space shuttle?

2. Why were the space shuttle-*Mir* docking missions so important?

3. What is the *International Space Station* used for? Describe how the *ISS* could help future space missions.

4. Describe Phase Three of the *International Space Station* program.

5. **Think Critically** What makes the space shuttle more versatile than earlier spacecraft?

Skill Builder Activities

6. **Making and Using Tables** Make a table of the discoveries from missions to the Moon and Mars. **For more help, refer to the Science Skill Handbook.**

7. **Communicating** Suppose you're in charge of assembling a crew for a new space station. Select 50 people to do a variety of jobs, such as farming, maintenance, scientific experimentation, and so on. In your Science Journal, list and explain your choices. **For more help, refer to the Science Skill Handbook.**

Star Sightings

Polaris ———

For thousands of years, humans have used the stars to learn about Earth. From star sightings, you can map the change of seasons, navigate the oceans, and even determine the size of Earth.

Polaris, or the North Star, has occupied an important place in human history. The location of Polaris is not affected by Earth's rotation. At any given observation point, it always appears at the same angle above the horizon. At Earth's north pole, Polaris appears directly overhead. At the equator, it is just above the northern horizon. Polaris provides a standard from which other locations can be measured. Such star sightings can be made using the astrolabe, an instrument used to measure the height of a star above the horizon.

Recognize the Problem

How can you determine the size of Earth?

Form a Hypothesis

Think about what you have learned about sightings of Polaris. How does this tell you that Earth is round? Knowing that Earth is round, form a hypothesis about how you can estimate the circumference of Earth based on star sightings.

Goals
- **Record** your sightings of Polaris.
- **Share** the data with other students to calculate the circumference of Earth.

Safety Precautions
WARNING: *Do not use the astrolabe during the daytime to observe the Sun.*

Data Sources
SCIENCE *Online* Go to the Glencoe Science Web site at **science.glencoe.com** to obtain instructions on how to make an astrolabe. Also visit the Web site for more information about the location of Polaris, and for data from other students.

Test Your Hypothesis

Plan

1. Obtain an astrolabe or construct one using the instructions posted on the Glencoe Science Web site.

2. **Design** a data table in your Science Journal similar to the one below.

Polaris Observations		
Your Location:		
Date	**Time**	**Astrolabe Reading**

3. Decide as a group how you will make your observations. Does it take more than one person to make each observation? When will it be easiest to see Polaris?

Do

1. Make sure your teacher approves your plan before you start.

2. Carry out your observations.

3. **Record** your observations in your data table.

4. Average your readings and post them in the table provided on the Glencoe Science Web site.

Analyze Your Data

1. **Research** the names of cities that are at approximately the same longitude as your hometown. Gather astrolabe readings at the Glencoe Science Web site from students in one of those cities.

2. **Compare** your astrolabe readings. Subtract the smaller reading from the larger one.

3. Determine the distance between your star sighting location and the other city.

4. **Calculate** the circumference of Earth using the following relationship.

Circumference = (360°) × (distance between locations)/ difference between readings

Draw Conclusions

1. How does the circumference of Earth that you calculated compare with the accepted value of 40,079 km?

2. What are some possible sources of error in this method of determining the size of Earth? What improvements would you suggest?

Communicating Your Data

SCIENCE Online Find this *Use the Internet* activity on the Glencoe Science Web site at **science.glencoe.com** Create a poster that includes a table of your data and data from students in other cities. Perform a sample circumference calculation for your class.

Cities in Space

Should the U.S. spend money to colonize space?

Humans have landed on the Moon, and spacecrafts have landed on Mars. But these space missions are just small steps that may lead to a giant new space program. As technology improves, humans may be able to visit and even live on other planets. The twenty-first century may turn science fiction into science fact. But is it worth the time and money involved?

Those in favor of living in space point to the International Space Station that already is orbiting Earth. It's an early step toward establishing floating cities where astronauts can live and work. The 94 billion dollar station may pave the way for "ordinary people" to live in space, too. As Earth's population continues to increase and there is less room on this planet, why not create ideal cities on another planet or a floating city in space? That reason, combined with the fact that there is little pollution in space, makes the idea appealing to many.

Critics of colonizing space think we should spend the hundreds of billions of dollars that it would cost to colonize space on projects to help improve people's lives here on Earth. Building better housing, developing ways to feed the hungry, finding cures for

diseases, and increasing funds for education should come first, these people say. And, critics continue, if people want to explore, why not explore right here on Earth? "The ocean floor is Earth's last frontier," says one person. "Why not explore that?"

If humans were to move permanently to space, the two most likely destinations would be Mars and the Moon, both bleak places.

But those in favor of moving to these places say humans could find a way to make them livable. They argue that humans have made homes in harsh climates and in rugged areas, and people can meet the challenges of living in space.

Choosing Mars

Mars may be the best place to live. Photos suggest that the planet once had liquid water on its surface. If that water is now frozen underground, humans may someday be able to tap into it.

NASA is studying whether it makes sense to send astronauts and scientists to explore Mars. An international team would live there for about 500 days, collecting and studying soil and rock samples for clues as to whether Mars is a planet that could be settled. NASA says this journey could begin as early as 2009.

But a longer-range dream to transform Mars into an Earthlike place with breathable air and usable water is just that—a dream. Some small steps are being taken to make that dream more realistic. Experimental plants are being developed that could absorb Mars' excess carbon dioxide and release oxygen. Solar mirrors, already available, could warm Mars' surface.

Those for and against colonizing space agree on one thing—setting up colonies on Mars or the Moon will take large amounts of money, research, and planning. It also will take the same spirit of adventure that has led history's pioneers into so many bold frontiers—deserts, the Poles, and the sky.

Is the International Space Station a small step toward colonizing space?

An early Mars colony might look something like this. Settlers would live in air-filled domes and even grow crops.

CONNECTIONS **Debate** Research further information about colonizing space. Make a list of the pros and cons for colonizing space. Do you think the United States should spend money to create space cities or use the money now to improve lives of people on Earth? Debate with your class.

SCIENCE *Online*
For more information, visit science.glencoe.com

Chapter **1** Study Guide

Section 1 Radiation from Space

1. The arrangement of electromagnetic waves according to their wavelengths is the electromagnetic spectrum.

2. Optical telescopes produce magnified images of objects. *What does this reflecting telescope use to focus light that produces an image?*

3. Radio telescopes collect and record radio waves given off by some space objects.

Section 2 Early Space Missions

1. A satellite is an object that revolves around another object. The moons of planets are natural satellites. Artificial satellites are those made by people.

2. A space probe travels into the solar system, gathers data, and sends them back to Earth. *How far can space probes, like the one pictured here, travel?*

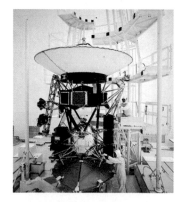

3. Early American piloted space programs included the Gemini and Apollo Projects.

Section 3 Recent and Future Space Missions

1. Space stations provide the opportunity to conduct research not possible on Earth. The *International Space Station* is being constructed in space with the cooperation of more than a dozen nations.

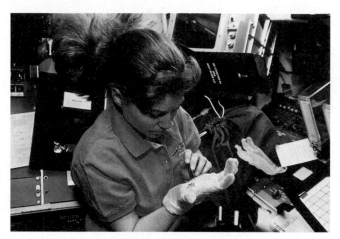

2. The space shuttle is a reusable spacecraft that carries astronauts, satellites, and other cargo to and from space. *What special obstacles must astronauts overcome when they conduct research in space?*

3. Space technology is used to solve problems on Earth not related to space travel. Advances in engineering related to space travel have led to problem solving in medicine and environmental sciences, among other fields.

FOLDABLES
Reading & Study Skills

After You Read

Use what you've learned to predict the future of space exploration. Record your predictions under the Future tab of your Foldable.

Visualizing Main Ideas

Complete the following concept map about the race to the Moon. Use the following phrases: first satellite, Project Gemini, Project Mercury, team of two astronauts orbits Earth, Project Apollo.

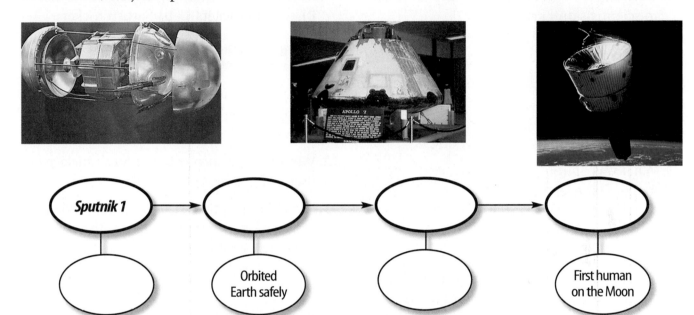

Sputnik 1 → ◯ → ◯ → ◯

| | Orbited Earth safely | | First human on the Moon |

Vocabulary Review

Vocabulary Words

a. electromagnetic spectrum
b. observatory
c. orbit
d. Project Apollo
e. Project Gemini
f. Project Mercury
g. radio telescope
h. reflecting telescope
i. refracting telescope
j. rocket
k. satellite
l. space probe
m. space shuttle
n. space station

THE PRINCETON REVIEW Study Tip

Without looking back at your textbook, write a summary of each section of a chapter after you've read it. If you write it in your own words, you will remember it better.

Using Vocabulary

Each of the following sentences is false. Make each sentence true by replacing the underlined word(s) with the correct vocabulary word(s).

1. A <u>radio</u> telescope uses lenses to bend light.

2. A <u>space probe</u> is an object that revolves around another object in space.

3. <u>Project Apollo</u> was the first piloted U.S. space program.

4. A <u>satellite</u> carries people and tools to and from space.

5. In the <u>space station</u>, electromagnetic waves are arranged according to their wavelengths.

Chapter (1) Assessment

Checking Concepts

Choose the word or phrase that best answers the question.

1. Which spacecraft has sent images of Venus to scientists on Earth?
   A) *Voyager*   C) *Apollo 11*
   B) *Viking*   D) *Magellan*

2. Which kind of telescope uses mirrors to collect light?
   A) radio   C) refracting
   B) electromagnetic   D) reflecting

3. What was *Sputnik I*?
   A) the first telescope
   B) the first artificial satellite
   C) the first observatory
   D) the first U.S. space probe

4. Which kind of telescope can be used during the day or night and during bad weather?
   A) radio   C) refracting
   B) electromagnetic   D) reflecting

5. When fully operational, what is the maximum number of people who will crew the *International Space Station?*
   A) 3   C) 15
   B) 7   D) 50

6. Which space mission's goal was to put a spacecraft into orbit and bring it back safely?
   A) Project Mercury   C) Project Gemini
   B) Project Apollo   D) *Viking I*

7. Which of the following is a natural satellite of Earth?
   A) *Skylab*   C) the Sun
   B) the space shuttle D) the Moon

8. What does the space shuttle use to place a satellite into space?
   A) liquid-fuel tank C) mechanical arm
   B) booster rocket   D) cargo bay

9. What was *Skylab?*
   A) a space probe   C) a space shuttle
   B) a space station   D) an optical telescope

10. What part of the space shuttle is reused?
    A) liquid-fuel tanks C) booster engines
    B) *Gemini* rockets D) Saturn rockets

Thinking Critically

11. Describe any advantages that a Moon-based telescope would have over an Earth-based telescope?

12. Would a space probe to the Sun's surface be useful? Explain.

13. Which do you think is a wiser method of exploration—space missions with people onboard or robotic space probes? Why?

14. Suppose two astronauts are outside the space shuttle orbiting Earth. The audio speaker in the helmet of one astronaut quits working. The other astronaut is 1 m away and shouts a message. Can the first astronaut hear the message? Explain.

15. Space probes have crossed Pluto's orbit, but never have visited the planet. Explain.

Developing Skills

16. **Making and Using Tables** Copy and complete the table below. Use information from several resources.

United States Space Probes		
Probe	Launch Date(s)	Planets or Objects Visited
Vikings 1 and *2*		
Galileo		
Lunar Prospector		
Pathfinder		

17. Concept Mapping Use the following phrases to complete the concept map about rocket launching: *thrust pushes rocket forward, rocket breaks free of Earth's gravity, propellant is ignited,* and *hot gases exert pressure on walls of burning chamber.*

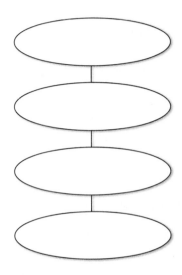

18. Classifying Classify the following as a satellite or a space probe: *Cassini, Sputnik I, Hubble Space Telescope,* space shuttle, and *Voyager 2.*

19. Comparing and Contrasting Compare and contrast space probes and satellites.

Performance Assessment

20. Poem Research a space probe launched within the last five years. Write a poem that includes its destination, the goals for its mission and something about the individuals who crewed the flight.

TECHNOLOGY

Go to the Glencoe Science Web site at **science.glencoe.com** or use the **Glencoe Science CD-ROM** for additional chapter assessment.

Test Practice

Scientists use several different kinds of telescopes to make observations about space. Information about some types of telescopes is listed in the table below.

1. According to the table, a refracting telescope focuses light using a _____.
- **A)** convex lens
- **B)** mirror
- **C)** dish
- **D)** receiver

Types of Telescopes		
Telescope	**Use**	**How it Works**
Optical Refracting Telescope	Produces magnified images of distant objects	Uses a convex lens to bend and focus light
Optical Reflecting Telescope	Produces magnified images of distant objects	Uses mirrors to reflect and focus light
Radio Telescope	Collects radio waves from space	Large dish reflects and focuses waves to receiver.

2. While in space, the *Hubble Space Telescope* needed its largest mirror repaired in 1993. While costly, the repair mission was a huge success. According to the chart, the *Hubble Space Telescope* is _____.
- **F)** an optical refracting telescope
- **G)** an optical reflecting telescope
- **H)** a radio telescope
- **J)** an optical radio receiver

The Sun-Earth-Moon System

Can you say with certainty that Earth is round? Why do you feel coldest when Earth is closest to the Sun? In this chapter, you will find the answers to these questions. You'll learn why the lengths of day and night change and why seasons occur. You'll also learn why the Moon's appearance changes throughout the month and why scientists think its surface might be a home for humans one day.

What do you think?

Science Journal Look at the picture below with a classmate. Discuss what this might be. Here's a hint: *It's behind the man in the Moon.* Write your best guess in your Science Journal.

he Sun rises in the morning. This occurs because Earth is moving through space. The movements of Earth cause day and night, as well as the seasons. In this activity, you will explore Earth's movements.

Model rotation and revolution

1. Hold a basketball with one finger at the top and one at the bottom. Have a classmate gently spin the ball.

2. Explain how this models rotation.

3. Continue to hold the basketball and walk one complete circle around another student in your class.

4. How does this model revolution?

Observe

In your Science Journal, compare and contrast rotation and revolution.

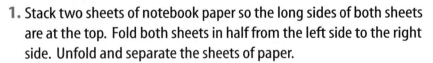

Before You Read

Making a Question Study Fold **Make the following Foldable to organize and answer questions as you read this chapter.**

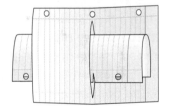

1. Stack two sheets of notebook paper so the long sides of both sheets are at the top. Fold both sheets in half from the left side to the right side. Unfold and separate the sheets of paper.

2. Take one sheet of paper and cut along the fold line, starting in the center of the fold and stopping at both margin lines as shown.

3. Place the second sheet in front so the long side is at the top. Cut along the fold line from the bottom and from the top, stopping at the margin lines.

4. Insert the second sheet into the cut of the first sheet. Unfold the inserted sheet; align the cuts along the fold of the other.

5. Fold both sheets in half to make a book as shown. On the first two pages, record questions you have about the Sun, on the middle two pages, questions about Earth, and on the last two pages, questions about the Moon. As you read the chapter, answer your questions.

Earth

As You Read

***What* You'll Learn**

- **Examine** Earth's physical characteristics.
- **Differentiate** between rotation and revolution.
- **Discuss** what causes seasons to change.

Vocabulary

sphere   ellipse
axis   solstice
rotation   equinox
revolution

***Why* It's Important**

Earth's movements cause night and day and the changing of seasons.

Figure 1
For many years, sailors have observed that the tops of ships coming across the horizon appear first. This suggests that Earth is spherical, not flat, as was once widely believed.

Properties of Earth

You awaken at daybreak to catch the Sun "rising" from the dark horizon. Then it begins its daily "journey" from east to west across the sky. Finally the Sun "sinks" out of view as night falls. Is the Sun moving—or are you?

It wasn't long ago that people thought Earth was the center of the universe. It was widely believed that the Sun revolved around Earth, which stood still. It is now common knowledge that the Sun only appears to be moving around Earth. Because Earth spins as it revolves around the Sun, it creates the illusion that the Sun is moving across the sky.

Another mistaken idea about Earth concerned its shape. Even as recently as the days of Christopher Columbus, many people believed Earth to be flat. Because of this, they were afraid that if they sailed far enough out to sea, they would fall off the edge of the world. How do you know this isn't true? How have scientists determined the true shape of Earth?

Spherical Shape A round, three-dimensional object is called a **sphere** (SFIHR). Its surface is the same distance from its center at all points. Some common examples of spheres are basketballs and tennis balls.

In the late twentieth century, artificial satellites and space probes sent back pictures showing that Earth is spherical. Much earlier, Aristotle, a Greek astronomer and philosopher who lived around 350 B.C., suspected that Earth was spherical. He observed that Earth cast a curved shadow on the Moon during an eclipse.

In addition to Aristotle, other individuals made observations that indicated Earth's spherical shape. Early sailors, for example, noticed that approaching ships came into view a little at a time, as shown in **Figure 1.**

Additional Evidence Sailors also noticed changes in how the night sky looked. As they sailed north or south, the North Star moved higher or lower in the sky. The best explanation was a spherical Earth.

Today, most people know that Earth is spherical. They also know all objects are attracted by gravity to the center of a spherical Earth. Astronauts have clearly seen the spherical shape of Earth. However, it bulges slightly at the equator and is somewhat flattened at the poles, so it is not a perfect sphere.

Rotation Earth's **axis** is the imaginary vertical line around which Earth spins. This line cuts directly through the center of Earth, as shown in the illustration accompanying **Table 1.** The poles are located at the north and south ends of Earth's axis. The spinning of Earth on its axis, called **rotation,** causes day and night to occur. Here is how it works. As Earth rotates, you can see the Sun come into view at daybreak. Earth continues to spin, making it seem as if the Sun moves across the sky until it sets at night. During night, your area of Earth has rotated so that it is on the opposite side as the Sun. Because of this, the Sun is no longer visible to you. Earth continues to rotate steadily, and eventually the Sun comes into view again the next morning. One complete rotation takes about 24 h, or one day. How many rotations does Earth complete during one year? As you can infer from **Table 1,** it completes about 365 rotations during its one-year journey around the Sun.

✔**Reading Check** *Why does the Sun seem to rise and set?*

Life Science
INTEGRATION

Suppose that Earth's rotation took twice as long as it does now. In your Science Journal, predict how conditions such as global temperatures, work schedules, plant growth, and other factors might change under these circumstances.

Axis

Rotation

Table 1 Physical Properties of Earth	
Diameter (pole to pole)	12,714 km
Diameter (equator)	12,756 km
Circumference (poles)	40,008 km
Circumference (equator)	40,075 km
Mass	5.98×10^{24} kg
Average Density	5.52 g/cm^3
Average Distance to the Sun	149,600,000 km
Period of Rotation (1 day)	23 h, 56 min
Period of Revolution (1 year)	365 days, 6 h, 9 min

Figure 2
Earth's magnetic field is similar to that of a bar magnet, almost as if Earth contained a giant magnet. Earth's magnetic axis is angled 11.5 degrees from its rotational axis.

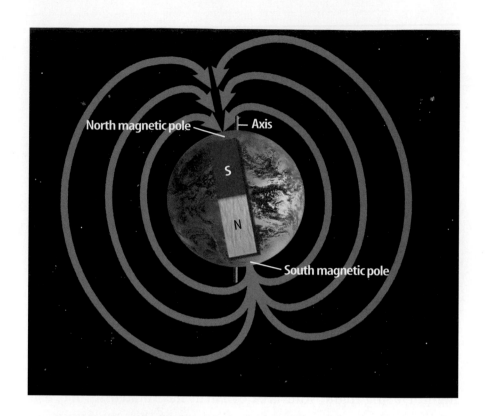

North magnetic pole — Axis

S

N

South magnetic pole

Making Your Own Compass

Procedure 🔧 🥽 🧤

WARNING: *Use care when handling sharp objects.*

1. Cut off the bottom of a **plastic foam cup** to make a polystyrene disk.
2. Magnetize a **sewing needle** by continuously stroking the needle in the same direction with a **magnet** for 1 min.
3. **Tape** the needle to the center of the foam disk.
4. Fill a **plate** with **water** and float the disk, needle side up, in the water.

Analysis

1. What happened to the needle and disk when you placed them in the water? Why did this happen?
2. Infer how ancient sailors might have used magnets to help them navigate on the open seas.

Physics
INTEGRATION

Magnetic Field Scientists hypothesize that the movement of material inside Earth's core, along with Earth's rotation, generates a magnetic field. This magnetic field is much like that of a bar magnet. Earth has a north and a south magnetic pole, just as a bar magnet has opposite magnetic poles at each of its ends. When you sprinkle iron shavings over a bar magnet, the shavings align with the magnetic field of the magnet. As you can see in **Figure 2,** Earth's magnetic field is similar—almost as if Earth contained a giant bar magnet. Earth's magnetic field protects you from harmful solar radiation by trapping many charged particles from the Sun.

Magnetic Axis When you observe a compass needle pointing north, you are seeing evidence of Earth's magnetic field. Earth's magnetic axis, the line joining its north and south magnetic poles, does not align with its rotational axis. The magnetic axis is inclined at an angle of 11.5° to the rotational axis. If you followed a compass needle, you would end up at the magnetic north pole rather than the rotational north pole.

The location of the magnetic poles has been shown to change slowly over time. The magnetic poles move around the rotational (geographic) poles in an irregular way. This movement can be significant over decades. Many maps include information about the position of the magnetic north pole at the time the map was made. Why would this information be important?

What causes changing seasons?

Flowers bloom as the days get warmer. The Sun appears higher in the sky, and daylight lasts longer. Spring seems like a fresh, new beginning. What causes these wonderful changes?

Orbiting the Sun You learned earlier that Earth's rotation causes day and night. Another important motion is **revolution,** which is Earth's yearly orbit around the Sun. Just as the Moon is Earth's satellite, Earth is a satellite of the Sun. If Earth's orbit were a circle with the Sun at the center, Earth would maintain a constant distance from the Sun. However, this is not the case. Earth's orbit is an **ellipse** (ee LIHPS)—an elongated, closed curve. The Sun is not at the center of the ellipse but is a little toward one end. Because of this, the distance between Earth and the Sun changes during Earth's yearlong orbit. Earth gets closest to the Sun—about 147 million km away—around January 3. The farthest Earth gets from the Sun is about 152 million km away. This happens around July 4 each year.

✔ **Reading Check** *What is an ellipse?*

Does this elliptical orbit cause seasonal temperatures on Earth? If it did, you would expect the warmest days to be in January. You know this isn't the case in the northern hemisphere, something else must cause the change.

Even though Earth is closest to the Sun in January, the change in distance is small. Earth is exposed to almost the same amount of Sun all year. But the amount of solar energy any one place on Earth receives varies greatly during the year. Next, you will learn why.

A Tilted Axis Earth's axis is tilted 23.5° from a line drawn perpendicular to the plane of its orbit. It is this tilt that causes seasons. Daylight hours are longer for the hemisphere, or half of Earth, that is tilted toward the Sun. Think of how early it gets dark in the winter compared to the summer. As shown in **Figure 3,** the hemisphere that is tilted toward the Sun receives more hours of sunlight each day than the hemisphere that is tilted away from the Sun. The longer period of sunlight is one reason summer is warmer than winter, but it is not the only reason.

SCIENCE Online

Research Visit the Glencoe Science Web site at **science.glencoe.com** for more information about ellipses. What special properties do they have? What effect does the shape of Earth's orbit have on incoming solar energy throughout the year? Present your findings to the class.

Figure 3
In summer, the northern hemisphere is tilted toward the Sun. Notice that the north pole is always lit during the summer. *Why are daylight hours longer in the summer than in the winter?*

North Pole

Radiation from the Sun Earth's tilt also causes the Sun's radiation to strike the hemispheres at different angles. The hemisphere tilted toward the Sun receives more direct rays, thus more total solar radiation than the hemisphere tilted away from the Sun. In the hemisphere tilted away from the Sun, the Sun appears low in the sky, and its rays are slanted.

Summer occurs in the hemisphere tilted toward the Sun, where the Sun appears high in the sky. Its radiation strikes Earth at a higher angle and for longer periods of time. The hemisphere receiving less radiation experiences winter.

Solstices

The **solstice** is the day when the Sun reaches its greatest distance north or south of the equator. In the northern hemisphere, the summer solstice occurs on June 21 or 22, and the winter solstice occurs on December 21 or 22. Both solstices are illustrated in **Figure 4.** In the southern hemisphere, the winter solstice is in June and the summer solstice is in December. Summer solstice is nearly the longest day of the year. After the summer solstice, days begin to get shorter. The winter solstice is nearly the shortest day of the year, but after the winter solstice, the period of sunlight grows longer each day.

Figure 4
During the summer solstice in the northern hemisphere, the Sun is directly over the tropic of Cancer, the latitude line at 23.5° N latitude. During the winter solstice, the Sun is directly over the tropic of Capricorn, the latitude line at 23.5° S latitude. At fall and spring equinoxes, the Sun is directly over the equator.

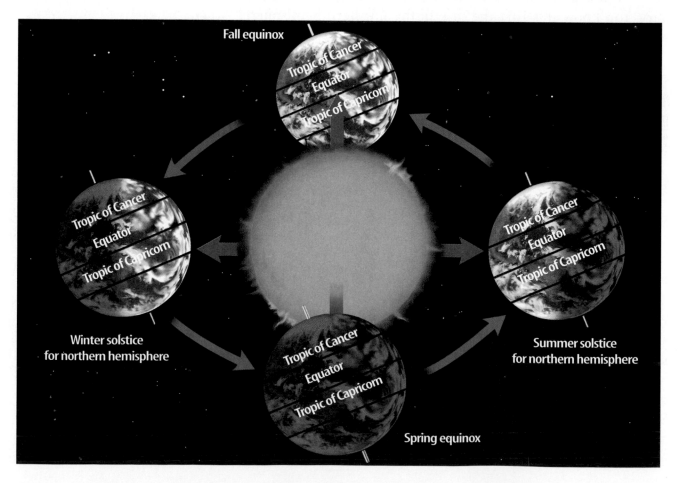

Fall equinox

Tropic of Cancer
Equator
Tropic of Capricorn

Tropic of Cancer
Equator
Tropic of Capricorn

Tropic of Cancer
Equator
Tropic of Capricorn

Winter solstice
for northern hemisphere

Summer solstice
for northern hemisphere

Tropic of Cancer
Equator
Tropic of Capricorn

Spring equinox

Equinoxes

An **equinox** (EE kwuh nahks) occurs when the Sun is directly above Earth's equator. Because of the tilt of Earth's axis, the Sun's position relative to the equator changes constantly. Most of the time, the Sun is either north or south of the equator, but two times each year it is directly over it, resulting in the spring and fall equinoxes. As you can see in **Figure 4,** on the equinox the Sun's most direct rays shine on the equator.

During an equinox, the number of daylight hours and night-time hours is nearly equal all over the world. Also at this time, neither the northern hemisphere nor the southern hemisphere is tilted toward the Sun.

In the northern hemisphere, the Sun reaches the spring equinox on March 20 or 21, and the fall equinox occurs on September 22 or 23. In the southern hemisphere, the equinoxes are reversed. Spring occurs in September and fall occurs in March.

Earth Data Review As you have learned, Earth is a sphere that rotates on a tilted axis. This rotation causes day and night. Earth's tilted axis and its revolution around the Sun cause the seasons. One Earth revolution takes one year. In the next section, you will read how the Moon rotates on its axis and revolves around Earth.

SCIENCE Online

Collect Data Visit the Glencoe Science Web site at **science.glencoe.com** for data about seasons. How are seasons different in other parts of the world? Make a poster summarizing what you learn.

Section Assessment

1. Why did Aristotle think Earth was spherical?

2. Compare and contrast rotation and revolution.

3. Describe how Earth's distance from the Sun changes throughout the year. When is Earth closest to the Sun?

4. Why is it summer in Earth's northern hemisphere at the same time it is winter in the southern hemisphere?

5. **Think Critically** **Table 1** lists Earth's distance from the Sun as an average. Why isn't an exact measurement available for this distance?

Skill Builder Activities

6. **Recognizing Cause and Effect** Answer these questions about the Sun-Earth-Moon relationship. **For more help, refer to the Science Skill Handbook.**
   a. What causes seasons on Earth?
   b. Why does the Sun appear to rise in the east and set in the west each day?

7. **Using an Electronic Spreadsheet** Create a table of Earth's physical properties. Show the following: *diameter, mass, period of rotation,* and *other data.* Then, write a description of Earth based on your table. **For more help, refer to the Technology Skill Handbook.**

The Moon— Earth's Satellite

Motions of the Moon

Doesn't it seem as if the Moon's shape changes night after night? Sometimes, just after sunset, you can see a full, round Moon low in the sky. Other times, only half of the Moon is visible, and it's high in the sky at sunset. At times, the Moon is even visible during the day. What causes the Moon to change in appearance and position in the sky?

Rotation and Revolution Just as Earth rotates on its axis and revolves around the Sun, the Moon rotates on its axis and revolves around Earth. The Moon's revolution around Earth is responsible for the changes in its appearance. If the Moon rotates on its axis, why can't you see it spin around in space? The reason is that the Moon's rotation takes 27.3 days—the same amount of time it takes to revolve once around Earth. Because these two motions take the same amount of time, the same side of the Moon always faces Earth, as shown in **Figure 5.**

You can demonstrate this by having a friend hold a ball in front of you. Direct your friend to move the ball in a circle around you while keeping the same side of it facing you. Everyone else in the room will see all sides of the ball. You will see only one side.

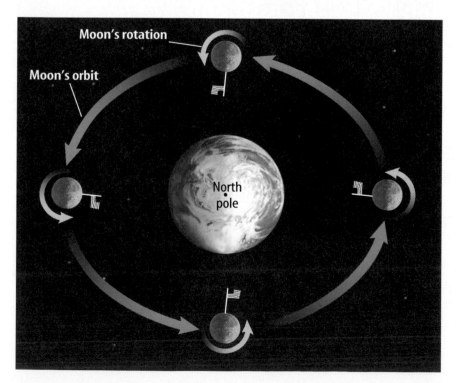

Figure 5
In about one month, the Moon orbits Earth. It also completes one rotation on its axis during the same period. *Does this affect which side of the Moon faces Earth? Explain.*

Reflection of the Sun The Moon seems to shine because its surface reflects sunlight. Just as half of Earth experiences day as the other half experiences night, half of the Moon is lighted while the other half is dark. As the Moon revolves around Earth, you see different portions of its lighted side, causing the Moon's appearance to change.

Phases of the Moon

Moon phases are the different forms that the Moon takes in its appearance from Earth. The phase depends on the relative positions of the Moon, Earth, and the Sun, as seen in **Figure 6** on the next page. A **new moon** occurs when the Moon is between Earth and the Sun. During a new moon, the lighted half of the Moon is facing the Sun and the dark side faces Earth. The Moon is in the sky, but it cannot be seen. The new moon rises and sets with the Sun.

✔ **Reading Check** *Why can't you see a new moon?*

Waxing Phases After a new moon, the phases begin waxing. **Waxing** means that more of the illuminated half of the Moon can be seen each night. About 24 h after a new moon, you can see a thin slice of the Moon. This phase is called the waxing crescent. About a week after a new moon, you can see half of the lighted side of the Moon, or one quarter of the Moon's surface. This is the first quarter phase.

The phases continue to wax. When more than one quarter is visible, it is called waxing *gibbous* after the Latin word for "humpbacked." A **full moon** occurs when all of the Moon's surface facing Earth reflects light.

Waning Phases After a full moon, the phases are said to be waning. When the Moon's phases are **waning,** you see less of its illuminated half each night. Waning gibbous begins just after a full moon. When you can see only half of the lighted side, it is the third-quarter phase. The Moon continues to appear to shrink. Waning crescent occurs just before another new moon. Once again, you can see only a small slice of the Moon.

It takes about 29.5 days for the Moon to complete its cycle of phases. Recall that it takes about 27.3 days for the Moon to revolve around Earth. The discrepancy between these two numbers is due to Earth's revolution. The roughly two extra days are what it takes for the Moon to keep up constantly with Earth as it orbits around the Sun.

Mini LAB

Comparing the Sun and the Moon

Procedure

1. Find an area where you can make a chalk mark on **pavement or another surface.**
2. Tie a piece of **chalk** to one end of a 400-cm-long **string.**
3. Hold the other end of the string to the pavement.
4. Have a friend pull the string tight and walk around you, leaving a mark (the Sun) on the pavement.
5. Draw a 1-cm-diameter circle in the middle of the larger circle (the Moon).

Analysis

1. How big is the Sun compared to the Moon?
2. The diameter of the Sun is 1.39 million km. The diameter of Earth is 12,756 km. Draw two new circles modeling the sizes of the Sun and Earth. What scale did you use?

Figure 6
The phases of the Moon change during a cycle that lasts about 29.5 days.

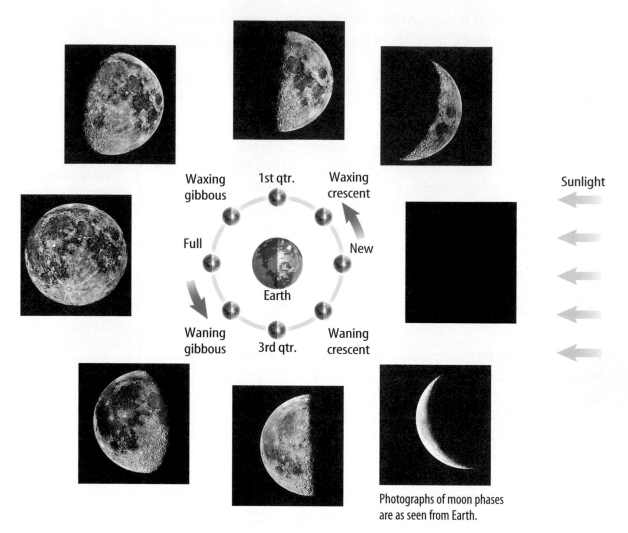

Waxing gibbous

1st qtr.

Waxing crescent

Full

New

Earth

Sunlight

Waning gibbous

3rd qtr.

Waning crescent

Photographs of moon phases are as seen from Earth.

Figure 7
Only the outer portion of the Sun's atmosphere is visible during a total solar eclipse. It looks like a halo around the Moon.

Eclipses

Imagine living 10,000 years ago. You are foraging for nuts and fruit when unexpectedly the Sun disappears from the sky. The darkness lasts only a short time, and the Sun soon returns to full brightness. You know something strange has happened, but you don't know why. It will be almost 8,000 years before anyone can explain what you just experienced.

The event just described was a total solar eclipse (ih KLIPS), shown in **Figure 7.** Today, most people know what causes such eclipses, but without this knowledge, they would have been terrifying events. During a solar eclipse, many animals act as if it is nighttime. Cows return to their barns and chickens go to sleep. What causes the day to become night and then change back into day?

✔ Reading Check *What happens during a total solar eclipse?*

What causes an eclipse? The revolution of the Moon causes eclipses. Eclipses occur when Earth or the Moon temporarily blocks the sunlight from reaching the other. Sometimes, during a new moon, the Moon's shadow falls on Earth and causes a solar eclipse. During a full moon, Earth's shadow can be cast on the Moon, resulting in a lunar eclipse.

An eclipse can occur only when the Sun, the Moon, and Earth are lined up perfectly. Because the Moon's orbit is not in the same plane as Earth's orbit around the Sun, eclipses occur only a few times each year.

Eclipses of the Sun A **solar eclipse** occurs when the Moon moves directly between the Sun and Earth and casts its shadow over part of Earth, as seen in **Figure 8.** Depending on where you are on Earth, you may experience a total eclipse or a partial eclipse. The darkest portion of the Moon's shadow is called the umbra (UM bruh). A person standing within the umbra experiences a total solar eclipse. During a total solar eclipse, the only visible portion of the Sun is a pearly white glow around the edge of the eclipsing Moon.

Surrounding the umbra is a lighter shadow on Earth's surface called the penumbra (puh NUM bruh). Persons standing in the penumbra experience a partial solar eclipse. **WARNING:** *Regardless of where you stand, never look directly at the Sun during an eclipse. The light can permanently damage your eyes.*

SCIENCE *Online*

Collect Data Visit the Glencoe Science Web site at **science.glencoe.com** for more information about solar and lunar eclipses due to occur over the next several years. Make a chart showing when and where they will occur.

Figure 8
Only a small area of Earth experiences a total solar eclipse during the eclipse event.

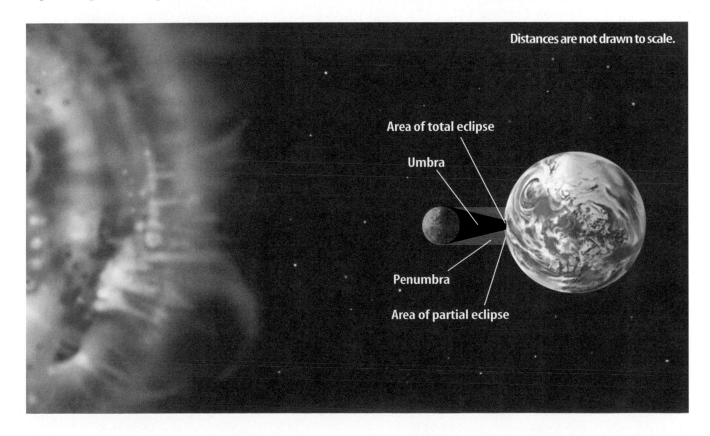

Distances are not drawn to scale.

Area of total eclipse

Umbra

Penumbra

Area of partial eclipse

Figure 9
These photographs show the Moon moving from right to left into Earth's umbra, then out again.

Figure 10
During a total lunar eclipse, Earth's shadow blocks light coming from the Sun.

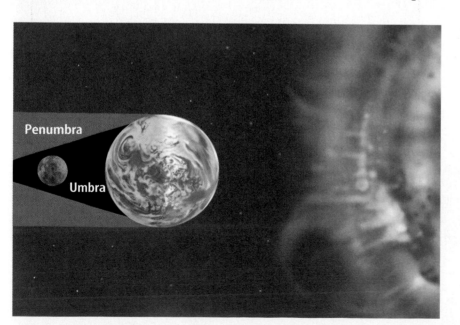

Penumbra

Umbra

Eclipses of the Moon When Earth's shadow falls on the Moon, a **lunar eclipse** occurs. A lunar eclipse begins when the Moon moves into Earth's penumbra. As the Moon continues to move, it enters Earth's umbra and you see a curved shadow on the Moon's surface, as in **Figure 9.** Upon moving completely into Earth's umbra, as shown in **Figure 10,** the Moon goes dark, signaling that a total lunar eclipse has occurred. Sometimes sunlight bent through Earth's atmosphere causes the eclipsed Moon to appear red.

A partial lunar eclipse occurs when only a portion of the Moon moves into Earth's umbra. The remainder of the Moon is in Earth's penumbra and, therefore, receives some direct sunlight. A penumbral lunar eclipse occurs when the Moon is totally within Earth's penumbra. However, it is difficult to tell when a penumbral lunar eclipse occurs because some direct sunlight is falling on the side of the Moon facing Earth.

A total lunar eclipse can be seen by anyone on the nighttime side of Earth where the Moon is not hidden by clouds. In contrast, only a lucky few people get to witness a total solar eclipse. Only those people in the small region where the Moon's umbra strikes Earth can witness one.

The Moon's Surface

When you look at the Moon, as shown in **Figure 12** on the next page, you can see many depressions called craters. Meteorites, asteroids, and comets striking the Moon's surface created most of these craters, which formed early in the Moon's history. Upon impact, cracks may have formed in the Moon's crust, allowing lava to reach the surface and fill up the large craters. The resulting dark, flat regions are called **maria** (MAHR ee uh). The igneous rocks of the maria are 3 billion to 4 billion years old. So far, they are the youngest rocks to be found on the Moon. This indicates that craters formed after the Moon's surface originally cooled. The maria formed early enough in the Moon's history that molten material still remained in the Moon's interior. The Moon once must have been as geologically active as Earth is today. Before the Moon cooled to the current condition, the interior separated into distinct layers.

Inside the Moon

Earthquakes allow scientists to learn about Earth's interior. In a similar way, scientists use instruments such as the one in **Figure 11A** to study moonquakes. The data they have received have led to the construction of several models of the Moon's interior. One such model, shown in **Figure 11B,** suggests that the Moon's crust is about 60 km thick on the side facing Earth. On the far side, it is thought to be about 150 km thick. Under the crust, a solid mantle may extend to a depth of 1,000 km. A partly molten zone of the mantle may extend even farther down. Below this mantle may lie a solid, iron-rich core.

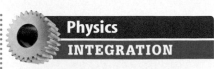

Physics
INTEGRATION

Waves generated by earthquakes and moonquakes change speeds when encountering materials with different physical properties. Research these waves to find out what factors affect their speed and direction. Infer how scientists might use this information to learn about the interiors of the Moon and Earth.

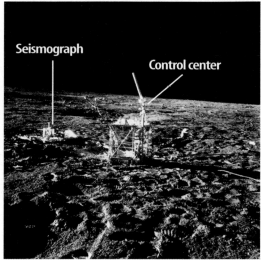

A

Seismograph

Control center

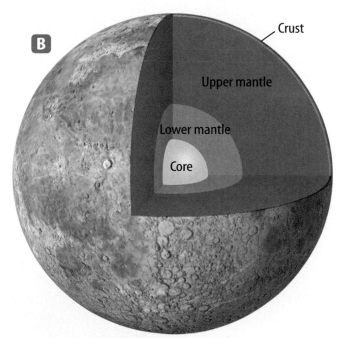

B

Crust

Upper mantle

Lower mantle

Core

Figure 11
A Equipment, such as the seismograph left on the Moon by the *Apollo 12* mission, helps scientists study moonquakes.
B Models of the Moon's interior were created from data obtained by scientists studying moonquakes.

Figure 12

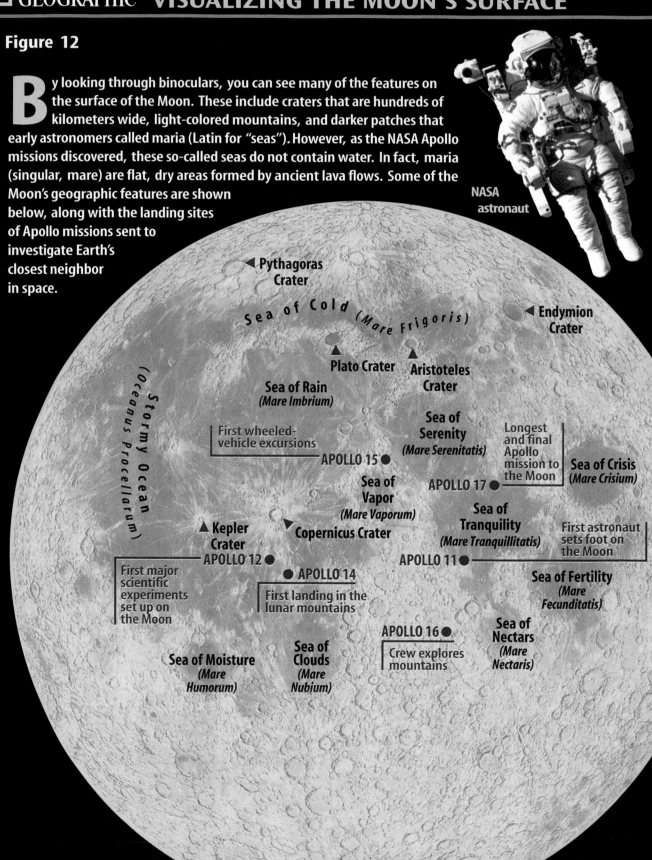

By looking through binoculars, you can see many of the features on the surface of the Moon. These include craters that are hundreds of kilometers wide, light-colored mountains, and darker patches that early astronomers called maria (Latin for "seas"). However, as the NASA Apollo missions discovered, these so-called seas do not contain water. In fact, maria (singular, mare) are flat, dry areas formed by ancient lava flows. Some of the Moon's geographic features are shown below, along with the landing sites of Apollo missions sent to investigate Earth's closest neighbor in space.

NASA astronaut

◄ Pythagoras Crater

Sea of Cold (Mare Frigoris)

◄ Endymion Crater

▲ Plato Crater   ▲ Aristoteles Crater

Sea of Rain (Mare Imbrium)

(Oceanus Procellarum) Stormy Ocean

Sea of Serenity (Mare Serenitatis)

Longest and final Apollo mission to the Moon

Sea of Crisis (Mare Crisium)

First wheeled-vehicle excursions

APOLLO 15 ●

Sea of Vapor (Mare Vaporum)

APOLLO 17 ●

Sea of Tranquility (Mare Tranquillitatis)

First astronaut sets foot on the Moon

▲ Kepler Crater

▼ Copernicus Crater

APOLLO 12 ●

First major scientific experiments set up on the Moon

● APOLLO 14

First landing in the lunar mountains

APOLLO 11 ●

Sea of Fertility (Mare Fecunditatis)

APOLLO 16 ●

Crew explores mountains

Sea of Nectars (Mare Nectaris)

Sea of Moisture (Mare Humorum)

Sea of Clouds (Mare Nubium)

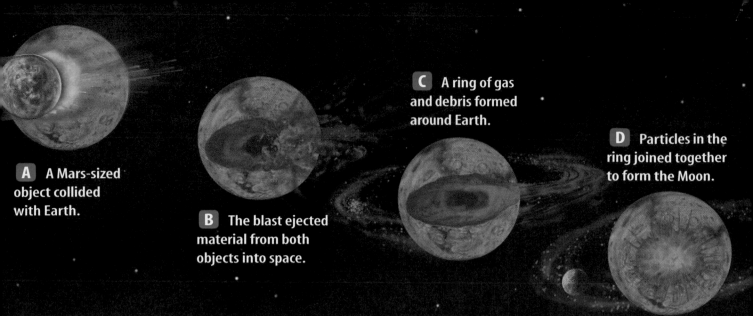

A A Mars-sized object collided with Earth.

B The blast ejected material from both objects into space.

C A ring of gas and debris formed around Earth.

D Particles in the ring joined together to form the Moon.

The Moon's Origin

Before the *Apollo* space missions in the 1960s and 1970s, there were three leading theories about the Moon's origin. According to one theory, the Moon was captured by Earth's gravity. Another held that material surrounding Earth condensed to produce the Moon. An alternative theory proposed that Earth ejected molten material that became the Moon.

The Impact Theory The data gathered by the *Apollo* missions have led many scientists to support a new theory, known as the impact theory. It states that the Moon formed billions of years ago from condensing gas and debris thrown off when Earth collided with a Mars-sized object as shown in **Figure 13**.

Figure 13
According to the impact theory, a Mars-sized object collided with Earth around 4.6 billion years ago. Vaporized materials ejected by the collision began orbiting Earth and quickly consolidated into the Moon.

Problem-Solving Activity

What will you use to survive on the Moon?

You have crash-landed on the Moon. It will take one day to reach a moon colony on foot. The side of the Moon that you are on will be facing away from the Sun during your entire trip. You manage to salvage the following items from your wrecked ship: food, rope, solar-powered heating unit, battery-operated heating unit, oxygen tanks, map of the constellations, compass, matches, water, solar-powered radio transmitter, three flashlights, signal mirror, and binoculars.

Identifying the Problem

The Moon lacks a magnetic field and has no atmosphere. How do the Moon's physical properties and the lack of sunlight affect your decisions?

Solving the Problem

1. Which items will be of no use to you? Which items will you take with you?
2. Describe why each of the salvaged items is useful or not useful.

Figure 14
Moon rocks collected by astronauts provide scientists with information about the Moon and Earth.

The Moon in History Regardless of how the Moon formed, it has played an important role. Studying the Moon's phases and eclipses led to the conclusion that both Earth and the Moon were in motion around the Sun. The curved shadow Earth casts on the Moon indicated to early scientists that Earth was spherical. When Galileo first turned his telescope toward the Moon, he found a surface scarred by craters and maria. Before that time, many people believed that all planetary bodies were perfectly smooth and lacking surface features.

 **Reading Check** *How has observing the Moon been important to science?*

More recently, actual Moon rocks became available for scientists to study, as seen in **Figure 14.** By doing so, they hope to learn more about Earth. The Moon was important in the past and promises to be important in the future, as well.

Section Assessment

1. How are the Sun, the Moon, and Earth positioned relative to each other during a new moon?

2. What do maria look like? How did they form?

3. What are the umbra and penumbra? How do they relate to eclipses?

4. What is the difference between a solar and a lunar eclipse? Explain what causes each and why more people see a lunar eclipse.

5. **Think Critically** What do the surface features of the Moon tell you about its history?

Skill Builder Activities

6. **Predicting** Look at a calendar or almanac to find out when the next new moon will occur. Using this information, predict when the first-quarter phase will begin. **For more help, refer to the Science Skill Handbook.**

7. **Communicating** Research the various theories about the Moon's origin in astronomy books and magazines. In your Science Journal, report on and make a diagram of each, including the impact theory. Evaluate the strengths and weaknesses of each theory. **For more help, refer to the Science Skill Handbook.**

Activity

Moon Phases and Eclipses

You have learned that Moon phases and eclipses result from the relative positions of the Sun, the Moon, and Earth. In this activity, you will demonstrate the positions of these bodies during certain phases and eclipses. You also will see why only a small portion of the people on Earth witness a total solar eclipse during a particular eclipse event.

What You'll Investigate

Can a model be devised to show the positions of the Sun, the Moon, and Earth during various phases and eclipses?

Materials

light source (unshaded)   globe
polystyrene ball   pencil

Goals

- **Model** moon phases.
- **Model** solar and lunar eclipses.

Procedure

1. Review the illustrations of Moon phases and eclipses shown in Section 2.

2. Use the light source as a Sun model and a polystyrene ball on a pencil as a Moon model. Move the Moon around the globe to duplicate the exact position that would have to occur for a lunar eclipse to take place.

3. Move the Moon to the position that would cause a solar eclipse.

4. Place the Moon at each of the following phases: first quarter, full moon, third quarter, and new moon. Identify which, if any, type of eclipse could occur during each phase. Record your data.

Moon Phase Observations	
Moon Phase	**Observations**
first quarter	
full moon	
third quarter	
new moon	

5. Place the Moon at the location where a lunar eclipse could occur. Move it slightly toward Earth, then away from Earth. Note the amount of change in the size of the shadow.

6. Repeat step 5 with the Moon in a position where a solar eclipse could occur.

Conclude and Apply

1. During which phase(s) of the Moon is it possible for an eclipse to occur?

2. **Describe** the effect of a small change in distance between Earth and the Moon on the size of the umbra and penumbra.

3. **Infer** why a lunar and a solar eclipse do not occur every month.

4. Why have only a few people experienced a total solar eclipse?

5. **Diagram** the positions of the Sun, Earth, and the Moon during a first quarter moon.

6. Why might it be better to call a full moon a half moon?

Communicating
Your Data

Communicate your answers to other students. **For more help, refer to the Science Skill Handbook.**

Exploring Earth's Moon

As You Read

What You'll Learn

- **Describe** recent discoveries about the Moon.
- **Examine** facts about the Moon that might influence future space travel.

Vocabulary

impact basin

Why It's Important

Continuing Moon missions may result in discoveries about Earth's origin.

Figure 15

This time line illustrates some of the most important events in the history of Moon exploration.

Missions to the Moon

The Moon has always fascinated humanity. People have made up stories about how it formed. Children's stories even suggested it was made of cheese. Of course, for centuries astronomers also have studied the Moon for clues to its makeup and origin. In 1959, the former Soviet Union launched the first *Luna* spacecraft, enabling up-close study of the Moon. Two years later, the United States began a similar program with the first *Ranger* spacecraft. Following the uncrewed *Ranger* missions, the United States launched a series of *Lunar Orbiters*. The spacecraft in these early missions took detailed photographs of the Moon. There also were seven *Surveyor* spacecraft designed to land on the Moon. Five of these spacecraft successfully touched down on the lunar surface. The *Surveyor* probes took detailed photographs and performed the first analysis of lunar soil. The goal of the program was to prepare for landing astronauts on the Moon. This goal was achieved in 1969 by the astronauts of *Apollo 11*. By 1972, when the *Apollo* missions ended, 12 U.S. astronauts had walked on the Moon. A time line of these important moon missions can be seen in **Figure 15.**

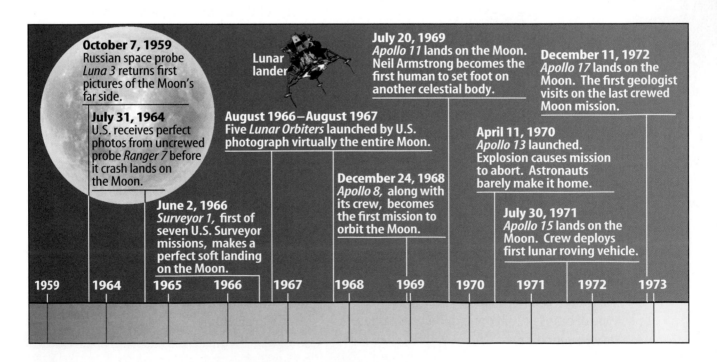

October 7, 1959
Russian space probe *Luna 3* returns first pictures of the Moon's far side.

July 31, 1964
U.S. receives perfect photos from uncrewed probe *Ranger 7* before it crash lands on the Moon.

June 2, 1966
Surveyor 1, first of seven U.S. Surveyor missions, makes a perfect soft landing on the Moon.

Lunar lander

August 1966–August 1967
Five *Lunar Orbiters* launched by U.S. photograph virtually the entire Moon.

December 24, 1968
Apollo 8, along with its crew, becomes the first mission to orbit the Moon.

July 20, 1969
Apollo 11 lands on the Moon. Neil Armstrong becomes the first human to set foot on another celestial body.

April 11, 1970
Apollo 13 launched. Explosion causes mission to abort. Astronauts barely make it home.

July 30, 1971
Apollo 15 lands on the Moon. Crew deploys first lunar roving vehicle.

December 11, 1972
Apollo 17 lands on the Moon. The first geologist visits on the last crewed Moon mission.

1959   1964   1965   1966   1967   1968   1969   1970   1971   1972   1973

Surveying the Moon More than 20 years passed before the United States resumed its studies of the Moon from space. In 1994, the *Clementine* was placed into lunar orbit. Its goal was to conduct a two-month survey of the Moon's surface. An important aspect of this study was collecting data on the mineral content of Moon rocks. In fact, this part of its mission was instrumental in naming the spacecraft. Clementine was the daughter of a miner in the ballad *My Darlin' Clementine*. While in orbit, *Clementine* also mapped features on the Moon's surface, including huge impact basins.

✔ **Reading Check**   *Why was Clementine placed in lunar orbit?*

Impact Basins When meteorites and other objects strike the Moon, they leave behind depressions in the Moon's surface. The depression left behind by an object striking the Moon is known as an **impact basin,** or impact crater. The South Pole-Aitken Basin is the oldest identifiable impact feature on the Moon's surface. At 12 km in depth and 2,500 km in diameter, it is also the largest and deepest impact basin in the solar system. Data returned by *Clementine* gave scientists the first set of high-resolution photographs of this area of the Moon. Because much of this basin stays in shadow throughout the Moon's rotation, a cold area has formed where ice deposits from impacting comets might have collected, as shown in **Figure 16.** A large plateau that is always in sunlight also was discovered in this area. If ice truly is near this plateau, as indicated by radio signals that *Clementine* reflected off the Moon to Earth, it would be the ideal location to build a moon colony powered by solar energy.

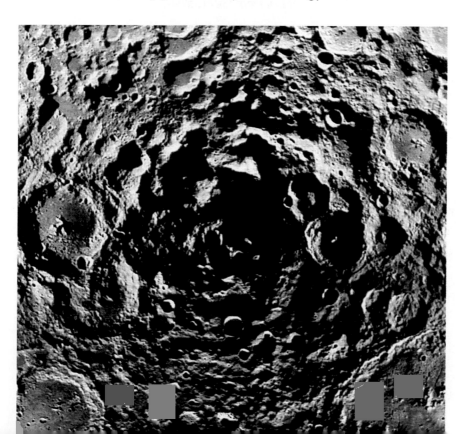

Figure 16
The South Pole-Aitken Basin is the largest of its kind found anywhere in the solar system. The deepest craters in the basin stay in shadow throughout the Moon's rotation. Ice deposits from impacting comets are thought to have collected at the bottom of these craters. This image shows the possible location of such ice.

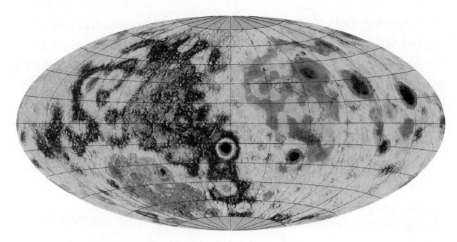

Figure 17
This computer-enhanced map based on *Clementine* data indicates the thickness of the Moon's crust. The crust of the side of the Moon facing Earth, shown mostly in red, is thinner than the crust on the far side of the Moon.

Mapping the Moon

A large part of *Clementine's* mission included taking high-resolution photographs so a detailed map of the Moon's surface could be compiled. Because the five cameras mounted on *Clementine* were able to resolve features as small as 200 m across, human knowledge of the Moon's surface increased immensely. One image resulting from other *Clementine* data is shown in **Figure 17.** It shows that the crust on the side of the Moon that faces Earth is much thinner than the crust on the far side. Additional information shows that the Moon's crust is thinnest under impact basins. Based on analysis of the light data received from *Clementine,* a global map of the Moon also was created that shows its composition, as seen in **Figure 18.**

✔ **Reading Check** *What information about the Moon did scientists learn from* Clementine?

The Lunar Prospector The success of *Clementine* at a relatively low cost opened the door for further Moon missions. In 1998, NASA launched the desk-sized *Lunar Prospector* into lunar orbit to collect more information about the lunar surface. The spacecraft spent a year orbiting the Moon from pole to pole, once every two hours. The resulting maps confirmed the *Clementine* data. The *Lunar Prospector* was scheduled to conduct a detailed study of the Moon from 100 km above the surface and to look for clues about its origin and makeup.

Figure 18
One of *Clementine's* main missions was to map the Moon. The different colors in this map represent the different types of lunar surface material, because not all parts of the Moon are made up of the same materials. This is the side of the Moon that faces Earth.

Icy Poles Early data from the *Lunar Prospector,* shown in **Figure 19,** indicate hydrogen is present in crater rocks at the Moon's poles. Hydrogen is one of the two elements in water. This information, combined with data from *Clementine,* has led scientists to hypothesize that ice may exist in the floors of craters at both Moon poles. These deep craters are cold because sunlight never reaches their floors. Temperatures are as low as −233°C. They are definitely cold enough to have preserved any ice that may have collected from colliding comets. Scientists estimate that 6 billion tons of ice might lie buried under 40 cm of crushed rock at the Moon's poles.

When the *Lunar Prospector* mission ended in July of 1999, it still was unknown whether the hydrogen was from water on the Moon or some other source, such as solar wind. NASA decided to crash the spacecraft into a crater at the Moon's south pole that might contain ice. The scientists hoped that the crash would release large quantities of water vapor that might be detected with special telescopes on Earth. The chance of this experiment working was considered slight, and the results were inconclusive. Water might exist on the Moon, but additional research will be needed before definite conclusions can be drawn. However, data from the *Lunar Prospector* have enabled scientists to confirm that the Moon has a small, iron-rich core about 600 km in diameter. The fact that the Moon has such a small core supports the impact theory of its origin because only small amounts of iron would have been blasted off the primitive Earth. Most of Earth's iron would have remained deep in the planet's interior.

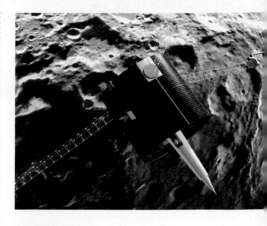

Figure 19
The *Lunar Prospector* provided data indicating that ice might exist at the Moon's poles. Further investigation will reveal whether or not this is true.

Section 3 Assessment

1. List two discoveries about the Moon made by *Clementine.*

2. What was the main mission of the *Lunar Prospector?*

3. How did studies of the Moon change after the 1950s?

4. What was the goal of the *Surveyor* and *Apollo* missions? How did these missions further scientists' studies of the Moon?

5. **Think Critically** Why would the discovery of ice at the Moon's poles be important to future space flights?

Skill Builder Activities

6. **Concept Mapping** Sequence the following Moon missions in the order they occurred: *Lunar Prospector, Apollo, Lunar Orbiter, Ranger,* and *Clementine.* **For more help, refer to the Science Skill Handbook.**

7. **Using Fractions** The Moon's orbit is tilted at an angle of 5° to Earth's orbit around the Sun. Using a protractor draw the Moon's orbit around Earth. What fraction of a full circle (360°) is 5°? **For more help, refer to the Math Skill Handbook.**

Activity

Tilt and Temperature

If you walk barefeet on blacktop pavement at noon, you can feel the effect of solar energy. The Sun's rays hit most directly at midday. Now consider the fact that Earth is tilted on its axis. How does this tilt affect how directly light rays strike an area on Earth? How is the angle of the light rays related to the amount of heat energy and the changing seasons?

What You'll Investigate

How does the angle at which light strikes Earth affect the amount of heat energy received by any area on Earth?

Materials

tape
black construction paper (one sheet)
gooseneck lamp with 75-watt bulb
celsius thermometer
watch
protractor

Goals

■ **Measure** the temperature change in a surface after light strikes it at different angles.
■ **Describe** how the angle of light relates to seasons on Earth.

Safety Precautions

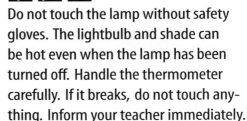

Do not touch the lamp without safety gloves. The lightbulb and shade can be hot even when the lamp has been turned off. Handle the thermometer carefully. If it breaks, do not touch anything. Inform your teacher immediately.

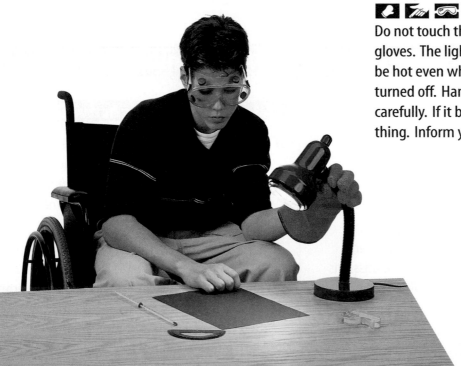

Procedure

1. Choose three angles that you will use to aim the light at the paper.

2. **Determine** how long you will shine the light at each angle before you measure the temperature. Measure the temperature at two times for each angle. Use the same time periods for each angle.

3. Copy the following data table into your Science Journal and fill in the temperature the paper reached at each angle and time.

4. Tape a sheet of black construction paper to a desk or the floor.

5. Using the protractor, set the gooseneck lamp so that it will shine on the paper at one of the angles you chose.

6. Turn on the lamp. Use the thermometer to measure the temperature of the paper at the end of the first time period. Continue shining the lamp on the paper until the second time period has passed. Measure the temperature again. Record your data in your data table.

7. Turn off the lamp until the paper cools to room temperature. Repeat steps 5 and 6 using your other two angles.

Temperature Data			
Angle of Lamp	Initial Temperature	Temperature at ____ Minutes/Seconds	Temperature at ____ Minutes/Seconds
First angle			
Second angle			
Third angle			

Conclude and Apply

1. **Describe** your experiment. Identify the variables in your experiment. Which were your independent and dependent variables?

2. **Graph** your data using a line graph. Describe what your graph tells you about the data.

3. What happened to the temperature of the paper as you changed the angle of light?

4. **Predict** how your results might have been different if you used white paper. Explain why.

5. **Describe** how the results of this experiment apply to seasons on Earth.

Communicating
Your Data

Compare your results with those of other students in your class. **Discuss** how the different angles and time periods affected the temperatures.

UNITED STATES

GULF OF MEXICO

North America

MEXICO

CUBA

Chichén Itzá

South America

Australia

An ancient people used many calendars to track time and to help them in everyday life

THE Mayan Calendar

Most people don't give the setup of calendars a second thought. They take for granted that a week is seven days, and that a year is 12 months. But this wasn't always the case. Roughly 1,750 years ago, in what is now south Mexico and Central America, the Mayan people invented a sophisticated calendar system. Their system used observations of Sun and Moon cycles to help them figure out time. They also developed a sophisticated mathematical system where single units are written with dots, and bars are used to represent five single units.

The Mayans had several calendars that they used at the same time. Two were most important. One was based on 260 days, the other on 365 days. The calendars were so accurate and useful that later civilizations, including the Aztecs, adopted them.

These glyphs represent four different days of the *Tzolkin* calendar.

The 260-Day Calendar

One calendar, called the *Tzolkin* (tz uhl KIN), was based on the planting, harvesting, drying, and storing of corn—the main crop of the Mayans. Each day of the *Tzolkin* had one of 20 names, as well as a number from 1 to 13. Each day also had a Mayan god associated with it.

Mayan priests used this calendar to determine the dates of religious festivals. The priests also used it to help decide when to go to war and what to name children. Just as important, the Mayans used the *Tzolkin* for timing their planting and harvesting.

The 365-Day Calendar

Another Mayan calendar was called the *Haab* (HAHB) and was based on the orbit of Earth around the Sun. It was divided into 18 months with 20 days each, plus five extra days at the end of each year. The 260-day *Tzolkin* calendar fit into the 365-day *Haab* year, so the Mayans used both calendars at once.

Used together, these calendars made the Mayans the most accurate reckoners of time before the modern period. In fact, they were only one day off every 6,000 years. Their idea of measuring time by Earth moving around the Sun is the basis for our calendar today.

This calendar was carved more than 1,000 years ago by an unknown Mayan.

Kukulkan (*left*), built around the year 1050, was used by the Mayans as a calendar. It had four stairways, each with 91 steps. Including the platform on top, the total number of steps is 365, the number of days in a year. You can see this pyramid if you visit Chichén Itzá in Mexico.

CONNECTIONS Drawing Symbols The Mayans created picture symbols for each day of their week. Historians call these symbols glyphs. Collaborate with another student to invent seven glyphs—one for each day of the week. Compare them with other glyphs on the Glencoe Science Web site.

Online
For more information, visit
science.glencoe.com

Reviewing Main Ideas

Section 1 Earth

1. Earth is a sphere that bulges slightly at its equator.

2. Earth rotates once per day and completes its orbit around the Sun in a little more than 365 days.

3. Earth has a magnetic field like that of a bar magnet.

4. Seasons on Earth are caused by the tilt of Earth's axis and its revolution around the Sun. Because Earth's axis is tilted, the amount of solar energy each hemisphere receives varies throughout the year, causing the seasons.

Section 2 The Moon—Earth's Satellite

1. Earth's Moon goes through phases that depend on the relative positions of the Sun, the Moon, and Earth. *What are the relative positions of the Sun, Earth, and the Moon during a new moon?*

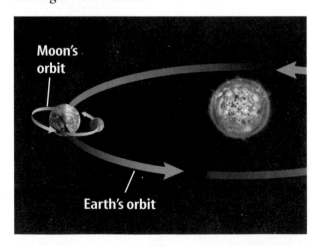

2. Eclipses occur when Earth or the Moon temporarily blocks sunlight from reaching the other. A solar eclipse occurs when the Moon moves directly between the Sun and Earth. A lunar eclipse occurs when Earth's shadow falls on the Moon.

3. The Moon's maria are the result of ancient lava flows. Craters on the Moon's surface formed from impacts with meteorites, asteroids, and comets. *What is the Moon's surface like?*

Section 3 Exploring Earth's Moon

1. The *Clementine* spacecraft took detailed, high-resolution photographs of the Moon's surface.

2. Data from *Clementine* indicate that the Moon's South Pole-Aitken Basin may contain ice deposits that could supply water for a Moon colony. *What could people living on the Moon do with water?*

3. NASA continued exploring the Moon with the *Lunar Prospector.* Data from *Lunar Prospector* lend support to the ice theory.

After You Read

FOLDABLES
Reading & Study Skills

Exchange Foldables with a classmate and quiz each other. Ask questions that can be answered with the information in your classmate's Foldable.

Visualizing Main Ideas

Complete the following concept map on Moon formation.

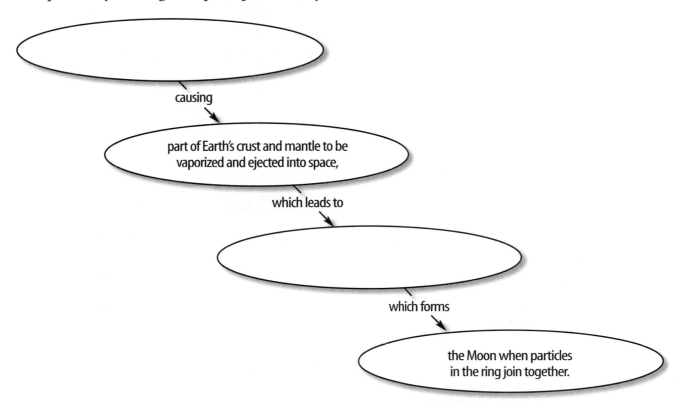

causing

part of Earth's crust and mantle to be vaporized and ejected into space,

which leads to

which forms

the Moon when particles in the ring join together.

Vocabulary Review

Vocabulary Words

a. axis
b. ellipse
c. equinox
d. full moon
e. impact basin
f. lunar eclipse
g. maria
h. moon phase
i. new moon
j. revolution
k. rotation
l. solar eclipse
m. solstice
n. sphere
o. waning
p. waxing

THE PRINCETON REVIEW **Study Tip**

Practice reading graphs and charts. Make a table that contains the same information that a graph does.

Using Vocabulary

Replace each underlined word with the correct vocabulary word.

1. The spinning of Earth around its axis is called <u>revolution</u>.

2. The <u>equinox</u> is the point at which the Sun reaches its greatest distance north or south of the equator.

3. The Moon is said to be <u>waxing</u> when the portion of the lighted side that can be seen becomes smaller.

4. The depression left behind by an object striking the Moon is called an <u>ellipse</u>.

5. Earth's orbit is an <u>eclipse</u>.

Chapter ② Assessment

Checking Concepts

Choose the word or phrase that best answers the question.

1. How long does it take for the Moon to rotate once?
   A) 24 hours
   C) 27.3 hours
   B) 365 days
   D) 27.3 days

2. Where is Earth's circumference greatest?
   A) equator
   C) poles
   B) mantle
   D) axis

3. During an equinox, the Sun is directly over what part of Earth?
   A) southern hemisphere
   B) northern hemisphere
   C) equator
   D) pole

4. What causes the Sun to appear to rise and set?
   A) Earth's revolution
   B) the Sun's revolution
   C) Earth's rotation
   D) Earth's elliptical orbit

5. How long does it take for the Moon to revolve once around Earth?
   A) 24 hours
   C) 27.3 hours
   B) 365 days
   D) 27.3 days

6. What is it called when the lighted portion of the Moon appears to get larger?
   A) waning
   C) rotating
   B) waxing
   D) crescent shaped

7. What kind of eclipse occurs when the Moon blocks sunlight from reaching Earth?
   A) solar
   C) full
   B) new
   D) lunar

8. What is the darkest part of the shadow during an eclipse?
   A) waxing gibbous
   C) waning gibbous
   B) umbra
   D) penumbra

9. What is the name for a depression on the Moon caused by an object striking its surface?
   A) eclipse
   C) phase
   B) moonquake
   D) impact basin

10. What fact does data gathered from the *Clementine* spacecraft support?
    A) The Moon rotates once in 29.5 days.
    B) The Moon has a thinner crust on the side facing Earth.
    C) The Moon revolves once in 29.5 days.
    D) The Moon has no crust.

Thinking Critically

11. How would the Moon appear to an observer in space during its revolution? Would phases be observable? Explain.

12. What would be the effect on Earth's seasons if the axis were tilted at 28.5° instead of 23.5°?

13. Seasons in the two hemispheres are opposite. Explain how this supports the statement that seasons are NOT caused by Earth's changing distance from the Sun.

14. How would solar eclipses be different if the Moon were twice as far from Earth? Explain.

15. Which observed motions of the Moon are real? Which are apparent? Explain.

Developing Skills

16. **Predicting** Predict how the information gathered by Moon missions could be helpful in the future for people wanting to establish a colony on the Moon.

17. **Using Variables, Constants, and Controls** Describe a simple activity to show how the Moon's rotation and revolution work to keep the same side facing Earth at all times.

18. Comparing and Contrasting Compare and contrast a waning moon and a waxing moon.

19. Concept Mapping Copy and complete the cycle concept map shown on this page. Show the sequence of the Moon's phases.

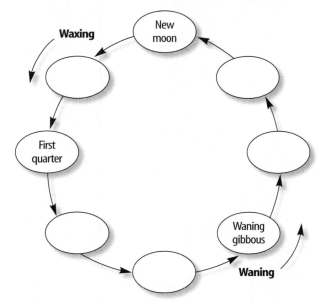

20. Hypothesizing Gravity is weaker on the Moon than it is on Earth. Use this fact to help you form a hypothesis as to why more craters are present on the far side of the Moon than on the side facing Earth.

Performance Assessment

21. Poem Write a poem in which you describe the various surface features of the Moon. Be sure to include information on how these features formed. Share your poem with others.

TECHNOLOGY

Go to the Glencoe Science Web site at **science.glencoe.com** or use the **Glencoe Science CD-ROM** for additional chapter assessment.

 **Test Practice**

The diagram below shows one complete lunar cycle.

1 **2** **3** **4** **5**

Study the picture and answer the following questions.

1. About how long does it take the Moon to complete the cycle shown above?
A) one hour
B) one day
C) one month
D) one year

2. Which phase of the Moon shown above does not reflect any sunlight toward Earth?
A) 1
B) 2
C) 3
D) 4

3. At which phase could a solar eclipse occur?
A) 1
B) 2
C) 3
D) 4

4. Which of the above phases is first quarter?
A) 1
B) 2
C) 3
D) 4

The Solar System

Did you know that some of the brightest objects in the night sky are not stars at all but other planets in the solar system? A planetarium, such as New York's Hayden Planetarium pictured here, is a place where people can go to learn about objects in space. In this chapter, you will learn about the solar system's planets and how they are being explored. You also will learn about other objects such as comets, meteoroids, and asteroids.

What do you think?

Science Journal Look at the picture below with a classmate. Discuss what you think this might be or what is happening. Here's a hint: *Death sometimes can foster new birth.* Write down your answer or best guess in your Science Journal.

The planets of the solar system are like neighbors in space, but to humans on Earth, they look like tiny points of light among the thousands of others visible on a clear night. With the help of telescopes and space probes, the points of light become giant spheres, some with rings and moons and others pitted with countless craters. In this activity, you'll explore how craters are formed on the surfaces of planets and moons.

Model crater formation

1. Place white flour into a metal cake pan to a depth of 3 cm, completely covering the bottom of the pan.

2. Cover the flour with 1 cm of colored powdered drink mix or different colors of gelatin powder.

3. From different heights ranging from 10 cm to 25 cm, drop various-sized objects into the pan. Use marbles, bolts, and nuts.

Observe

In your Science Journal, make a drawing that shows what happened to the surface of the powder in the pan when each object was dropped from different heights.

Before You Read

FOLDABLES
Reading & Study Skills

Making a Compare and Contrast Study Fold As you study this chapter, use this Foldable to compare and contrast inner planets and outer planets. When you compare two things, you say how they are similar. When you contrast two things, you say how they are different.

INNER PLANETS   OUTER PLANETS

1. Place a sheet of paper in front of you so the long side is at the top. Fold the paper in half from the left side to the right side and then unfold.

2. Fold each side in to the centerfold line to divide the paper into fourths.

3. Write "Inner Planets" on one flap and "Outer Planets" on the other.

4. On the back of each flap, contrast inner planets and outer planets.

5. Under the flaps in the center section, compare inner planets and outer planets.

The Solar System

Ideas About the Solar System

On a clear night, gazing at the sky can be an awe-inspiring experience. Early observers who noted the changing positions of the planets presented differing ideas about the solar system based on their observations and beliefs. Today, people know that the Sun and the stars only appear to move through the sky because Earth is moving. This wasn't always an accepted fact.

Earth-Centered Model Many early Greek scientists thought the planets, the Sun, and the Moon were fixed in separate spheres that rotated around Earth. The stars were thought to be fixed in another sphere that also rotated around Earth.

This is called the Earth-centered model of the solar system. It included Earth, the Moon, the Sun, five planets—Mercury, Venus, Mars, Jupiter, and Saturn—and the sphere of stars.

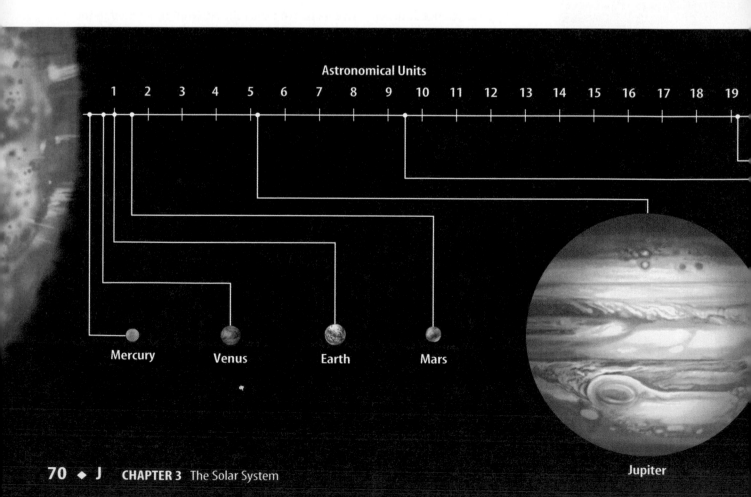

Astronomical Units

| 1 | 2 | 3 | 4 | 5 | 6 | 7 | 8 | 9 | 10 | 11 | 12 | 13 | 14 | 15 | 16 | 17 | 18 | 19 |

Mercury Venus Earth Mars

Jupiter

Sun-Centered Model People believed the idea of an Earth-centered solar system for centuries. Then in 1543, Polish astronomer Nicholas Copernicus published a different view.

Copernicus stated that the Moon revolved around Earth and that Earth and the other planets revolved around the Sun. He also stated that the daily movement of the planets and the stars was due to Earth's rotation. This is the Sun-centered model of the solar system.

Using his telescope, Italian astronomer Galileo Galilei observed that Venus went through a full cycle of phases like the Moon's, which could be explained only if Venus were orbiting the Sun. From this, he concluded that Venus revolves around the Sun and that the Sun is the center of the solar system.

Modern View of the Solar System We now know that the **solar system** is made up of nine planets, including Earth, and many smaller objects that orbit the Sun. The nine planets and the Sun are shown in **Figure 1.** Notice how small Earth is compared with some of the other planets and the Sun.

The solar system includes a huge volume of space that stretches in all directions from the Sun. The Sun contains 99.86 percent of the mass of the solar system. Because of its gravitational pull, the Sun is the central object in the solar system. All other objects in the solar system revolve around the Sun.

Figure 1
Each of the nine planets in the solar system is unique. The distances between the planets and the Sun are shown on the scale. One astronomical unit (AU) is the average distance between Earth and the Sun.

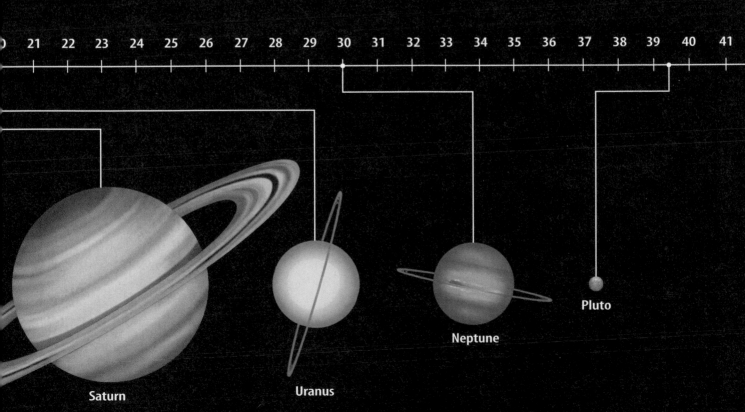

Saturn   Uranus   Neptune   Pluto

How the Solar System Formed

Scientists hypothesize that the solar system formed from part of a nebula of gas, ice, and dust, like the one shown in **Figure 2,** about 4.6 billion years ago. Follow the steps shown in **Figures 3A** through **3D,** which illustrate how this might have happened. A cloud of material in this nebula was rotating slowly in space. A nearby star might have exploded, and the shock waves from this event could have caused the cloud to start contracting. As it contracted, the matter in the cloud was squeezed into less space. The cloud's density became greater, and the attraction of gravity pulled more gas and dust toward the cloud center. This caused the cloud to rotate faster, which in turn caused it to flatten into a disk with a dense center.

As the cloud contracted, its temperature began to increase. Eventually, the temperature in the core of the cloud reached about 10 million degrees Celsius and nuclear fusion began. A star was born—the beginning of the Sun.

Nuclear fusion occurs when atoms with low mass, such as hydrogen, combine to form heavier elements, such as helium. The new, heavier element contains slightly less mass than the sum of the lighter atoms that formed it. The "lost" mass is converted into energy.

✔ **Reading Check** *At what temperature does nuclear fusion begin?*

Planet Formation Not all of the nearby gas, ice, and dust was drawn into the core of the cloud. The matter that did not get pulled into the cloud's center collided and stuck together to form the planets and asteroids. Close to the Sun, the temperature was hot, and the easily vaporized elements could not condense into solids. This is why lighter elements are scarcer in the planets near the Sun than in planets farther out in the solar system.

The inner planets of the solar system—Mercury, Venus, Earth, and Mars—are small, rocky planets with iron cores. The outer planets are Jupiter, Saturn, Uranus, Neptune, and Pluto. Pluto, a small planet, is the only outer planet made mostly of rock and ice. The other outer planets are much larger and are made mostly of lighter substances such as hydrogen, helium, methane, and ammonia.

Figure 2
Systems of planets such as the solar system form in areas of space like this, called a nebula.

Figure 3

Through careful observations, astronomers have found clues that help explain how the solar system may have formed. **A** About 4.6 billion years ago, the solar system was a vast, swirling cloud of gas, ice, and dust. **B** Gradually, part of the nebula contracted into a large, tightly packed, spinning disk. The disk's center was so hot and dense that nuclear fusion reactions began to occur, and the Sun was born. **C** Eventually, the rest of the material in the disk cooled enough to clump into scattered solids. **D** Finally, these clumps collided and combined to become the nine planets that make up the solar system today.

Table 1 Average Orbital Speed

Planet	Average Orbital Speed (km/s)
Mercury	48
Venus	35
Earth	30
Mars	24
Jupiter	13
Saturn	9.7
Uranus	6.8
Neptune	5.4
Pluto	4.7

Motions of the Planets

Physics INTEGRATION

When Nicholas Copernicus developed his Sun-centered model of the solar system, he thought that the planets orbited the Sun in circles. In the early 1600s, German mathematician Johannes Kepler began studying the orbits of the planets. He discovered that the shapes of the orbits are not circular. They are oval shaped, or elliptical.

His calculations further showed that the Sun is not at the center of the orbits but is slightly offset.

Kepler also discovered that the planets travel at different speeds in their orbits around the Sun, as shown in **Table 1.** By studying these speeds, you can see that the planets closer to the Sun travel faster than planets farther away from the Sun. Because of their slower speeds and the longer distance they must travel, the outer planets take much longer to orbit the Sun than the inner planets do.

Copernicus's ideas, considered radical at the time, led to the birth of modern astronomy. Early scientists didn't have technology such as computers and space probes to perform rapid calculations and learn about the planets. Nevertheless, they developed theories about the solar system that still are used today.

Johannes Kepler

Section Assessment

1. Describe the Sun-centered model of the solar system.

2. How do most scientists hypothesize that the solar system formed?

3. The outer planets are rich in water, methane, and ammonia—the materials needed for life. Yet life is unlikely on these planets. Explain.

4. Why do the outer planets take longer to orbit the Sun than the inner planets do?

5. **Think Critically** Would a year on the planet Neptune be longer or shorter than an Earth year? Explain.

Skill Builder Activities

6. **Concept Mapping** Make a concept map that compares and contrasts the Earth-centered model with the Sun-centered model of the solar system. **For more help, refer to the Science Skill Handbook.**

7. **Solving One-Step Equations** Use the average-orbital-speed data in **Table 1** to determine how much faster Mercury travels in its orbit than Earth travels in its orbit. How much faster does Mars travel than Neptune? How much faster does Earth travel than Pluto? **For more help, refer to the Math Skill Handbook.**

Activity

Planetary Orbits

Planets travel around the Sun along fixed paths called orbits. As you construct a model of a planetary orbit, you will observe that the shape of planetary orbits is an ellipse.

What You'll Investigate
How can you model planetary orbits?

Materials
thumbtacks or pins (2)   metric ruler
cardboard (23 cm × 30 cm)   string (25 cm)
paper (21.5 cm × 28 cm)   pencil

Goals
■ **Model** planetary orbits.
■ **Calculate** changes in ellipses.

Safety Precautions

Procedure

1. Place a blank sheet of paper on top of the cardboard and insert two thumbtacks or pins about 3 cm apart.

2. Tie the string into a circle with a circumference of 15 cm to 20 cm. Loop the string around the thumbtacks. With someone holding the tacks or pins, place your pencil inside the loop and pull it tight.

3. Moving the pencil around the tacks and keeping the string tight, mark a line until you have completed a smooth, closed curve, called an ellipse.

4. Repeat steps 1 through 3 several times. First, vary the distance between the tacks, then vary the length of the string. However, change only one of these each time. Make a data table to record the changes in the sizes and shapes of the ellipses.

5. Orbits usually are described in terms of eccentricity, *e.* The eccentricity of any ellipse is determined by dividing the distance, *d,* between the foci (fixed points—here, the tacks) by the length, *l,* of the major axis. See the diagram below.

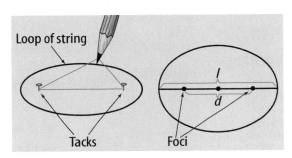

6. **Calculate** and record the eccentricity of the ellipses that you constructed.

7. **Research** the eccentricities of planetary orbits. Construct an ellipse with the same eccentricity as Earth's orbit.

Conclude and Apply

1. **Analyze** the effect that a change in the length of the string or the distance between the tacks has on the shape of the ellipse.

2. **Hypothesize** what must be done to the string or placement of tacks to decrease the eccentricity of a constructed ellipse.

3. **Describe** the shape of Earth's orbit. Where is the Sun located within the orbit?

Compare your results with those of other students. **For more help, refer to the Science Skill Handbook.**

The Inner Planets

What You'll Learn
- **List** the inner planets in their relative order from the Sun.
- **Describe** important characteristics of each inner planet.
- **Compare and contrast** Venus and Earth.

Vocabulary
Mercury   Earth
Venus   Mars

Why It's Important
The planet you live on is uniquely capable of sustaining life.

Figure 4
Large cliffs on Mercury might have formed when the crust of the planet broke as the planet contracted.

Inner Planets

Today, people know more about the solar system than ever before. Better telescopes allow astronomers to observe the planets from Earth and space. In addition, space probes have explored much of the solar system. Prepare to take a tour of the solar system through the eyes of some space probes.

Mercury The closest planet to the Sun is **Mercury.** It is also the second-smallest planet. The first American spacecraft mission to Mercury was in 1974–1975 by *Mariner 10*. The spacecraft flew by the planet and sent pictures back to Earth. *Mariner 10* photographed only 45 percent of Mercury's surface, so scientists don't know what the other 55 percent looks like. What they do know is that the surface of Mercury has many craters and looks much like Earth's Moon. It also has cliffs as high as 3 km on its surface. These cliffs may have formed at a time when Mercury apparently shrank in diameter, as seen in **Figure 4.**

Why would Mercury have shrunk? *Mariner 10* detected a weak magnetic field around Mercury. This indicates that the planet has an iron core. Some scientists hypothesize that the crust of Mercury solidified while the iron core was still hot and molten.

As the core cooled and solidified, it contracted. The cliffs might have resulted from breaks in the crust caused by this contraction.

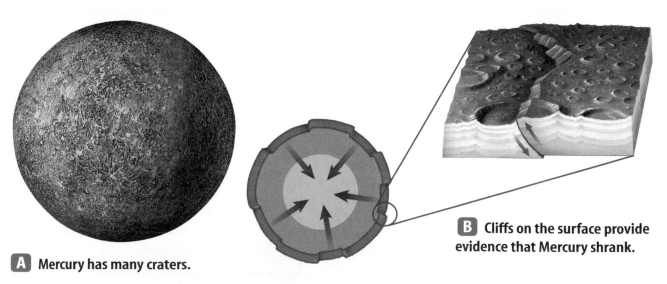

A Mercury has many craters.

B Cliffs on the surface provide evidence that Mercury shrank.

Does Mercury have an atmosphere? Because of Mercury's small size and low gravitational pull, most gases that could form an atmosphere escape into space. *Mariner 10* found traces of gases that were first thought to be an atmosphere. However, these gases are now known to be temporarily trapped hydrogen and helium from the solar wind. Mercury traps these gases and holds them for just a few weeks.

Earth-based observations have also found traces of sodium and potassium around Mercury. Scientists think that these atoms come from rocks in the planet's crust. Therefore, Mercury has no true atmosphere. This lack of atmosphere and the nearness of Mercury to the Sun cause this planet to have great extremes in temperature. Mercury's surface temperature can reach 425°C during the day and it can drop to −170°C at night.

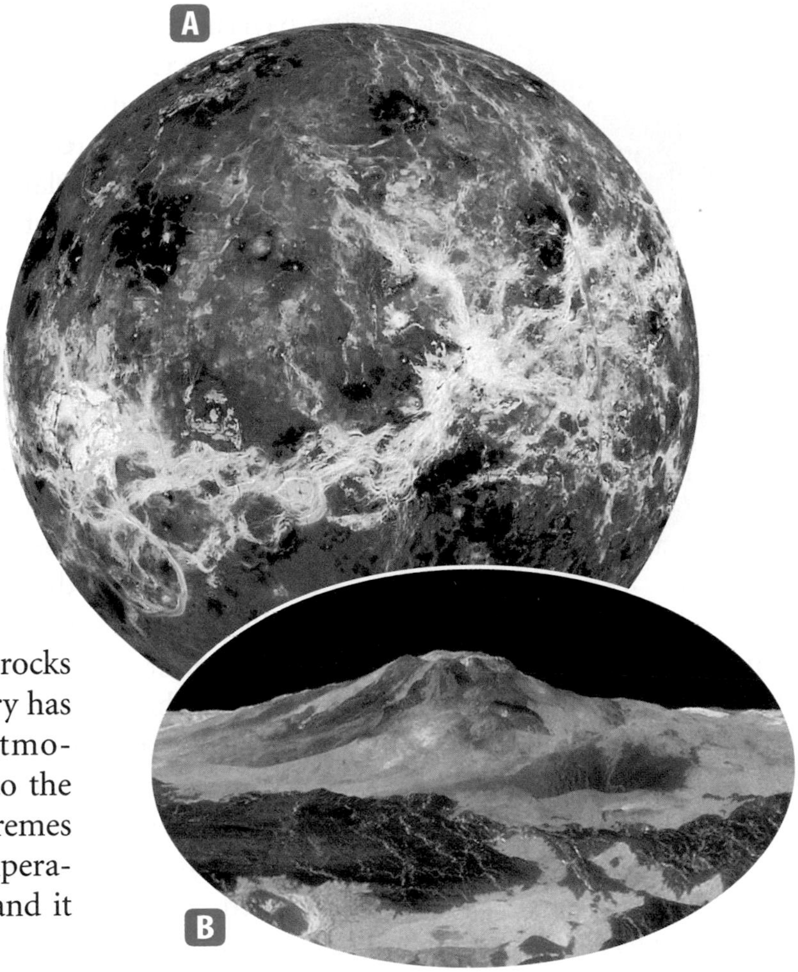

Venus The second planet from the Sun is **Venus,** shown in **Figure 5A.** Venus is sometimes called Earth's twin because its size and mass are similar to Earth's. In 1962, *Mariner 2* flew within 34,400 km of Venus and sent back information about Venus's atmosphere and rotation. The former Soviet Union landed the first probe on the surface of Venus in 1970. *Venera 7,* however, stopped working in less than an hour because of the high temperature and pressure. Additional *Venera* probes photographed and mapped the surface of Venus using cameras and radar. Between 1990 and 1994, the U.S. *Magellan* probe used its radar to make the most detailed maps yet of Venus's surface. It collected radar images of 98 percent of Venus's surface. Notice the huge volcano with visible lava flows shown in **Figure 5B.**

Clouds on Venus are so dense that only a small percentage of the sunlight that strikes the top of the clouds reaches the planet's surface. Much of the solar energy that does reach the surface is trapped by carbon dioxide gas in Venus's atmosphere. This causes a greenhouse effect similar to, but more intense than, Earth's greenhouse effect. Due to this intense greenhouse effect, the temperature on the surface of Venus is between 450°C and 475°C.

Figure 5
A This radar image of Venus's surface was made from data acquired by *Magellan*. **B** Maat Mons is the highest volcano on Venus. Lava flows extend for hundreds of kilometers across the plains.

Mars's Atmosphere The *Viking* and *Global Surveyor* probes analyzed gases in the Martian atmosphere and determined atmospheric pressure and temperature. They found that Mars's atmosphere is much thinner than Earth's. It is composed mostly of carbon dioxide, with some nitrogen and argon. Surface temperatures range from −125°C to 35°C. The temperature difference between day and night results in strong winds on the planet, which can cause global dust storms during certain seasons. This information will help in planning possible human exploration of Mars in the future.

Martian Seasons Mars is tilted on its axis by 25°, which is close to Earth's tilt of 23.5°. Because of this, Mars goes through seasons as it orbits the Sun, just like Earth does. The polar ice caps get larger during the Martian winter as ice collects on their surface. The ice caps shrink during the summer. As one ice cap shrinks, the other expands, and both their surfaces change color during different seasons. Wind causes this seasonal change in the coloration of the Martian surface. When the seasons change, winds blow the dust around on the planet's surface. As dust blows off one area, it might look darker.

Math Skills Activity

Calculating with Percentages

Example Problem

The diameter of Earth is 12,756 km. The diameter of Mars is 53.3 percent of the diameter of Earth. Calculate the diameter of Mars.

Solution

1 *This is what you know:*

diameter of Earth: 12,756 km
percent of Earth's diameter: 53.3%
decimal equivalent: 0.533 (53.3% ÷ 100)

2 *This is what you need to find:*   diameter of Mars

3 *This is the equation you need to use:*   (diameter of Earth) × (decimal equivalent) = diameter of Mars

4 *Solve the equation for the diameter of Mars:*   (12,756 km) × (0.533) = 6,799 km

> **Practice Problem**
>
> Use the same procedure to calculate the diameter of Venus. Its diameter is 94.9 percent of the diameter of Earth.

For more help, refer to the Math Skill Handbook.

Martian Moons Mars has two small, irregularly shaped moons that are heavily cratered. Phobos, shown in **Figure 9,** is about 25 km in length, and Deimos is about 13 km in length. Deimos orbits Mars once every 31 h, while Phobos speeds around Mars once every 7 h.

Phobos has grooves on its surface that seem to radiate out in all directions from the giant Stickney Crater. Some of the grooves are 700 m across and 90 m deep. Phobos's orbit is spiraling slowly inward toward Mars. It is expected to crash into the Martian surface in about 50 million years.

Deimos is the outer of Mars's two moons. It is among the smallest known moons in the solar system. Its surface is smoother in appearance than that of Phobos because some of its craters have partially filled with soil and rock.

As you toured the inner planets through the eyes of the space probes, you saw how each planet is unique. Refer to **Table 3** following Section 3 for a summary of the planets. Mercury, Venus, Earth, and Mars are different from the outer planets, which you'll explore in the next section.

Figure 9
Phobos orbits Mars once every 7 h. *Why does Phobos have so many craters?*

Section Assessment

1. How are Mercury and Earth's Moon similar?
2. List one important characteristic of each inner planet.
3. Although Venus often is called Earth's twin, why would life as you know it be unlikely on Venus?
4. Name the inner planets in order from the Sun.
5. **Think Critically** Do the closest planets to the Sun always have the hottest surface temperatures? Explain.

Skill Builder Activities

6. **Interpreting Data** Using the information in this section, explain how Mars is like Earth. How are they different? **For more help, refer to the Science Skill Handbook.**

7. **Communicating** Use textbooks and NASA materials to investigate NASA's missions to Mars. In your Science Journal, report on the possibility of life on Mars and the tests that have been conducted to see whether life-forms exist. **For more help, refer to the Science Skill Handbook.**

The Outer Planets

As You Read

What You'll Learn

- **Describe** the major characteristics of Jupiter, Saturn, Uranus, and Neptune.
- **Explain** how Pluto differs from the other outer planets.

Vocabulary

Jupiter	Uranus
Great Red Spot	Neptune
Saturn	Pluto

Why It's Important

Studying the outer planets might help scientists better understand Earth.

Figure 10
A Jupiter is the largest planet in the solar system, containing more mass than all of the other planets combined. **B** The Great Red Spot is a giant storm about 25,000 km in size from east to west.

Outer Planets

You may have heard about the *Voyager* and *Galileo* spacecrafts. They were not the first probes to the outer planets, but they gathered a lot of new information about them. Follow the spacecrafts as you read about their journeys to the outer planets.

Jupiter In 1979, *Voyager 1* and *Voyager 2* flew past **Jupiter,** the largest planet and the fifth planet from the Sun. *Galileo* reached Jupiter in 1995. The spacecrafts gathered new information about Jupiter's atmosphere and discovered three new moons. *Voyager* probes also revealed that Jupiter has faint dust rings around it and that one of its moons has volcanoes on it.

Jupiter's Atmosphere Jupiter is composed mostly of hydrogen and helium, with some ammonia, methane, and water vapor. Scientists hypothesize that the atmosphere of hydrogen and helium gradually changes to a planetwide ocean of liquid hydrogen and helium toward the middle of the planet. Below this liquid layer might be a solid rocky core. The extreme pressure and temperature, however, would make the core different from any rock on Earth.

You've probably seen pictures from the probes of Jupiter's colorful clouds. In **Figure 10,** you can see bands of white, red, tan, and brown clouds in its atmosphere. Continuous storms of swirling, high-pressure gas have been observed on Jupiter. The **Great Red Spot** is the most spectacular of these storms. Lightning also has been observed within Jupiter's clouds.

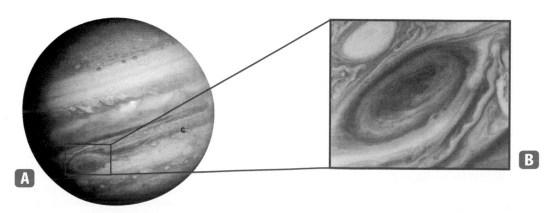

Table 2 Large Moons of Jupiter

 **Io** The most volcanically active object in the solar system; sulfurous compounds give it its distinctive reddish and orange colors; has a thin oxygen, sulfur, and sulfur dioxide atmosphere.

 **Europa** Rocky interior is covered by a 100-km-thick crust of ice, which has a network of cracks, indicating tectonic activity; an ocean might exist under the ice crust; has a thin oxygen atmosphere.

 **Ganymede** Has a crust of ice about 100 km thick, covered with grooves; crust might surround an ocean of water or slushy ice; has a rocky core and a thin oxygen atmosphere.

 **Callisto** Has a heavily cratered crust of ice and rock several hundred kilometers thick; crust might surround a salty ocean around a rock core; has a thin atmosphere of carbon dioxide.

Moons of Jupiter At least 28 moons orbit Jupiter. In 1610, the astronomer Galileo Galilei was the first person to see Jupiter's four largest moons, shown in **Table 2.** Io (I oh) is the closest large moon to Jupiter. Jupiter's tremendous gravitational force and the gravity of Europa, Jupiter's next large moon, pull on Io. This force heats up Io, causing it to be the most volcanically active object in the solar system. You can see a volcano erupting on Io in **Figure 11.** Europa is composed mostly of rock with a thick, smooth crust of ice. Under the ice might be an ocean as deep as 50 km. If this ocean of water exists, it will be the only place in the solar system, other than Earth and possibly Ganymede and Callisto, where liquid water exists in large quantities. Next is Ganymede, the largest moon in the solar system—larger even than the planet Mercury. Callisto, the last of Jupiter's large moons, is composed mostly of ice and rock. Studying these moons adds to knowledge about the origin of Earth and the rest of the solar system.

Figure 11
Voyager 2 photographed the eruption of this volcano on Io in July 1979.

Figure 12
Saturn's rings are composed of pieces of rock and ice.

Modeling Planets

Procedure
1. Research the planets to determine how the sizes of the planets in the solar system compare with each other.
2. Select a scale for the diameter of Earth.
3. Make a model by drawing a circle with this diameter on **paper.**
4. Using Earth's diameter as 1.0 unit, draw each of the other planets to scale.

Analysis
1. What would 1 AU be equal to in this model?
2. Using a scale of 1 AU = 2 m, how large would the models have to be to remain in scale?

Saturn The *Voyager* probes next surveyed Saturn in 1980 and 1981. **Saturn** is the sixth planet from the Sun. It is the second-largest planet in the solar system, but it has the lowest density. Its density is so low that the planet would float in water.

Saturn's Atmosphere Similar to Jupiter, Saturn is a large, gaseous planet. It has a thick outer atmosphere composed mostly of hydrogen and helium. Saturn's atmosphere also contains ammonia, methane, and water vapor. As you go deeper into Saturn's atmosphere, the gases gradually change to liquid hydrogen and helium. Below its atmosphere and liquid layer, Saturn might have a small, rocky core.

Rings and Moons The *Voyager* probes gathered new information about Saturn's ring system and its moons. The probes showed that Saturn has several broad rings. Each large ring is composed of thousands of thin ringlets. **Figure 12** shows that they are composed of countless ice and rock particles. These particles range in size from a speck of dust to tens of meters across. This makes Saturn's ring system the most complex of all the outer gaseous planets.

At least 30 moons orbit Saturn. The latest moons to be discovered orbiting Saturn were found using telescopes in Chile and Hawaii. Some scientists suggest that Saturn's gravity captured several of these moons as they passed nearby. The largest of Saturn's moons, Titan, is larger than the planet Mercury. It has an atmosphere of nitrogen, argon, and methane. Thick clouds prevent scientists from seeing the surface of Titan.

Uranus Beyond Saturn, Voyager 2 flew by Uranus in 1986. Uranus (YOOR uh nus) is the seventh planet from the Sun and was discovered in 1781. It is a large, gaseous planet with 21 satellites and a system of thin, dark rings. Three of its satellites were identified in 1999 from Earth-based observations. Most of the rings of Uranus are less than 10 km across. Two of Uranus's moons, Cordelia and Ophelia, keep the outer ring from dispersing into space.

Uranus's Characteristics The atmosphere of Uranus is composed of hydrogen, helium, and some methane. Methane gives the planet the bluish-green color that you see in **Figure 13.** Methane absorbs the red and yellow light, and the clouds reflect the green and blue. Few cloud bands and storm systems can be seen on Uranus. Evidence suggests that under its atmosphere, Uranus has a mantle of liquid and solid water, methane, and ammonia surrounding a rocky core.

Figure 14 shows one of the most unusual features of Uranus. Its axis of rotation is tilted on its side compared with the other planets. The axes of rotation of the other planets, except Pluto, are nearly perpendicular to the planes of their orbits. However, Uranus's axis of rotation is nearly parallel to the plane of its orbit. Some scientists believe a collision with another object tipped Uranus on its side.

Figure 13
The atmosphere of Uranus gives the planet its distinct bluish-green color.

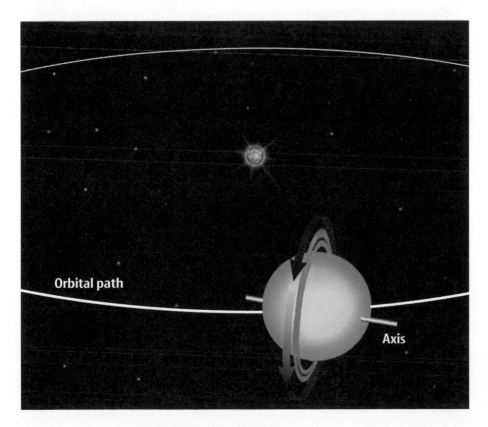

Orbital path

Axis

Figure 14
Uranus rotates on an axis nearly parallel to the plane of its orbit. During its revolution around the Sun, one of the poles, at times, points almost directly at the Sun.

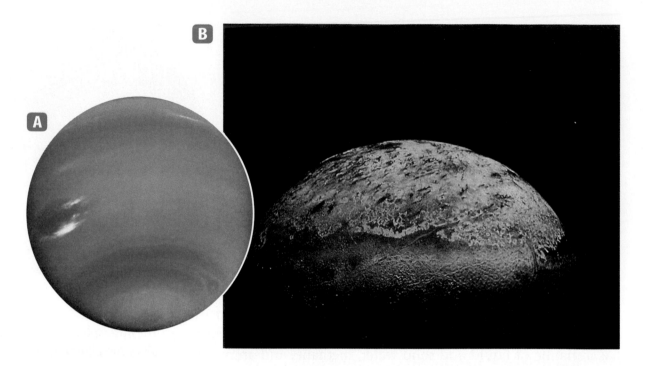

Figure 15

A Neptune has a distinctive bluish-green color. **B** The pinkish hue of Neptune's largest moon, Triton, is thought to come from an evaporating layer of nitrogen ice.

Physics INTEGRATION

All change requires energy. On Earth energy from the Sun powers hurricanes. However, hurricanes on Neptune probably get most of their energy from Neptune's interior. Do research and write a short paragraph comparing and contrasting hurricanes on Earth and storms on Neptune.

Neptune Passing Uranus, *Voyager 2* traveled to Neptune, another large, gaseous planet. Discovered in 1846, **Neptune** is usually the eighth planet from the Sun. However, Pluto's orbit crosses inside Neptune's during part of its voyage around the Sun. Between 1979 and 1999, Pluto was closer to the Sun than was Neptune. Early in 1999, Pluto once again became the farthest planet from the Sun.

Neptune's Characteristics Neptune's atmosphere is similar to Uranus's atmosphere. The methane content gives Neptune, shown in **Figure 15A,** its distinctive bluish-green color, just as it does for Uranus.

✔ **Reading Check** *What gives Neptune its bluish-green color?*

Neptune has dark-colored storms in its atmosphere that are similar to the Great Red Spot on Jupiter. One discovered by *Voyager 2* in 1989 was called the Great Dark Spot. It was about the size of Earth. However, observations by the *Hubble Space Telescope* in 1994 showed that the Great Dark Spot had disappeared. Bright clouds also form, then disappear in several hours. This shows that Neptune's atmosphere is active and changes rapidly.

Under its atmosphere, Neptune is thought to have a layer of liquid water, methane, and ammonia that might change to solid ice. Neptune probably has a rocky core.

Voyager 2 detected six new moons, so the total number of Neptune's known moons is now eight. Triton, shown in **Figure 15B,** is the largest. It has a thin atmosphere composed mostly of nitrogen.

Pluto The smallest planet in the solar system, and the one scientists know the least about, is Pluto. For 20 years of its 249-year orbit, Pluto is closer to the Sun than Neptune. However, because **Pluto** is farther from the Sun than Neptune during most of its orbit, it is considered to be the ninth planet from the Sun. From Pluto's surface, the Sun would appear as only a bright star. Pluto is vastly different from the other outer planets. It's surrounded by only a thin atmosphere, and it's the only outer planet with a solid, icy-rock surface.

Pluto's Moon Pluto's single moon, Charon, has a diameter about half the size of Pluto's. It was discovered in 1978 when a bulge was noticed on a photograph of the planet. Later photographs, taken with improved telescopes, showed that the bulge was a moon. Pluto and Charon are shown in **Figure 16.** Because of their close size and orbit, some scientists consider them to be a double planet.

Data from the *Hubble Space Telescope* indicate the presence of a vast disk of icy comets called the Kuiper Belt near Neptune's orbit. Some of the comets are hundreds of kilometers in diameter. Are Pluto and Charon members of this belt? Or did they simply form at the distance where they are? Scientists might not find out until a probe is sent to Pluto.

Figure 16
The *Hubble Space Telescope* gave astronomers their first clear view of Pluto and Charon as distinct objects.

Section Assessment

1. Describe the main differences between the outer planets and the inner planets.

2. Are any moons in the solar system larger than any planets? If so, which ones?

3. How does Pluto differ from the other outer planets? How is it similar to the inner planets?

4. Why are Pluto and Charon sometimes considered a double planet?

5. **Think Critically** Some scientists think life could exist on one of Jupiter's moons. On which moons would you look for life? Why?

Skill Builder Activities

6. **Recognizing Cause and Effect** Answer the following questions about Jupiter. **For more help, refer to the Science Skill Handbook.**
   a. How is the Great Red Spot affected by Jupiter's rotation?
   b. How does Jupiter's mass affect its gravitational force?

7. **Using Graphics Software** Use graphing software to plot each planet's average speed against its distance from the Sun. Describe the type of curve that is produced. **For more help, refer to the Technology Skill Handbook.**

Table 3 Planets

Mercury

- closest to the Sun
- second-smallest planet
- surface has many craters and high cliffs
- no atmosphere
- temperatures range from 425°C during the day to −170°C at night
- has no moons

Venus

- similar to Earth in size and mass
- thick atmosphere made mostly of carbon dioxide
- droplets of sulfuric acid in atmosphere give clouds a yellowish color
- surface has craters, faultlike cracks, and volcanoes
- greenhouse effect causes surface temperatures of 450°C to 475°C
- has no moons

Earth

- atmosphere protects life
- surface temperatures allow water to exist as solid, liquid, and gas
- only planet where life is known to exist
- has one large moon

Mars

- surface appears reddish-yellow because of iron oxide in rocks
- ice caps are made of frozen carbon dioxide and water
- channels indicate that water has flowed on the surface; has large volcanoes and valleys
- has a thin atmosphere composed mostly of carbon dioxide
- surface temperatures range from −125°C to 35°C
- huge dust storms often blanket the planet
- has two small moons

Jupiter

- largest planet
- has faint rings
- atmosphere is mostly hydrogen and helium; continuous storms swirl on the planet—the largest is the Great Red Spot
- has four large moons and at least 24 smaller moons; one of its moons, Io, has active volcanoes

Saturn

- second-largest planet
- thick atmosphere is mostly hydrogen and helium
- has a complex ring system
- has at least 30 moons—the largest, Titan, is larger than Mercury

Uranus

- large, gaseous planet with thin, dark rings
- atmosphere is hydrogen, helium, and methane
- axis of rotation is parallel to plane of orbit
- has at least 21 moons

Neptune

- large, gaseous planet with rings that vary in thickness
- is sometimes farther from the Sun than Pluto is
- methane in atmosphere causes its bluish-green color
- has dark-colored storms in atmosphere
- has eight moons

Pluto

- small, icy-rock planet with thin atmosphere
- single moon, Charon, is half the diameter of the planet

SECTION

4 Other Objects in the Solar System

As You Read

What You'll Learn
- **Describe** where comets come from and how a comet develops as it approaches the Sun.
- **Distinguish** among comets, meteoroids, and asteroids.

Vocabulary

comet   meteorite
meteor   asteroid

Why It's Important
Comets, meteoroids, and asteroids might be composed of material that formed early in the history of the solar system.

Figure 17
Comet Hale-Bopp was most visible in March and April 1997.

Comets

The planets and their moons are the most noticeable members of the Sun's family, but many other objects also orbit the Sun. Comets, meteoroids, and asteroids are important other objects in the solar system.

You might have heard of Halley's comet. A **comet** is composed of dust and rock particles mixed with frozen water, methane, and ammonia. Halley's comet was last seen from Earth in 1986. English astronomer Edmund Halley realized that comet sightings that had taken place about every 76 years were really sightings of the same comet. This comet, which takes about 76 years to orbit the Sun, was named after him. Halley's comet is just one example of the many other objects in the solar system besides the planets.

Oort Cloud Dutch astronomer Jan Oort proposed the idea that a large collection of comets lies in a cloud that completely surrounds the solar system. This cloud, called the Oort Cloud, is located beyond the orbit of Pluto. Oort suggested that the gravities of the Sun and nearby stars interact with comets in the Oort Cloud. Comets either escape from the solar system or get captured into smaller orbits.

Comet Hale-Bopp On July 23, 1995, two amateur astronomers made an exciting discovery. A new comet, Comet Hale-Bopp, was headed toward the Sun. Larger than most that approach the Sun, it was the brightest comet visible from Earth in 20 years. Shown in **Figure 17,** Comet Hale-Bopp was at its brightest in March and April 1997.

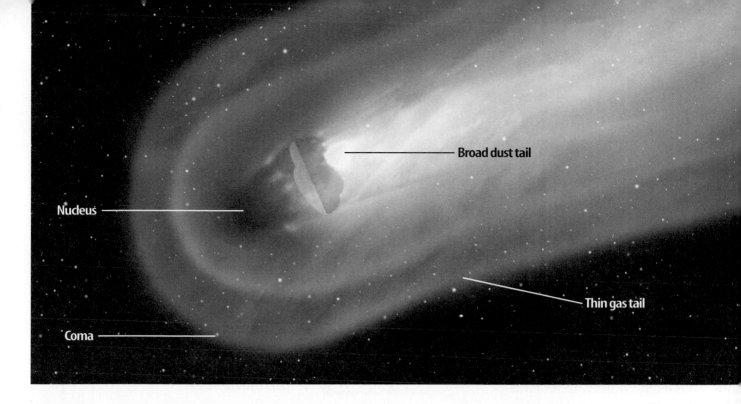

Nucleus

Broad dust tail

Thin gas tail

Coma

Structure of Comets

The *Hubble Space Telescope*, satellites orbiting Earth, and spacecrafts such as the *International Cometary Explorer* have all gathered information about comets. Notice the structure of a comet shown in **Figure 18.** It is like a large, dirty snowball or a mass of frozen ice and rock.

As the comet approaches the Sun, it starts to change. Ices of water, methane, and ammonia begin to vaporize because of the heat from the Sun, releasing dust and bits of rock. The vaporized gases and released dust form a bright cloud called a coma around the nucleus, or solid part, of the comet. The solar wind pushes on the gases and released dust in the coma, causing the particles to form tails that always point away from the Sun.

After many trips around the Sun, most of the frozen ice in a comet's nucleus has vaporized. All that's left are the small particles, which are spread throughout the orbit of the original comet.

Meteoroids, Meteors, and Meteorites

You learned that comets tend to vaporize and break up after they have passed close to the Sun many times. The small pieces of the comet's nucleus spread out into a loose group within the original orbit of the comet. These smaller pieces, along with particles derived from other sources, are called meteoroids.

Sometimes the path of a meteoroid crosses the position of Earth, and it enters Earth's atmosphere at speeds of 15 km/s to 70 km/s. Most meteoroids are so small that they completely burn up in Earth's atmosphere. A meteoroid that burns up in Earth's atmosphere is called a **meteor.** People often see meteors like the one in **Figure 19** and call them shooting stars.

Figure 18
A comet consists of a nucleus, a coma, a dust tail, and a gas tail.

Figure 19
A meteoroid that burns up in Earth's atmosphere is called a meteor.

Figure 20
Meteorites occasionally strike Earth's surface. A large meteorite struck Arizona, forming a crater about 1.2 km in diameter and about 200 m deep.

Meteor Showers Each time Earth passes through the loose group of particles within the old orbit of a comet, many small particles of rock and dust enter the atmosphere. Because more meteors than usual are seen, the event is called a meteor shower.

When a meteoroid is large enough, it might not burn up completely in the atmosphere. If it strikes Earth, it is called a **meteorite.** Barringer Crater in Arizona, shown in **Figure 20,** was formed when a large meteorite struck Earth about 50,000 years ago. Most meteorites are probably debris from asteroid collisions or broken-up comets, but some originate from the Moon and Mars.

 **Reading Check** *What is a meteorite?*

Asteroids

An **asteroid** is a piece of rock similar to the material that formed into the planets. Most asteroids are located in an area between the orbits of Mars and Jupiter called the asteroid belt. Find the asteroid belt in **Figure 21.** Why are they located there? The gravity of Jupiter might have kept a planet from forming in the area where the asteroid belt is located now.

Other asteroids are scattered throughout the solar system. They might have been thrown out of the belt by Jupiter's gravity. Some may have since been captured as moons around other planets. Some scientists think that Mars's moons are captured asteroids.

Figure 21
The asteroid belt lies between the orbits of Mars and Jupiter.

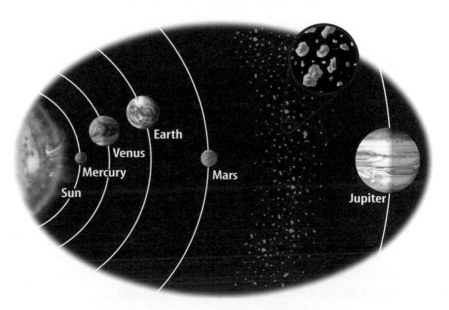

Exploring Asteroids The sizes of the asteroids in the asteroid belt range from tiny particles to objects 940 km in diameter. Ceres is the largest and the first one discovered. The next three in order of size are Vesta (530 km), Pallas (522 km), and 10 Hygiea (430 km). Two asteroids, Ida and Gaspra, shown in **Figure 22,** were photographed by *Galileo* on its way to Jupiter.

NEAR On February 14, 2000, the *Near Earth Asteroid Rendezvous (NEAR)* spacecraft went into orbit around the asteroid 433 Eros and successfully began its one-year mission of data gathering. Data from the spacecraft show that Eros's surface has a large number of craters. Other data indicate that Eros might be similar to the most common type of meteorite that strikes Earth. On February 12, 2001, *NEAR* ended its mission by becoming the first spacecraft to land softly on an asteroid.

Comets, meteoroids, and asteroids probably are composed of material that formed early in the history of the solar system. Scientists study the structure and composition of these space objects in order to learn what the solar system might have been like long ago. Understanding this could help scientists better understand how Earth formed.

Figure 22
A The asteroid Ida is about 56 km long. **B** Gaspra is about 20 km long.

Section Assessment

1. Why does a comet's tail form as it approaches the Sun?

2. What type of feature might be formed on Earth if a large meteorite reached its surface?

3. Describe differences among comets, meteoroids, and asteroids.

4. What was the mission of the *NEAR* spacecraft?

5. **Think Critically** What is the chemical composition of comets? Are comets more similar to the inner or the outer planets?

Skill Builder Activities

6. **Forming a Hypothesis** A meteorite found in Antarctica in 1979 is thought to have originated on Mars about 16 million years ago. Write a hypothesis to explain how a piece of Mars might have ended up on Earth. **For more help, refer to the Science Skill Handbook.**

7. **Communicating** The asteroid belt contains many objects—from tiny particles to objects 940 km in diameter. In your Science Journal, describe how mining the asteroids for valuable minerals might be accomplished. **For more help, refer to the Science Skill Handbook.**

Activity
Model and Invent

Solar System Distance Model

Distances between the planets of the solar system are large. Can you design a model that will demonstrate these large distances?

Recognize the Problem

Can a model be designed to show relative distances in the solar system?

Thinking Critically

How can you design a model of a reasonable size that will demonstrate the distances between and among the Sun and planets of the solar system?

Possible Materials

meterstick	string (several meters)
scissors	notebook paper
pencil	(several sheets)

Safety Precautions

Use care when handling scissors.

Data Source

SCIENCE*Online* Go to the Glencoe Science Web site at **science.glencoe.com** to find information about distances in the solar system.

Goals

■ **Design** a table of scale distances and model the distances between and among the Sun and the planets.

Planetary Distances				
Planet	**Distance to Sun (km)**	**Distance to Sun (AU)**	**Scale Distance (1 AU = 10 cm)**	**Scale Distance (1 AU = 2 m)**
Mercury				
Venus				
Earth				
Mars				
Jupiter				
Saturn				
Uranus				
Neptune				
Pluto				

Test Your Hypothesis

Planning the Model

1. **List** the steps that you need to take in making your model. Be specific, describing exactly what you will do at each step.

2. **List** the materials that you will need to complete your model.

3. **Make a table** of scale distances you will use in your model.

4. **Write** a description of how you will build your model, explaining how it will demonstrate relative distances between and among the Sun and planets of the solar system.

Check the Model Plans

1. **Compare** your scale distances with those of other students. Discuss why each of you chose the scale you did.

2. Make sure your teacher approves your plan before you start.

Making the Model

1. **Construct** the model using your scale distances.

2. While constructing the model, write any observations that you or other members of your group make, and complete the data table in your Science Journal. Calculate the scale distances that would be used in your model if 1 AU = 2 m.

Analyzing and Applying Results

1. **Explain** how a scale distance is determined.

2. Was it possible to work with your scale? Explain why or why not.

3. How much string would be required to construct a model with a scale distance of 1 AU = 2 m?

4. Proxima Centauri, the closest star to the Sun, is about 270,000 AU from the Sun. Based on your scale, how much string would you need to place this star on your model?

Your Data

Compare your scale model with those of other students. Discuss any differences. **For more help, refer to the Science Skill Handbook.**

Oops! Accidents in SCIENCE

SOMETIMES GREAT DISCOVERIES HAPPEN BY ACCIDENT!

IT CAME FROM OUTER

An unexpected visitor crashes into
"Old Kentucky Home"

On September 4, 1990, Frances Pegg had just returned from grocery shopping and was unloading bags of groceries in her kitchen in Burnwell, Kentucky. Suddenly and unexpectedly, she heard a loud crashing sound. Her husband, Arthur, had heard the same sound. Before it, however, he had heard another sound—one that was similar to a noise a helicopter makes. The sound frightened the couple's goat and horse. The noise had come from an object that had crashed through the Peggs' roof, their ceiling, and the floor of their porch. They couldn't see what the object was, but the noise sounded like a gunshot, and pieces of wood from their home flew everywhere.

The Burnwell meteorite crashed into the Peggs' home and landed in their basement on the right.

Frances and Arthur Pegg were not hurt, but they certainly were puzzled.

They thought that perhaps a part of an airplane had fallen off as it flew overhead. The next day the couple looked under their front porch and found the culprit—a chunk of rock from outer space. It was a meteorite!

SPACE!

Actual size

When the Burnwell meteorite entered Earth's atmosphere, it became covered in a shiny black crust. Its mass is about 2 kilograms.

For seven years, the Peggs kept their "space rock" at home, making them local celebrities. The rock appeared on TV, and the couple were interviewed by newspaper reporters. In 1997, the Peggs sold the meteorite to the National Museum of Natural History in Washington, D.C., which has a collection of over 9,000 meteorites. Scientists there study meteorites to learn more about space and the beginnings of the solar system. One astronomer explained, "Meteorites were formed at about the same time as the solar system, about 4.6 billion years ago, though some are younger."

Scientists especially are interested in the Burnwell meteorite because its chemical make up is different from other meteorites previously studied. Meteorites are made of various amounts of minerals and metals, including iron, cobalt, and nickel. The Burnwell meteorite is richer in metallic iron and nickel than other known meteorites and is less rich in some metals such as cobalt. Scientists are comparing the rare Burnwell rock with data from NASA space probes to find out if there are more meteorites like the one that fell on the Peggs' roof. But so far, it seems the Peggs' visitor from outer space is one-of-a-kind.

CONNECTIONS

Research the latest information on meteorites. How do they give clues to how our solar system was formed? Visit the Glencoe Science Web site. Report to the class.

SCIENCE
Online

For more information, visit
science.glencoe.com

Reviewing Main Ideas

Section 1 The Solar System

1. Early astronomers thought that the planets, the Moon, the Sun, and the stars were fixed in separate spheres that rotated around Earth.

2. The Sun-centered model of the solar system states that the Sun is the center of the solar system. Earth and the other planets revolve around the Sun.

3. Scientists think the solar system formed from a cloud of gas, ice, and dust about 4.6 billion years ago.

4. Johannes Kepler discovered that the planets orbit the Sun in elliptical, not circular, orbits.

Section 2 The Inner Planets

1. The moonlike planet Mercury has craters and cliffs on its surface.

2. Venus and Earth are similar in size and mass. Venus has a dense atmosphere.

3. On Earth, surface temperatures allow water to exist as a solid, liquid, and gas. Earth's atmosphere protects life-forms from the Sun's radiation.

4. Mars appears to be reddish-yellow due to the iron oxide content of its weathered rocks. Recent studies by *Global Surveyor* indicate that Mars's surface once had large amounts of water flowing over it. *Why do the polar ice caps of Mars, shown here, change size?*

Section 3 The Outer Planets

1. Faint rings and at least 28 moons orbit the gaseous planet Jupiter.

2. Saturn has pronounced rings. *What are Saturn's rings, shown here, made of?*

3. Uranus is a large, gaseous planet with many moons and several rings. Neptune is similar to Uranus in size, composition, and storm-like features.

4. Pluto has a surface of icy rock.

Section 4 Other Objects in the Solar System

1. As a comet approaches the Sun, a bright coma of dust and gas forms. *Why do comet tails always point away from the Sun?*

2. Meteoroids and asteroids are relatively small objects within the solar system. Meteoroids form when asteroids collide, when comets break up, or when meteorites collide with the Moon or planets.

FOLDABLES
Reading & Study Skills

After You Read

To help you review the similarities and differences among inner planets and outer planets, use the Foldable you made at the beginning of the chapter.

Visualizing Main Ideas

Complete the following concept map on the solar system.

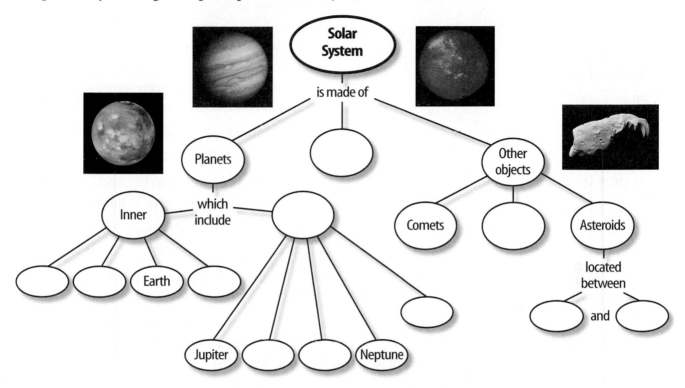

Vocabulary Review

Vocabulary Words

a. asteroid
b. comet
c. Earth
d. Great Red Spot
e. Jupiter
f. Mars
g. Mercury
h. meteor

i. meteorite
j. Neptune
k. Pluto
l. Saturn
m. solar system
n. Uranus
o. Venus

Study Tip

Practice reading tables. See if you can devise a graph that shows the same information that a table does.

Using Vocabulary

Replace the underlined words with the correct vocabulary words.

1. A meteoroid that burns up in Earth's atmosphere is called a <u>meteorite</u>.

2. The axis of rotation of <u>Neptune</u> is tilted on its side compared with the other planets.

3. <u>Uranus</u> is the second-largest planet in the solar system, but it has the lowest density.

4. The *Viking 1* and *2* orbiters photographed the entire surface of <u>Venus</u> from orbit.

5. One of the moons of <u>Mars</u> has volcanoes on it.

Checking Concepts

Choose the word or phrase that best answers the question.

1. Who proposed a Sun-centered solar system?
   A) Ptolemy
   C) Galileo
   B) Copernicus
   D) Oort

2. How does the Sun produce energy?
   A) magnetism
   B) nuclear fission
   C) nuclear fusion
   D) the greenhouse effect

3. What is the shape of planetary orbits?
   A) circles
   C) squares
   B) ellipses
   D) rectangles

4. Which planet has extreme temperatures because it has no atmosphere?
   A) Earth
   C) Saturn
   B) Jupiter
   D) Mercury

5. Water is a solid, liquid, and gas on which planet?
   A) Pluto
   C) Saturn
   B) Uranus
   D) Earth

6. Where is the largest known volcano in the solar system?
   A) Earth
   C) Mars
   B) Jupiter
   D) Uranus

7. What do scientists call a rock that strikes Earth's surface?
   A) asteroid
   C) meteorite
   B) comet
   D) meteoroid

8. Which planet has a complex ring system made of thousands of ringlets?
   A) Pluto
   C) Uranus
   B) Saturn
   D) Mars

9. Which planet has a Great Red Spot?
   A) Uranus
   C) Jupiter
   B) Earth
   D) Pluto

10. In what direction do comet tails always point?
    A) toward the Sun
    B) away from the Sun
    C) toward Earth
    D) away from the Oort Cloud

Thinking Critically

11. Why is the surface temperature on Venus so much higher than that on Earth?

12. Describe a relationship between a planet's mass and the number of satellites it has.

13. Why are probe landings on Jupiter or Saturn unlikely events?

14. What evidence suggests that water is or once was present on Mars?

15. An observer on Earth can watch Venus go through phases much like Earth's Moon does. Explain.

Developing Skills

16. **Making and Using Graphs** Use the graph below to explain how the time of a planet's revolution is related to its distance from the Sun.

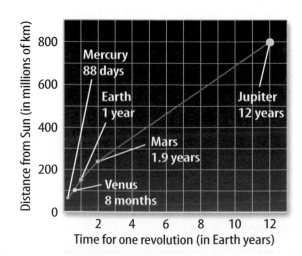

17. Forming a Hypothesis Mercury is the closest planet to the Sun, yet it does not reflect much of the Sun's light. What can you say about Mercury's color?

18. Concept Mapping Complete the concept map on this page to show how a comet changes as it travels through space.

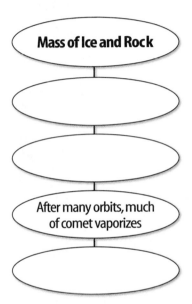

Mass of Ice and Rock

After many orbits, much of comet vaporizes

Performance Assessment

19. Display Mercury, Venus, Mars, Jupiter, and Saturn can be observed with the unaided eye. Research where in the sky these planets can be observed in the next year. Construct a display with your findings. Include time of day, day of the year, and locations with respect to known landmarks in your area on your display.

TECHNOLOGY

Go to the Glencoe Science Web site at **science.glencoe.com** or use the **Glencoe Science CD-ROM** for additional chapter assessment.

THE PRINCETON REVIEW — Test Practice

The table below presents data about the four inner planets of the solar system.

The Inner Planets

Planet	Diameter (km)	Distance from the Sun (millions of km)	Period of Revolution (days)
Mercury	4,880	58	88
Venus	12,104	108	225
Earth	12,756	150	365
Mars	6,799	228	687

Study the table and answer the following questions.

1. How many millions of kilometers farther from the Sun is Venus than Mercury?
A) 150   **C)** 58
B) 108   **D)** 50

2. The best conclusion to be made from these data is that _____.
F) Mercury is a larger planet than Mars
G) the period of a planet's revolution increases with increasing distance from the Sun
H) over time, the planets are gradually moving farther and farther away from the Sun
J) the size of a planet increases with increasing period of revolution

CHAPTER 4

Stars and Galaxies

When you look at stars, do you ever wonder why some stars appear brighter than others do? How do you know how far stars are from Earth and what they are made of? How does the Sun compare to the other stars you see? In this chapter, you will find the answers to these questions. You'll also learn how stars are classified and about the different kinds of galaxies that stars are grouped into. In addition, you'll learn about the Big Bang theory, which most astronomers believe is the most likely way that the universe began.

What do you think?

Science Journal Look at the picture below with a classmate. Discuss what this might be or what is happening. Here's a hint: *When it comes to space, two is sometimes better than one.* Write down your answer or best guess in your Science Journal.

This photo may look like a scene from the latest science fiction movie, but it shows a real event— two galaxies colliding. However, don't be worried. Most clusters of galaxies are not moving toward each other. They are moving apart, and astronomers have concluded that the universe is expanding in all directions. In the following activity, model how the universe might be expanding.

Model the universe

1. Partially inflate a balloon. Clip the neck shut with a clothespin.

2. Draw six evenly spaced dots on the balloon with a felt-tip marker. Label the dots A through F.

3. Use a string and ruler to measure the distance, in millimeters, from dot A to each of the other dots.

4. Inflate the balloon some more.

5. Measure the distances from dot A again.

6. Inflate the balloon again and take new measurements.

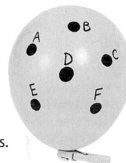

Observe

If each dot represents a cluster of galaxies and the balloon represents the universe, describe in your Science Journal the motion of the clusters relative to one another.

Before You Read

Making a Concept Map Study Fold
A concept map is a diagram that shows how concepts or ideas are related and organizes information. Make this Foldable to show what you already know about stars, galaxies, and the Universe.

1. Place a sheet of paper in front of you so the short side is at the top. Fold the paper in half from the left side to the right side.

2. Fold the top and bottom in to divide the paper into thirds. Unfold the paper so three columns show.

3. Through the top thickness of paper, cut along each of the fold lines to the left fold, forming three tabs. Label the tabs "Stars," "Galaxies," and "Universe," as shown.

4. Before you read the chapter, write what you already know about stars, galaxies, and the Universe under the tabs.

5. As you read the chapter, add to or correct what you have written under the tabs.

Stars

What You'll Learn

- **Explain** why the positions of constellations change throughout the year.
- **Distinguish** between absolute magnitude and apparent magnitude.
- **Describe** how parallax is used to determine distance.

Vocabulary

constellation
absolute magnitude
apparent magnitude
light-year

Why It's Important

Each of the thousands of stars you see in the night sky is a sun.

Constellations

It's fun to look at cloud formations and find ones that remind you of animals, people, or objects that you recognize. It takes much more imagination to play this game with celestial bodies. Ancient Greeks, Romans, and other early cultures observed patterns of stars in the sky called **constellations** and imagined that they represented mythological characters, animals, or familiar objects.

From Earth, a constellation looks like spots of light arranged in a particular shape against the dark night sky. **Figure 1** shows how the constellation of the mythological Greek hunter Orion appears from Earth. It also shows how stars in the constellation have no relationship to each other in space.

Stars in the sky can be found at specific locations within a constellation. For example, you can find the star Betelgeuse (BEE tul jooz) in the shoulder of the mighty hunter Orion. Orion's faithful companion is his dog, Canis Major. Sirius, the brightest star visible from the northern hemisphere, is in Canis Major.

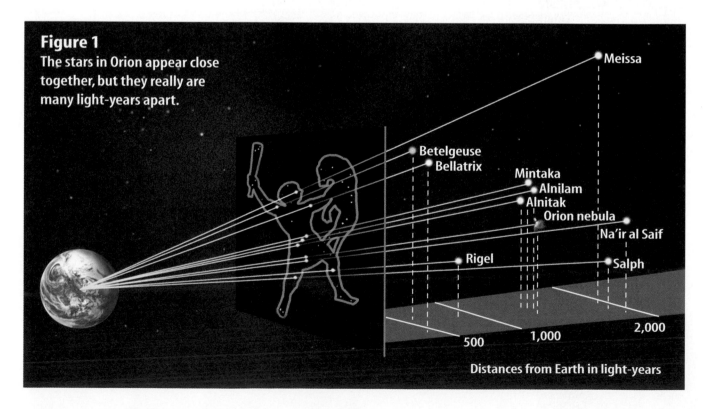

Figure 1
The stars in Orion appear close together, but they really are many light-years apart.

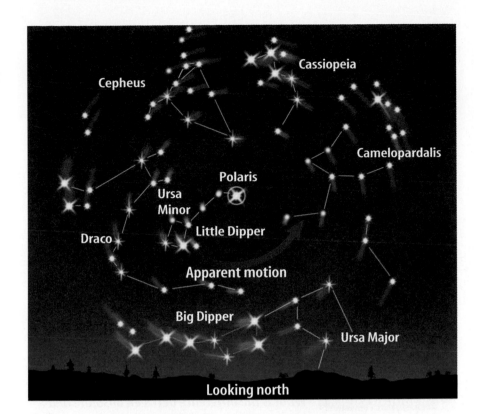

Looking north

Figure 2
The Big Dipper, in red, is part of the constellation Ursa Major. It is visible year-round in the northern hemisphere. Constellations close to Polaris rotate around Polaris, which is almost directly over the north pole.

Modern Constellations

Modern astronomy divides the sky into 88 constellations, many of which were named by early astronomers. You probably know some of them. Can you recognize the Big Dipper? It's part of the constellation Ursa Major, shown in **Figure 2.** Notice how the front two stars of the Big Dipper point almost directly at the North Star, Polaris, which is located at the end of the Little Dipper in the constellation Ursa Minor. Polaris is positioned almost directly over Earth's north pole.

Circumpolar Constellations

As Earth rotates, Ursa Major, Ursa Minor, and other constellations in the northern sky circle around Polaris. Because of this, they are called circumpolar constellations. The constellations appear to move, as shown in **Figure 2,** because Earth is in motion. The stars appear to complete one full circle in the sky in less than 24 h as Earth rotates on its axis. One circumpolar constellation that's easy to find is Cassiopeia (kas ee uh PEE uh). You can look for five bright stars that form a big W or a big M in the northern sky, depending on the season. In spring and summer, Cassiopeia forms an M, and in fall and winter, it forms a W.

As Earth orbits the Sun, different constellations come into view while others disappear. Because of their unique position, circumpolar constellations are visible all year long. Other constellations are not. Orion, which is visible in the winter in the northern hemisphere, can't be seen there in the summer because the daytime side of Earth is facing it.

TRY AT HOME
Mini LAB

Observing Star Patterns

Procedure
1. On a clear night, go outside after dark and study the stars. Take an adult with you and help each other find some common constellations.
2. Let your imagination flow to find patterns of stars that look like something familiar.
3. Draw the stars you see, note their positions, and include a drawing of what you think each star pattern resembles.

Analysis
1. Which of your constellations match those observed by your classmates?
2. How can recognizing star patterns be useful?

Absolute and Apparent Magnitudes

When you look at constellations, you'll notice that some stars are brighter than others. For example, Sirius looks much brighter than Rigel. Is Sirius a brighter star, or is it just closer to Earth, making it appear to be brighter? As it turns out, Sirius is 100 times closer to Earth than Rigel is. If Sirius and Rigel were the same distance from Earth, Rigel would appear much brighter in the night sky than Sirius would.

When you refer to the brightness of a star, you can refer to its absolute magnitude or its apparent magnitude. The **absolute magnitude** of a star is a measure of the amount of light it gives off. A measure of the amount of light received on Earth is called the **apparent magnitude.** A star that's rather dim can appear bright in the sky if it's close to Earth, and a star that's bright can appear dim if it's far away. If two stars are the same distance away, what might cause one of them to be brighter than the other?

 **Reading Check** *What is the difference between absolute and apparent magnitude?*

Which constellations are visible during different seasons? To find out, see the **Backyard Astronomy Field Guide** at the back of the book.

Problem-Solving Activity

Are distance and brightness related?

The apparent magnitude of a star is affected by its distance from Earth. This activity will help you determine the relationship between distance and brightness.

Identifying the Problem

Luisa conducted an experiment to determine the relationship between distance and the brightness of stars. She used a meterstick, a light meter, and a lightbulb. She placed the bulb at the zero end of the meterstick, then placed the light meter at the 20-cm mark and recorded the distance and the light-meter reading in her data table. Readings are in luxes, which are units for measuring light intensity. Luisa then increased the distance from the bulb to the light meter and took more readings. By examining the data in the table, can you see a relationship between the two variables?

Effect of Distance on Light	
Distance (cm)	Meter Reading (luxes)
20	4150.0
40	1037.5
60	461.1
80	259.4

Solving the Problem

1. What happened to the amount of light recorded when the distance was increased from 20 cm to 40 cm? When the distance was increased from 20 cm to 60 cm?

2. What does this indicate about the relationship between light intensity and distance? What would the light intensity be at 100 cm? Would making a graph help you visualize the relationship?

Measurement in Space

How do scientists determine distance to stars from the solar system that Earth is part of? One way is to measure its parallax—the apparent shift in the position of an object when viewed from two different positions. Extend your arm and look at your thumb first with your left eye closed and then with your right eye closed, as the girl in **Figure 3A** is doing. Your thumb appears to change position with respect to the background. Now do the same experiment with your thumb closer to your face, as shown in **Figure 3B.** What do you observe? The nearer an object is to the observer, the greater its parallax is.

Astronomers can measure the parallax of relatively close stars to determine their distances from Earth. **Figure 4** shows how a close star's position appears to change. Knowing the angle that the star's position changes and the size of Earth's orbit, astronomers can calculate the distance of the star from Earth.

Because space is so vast, a special unit of measure is needed to record distances. Distances between stars and galaxies are measured in light-years. A **light-year** is the distance that light travels in one year. Light travels at 300,000 km/s, or about 9.5 trillion km in one year. The nearest star to Earth, other than the Sun, is Proxima Centauri. Proxima Centauri is a mere 4.3 light-years away, or about 40 trillion km.

A

B

Figure 3
A Your thumb appears to move less against the background when it is farther away.
B It appears to move more when it is closer.

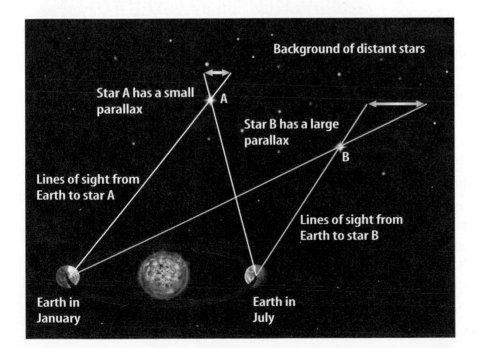

Figure 4
Parallax can be seen if you observe the same star when Earth is at two different points during its orbit around the Sun. The star's position relative to more distant background stars will appear to change. *Is star* **A** *or* **B** *farther from Earth?*

Figure 5
These star spectra were made by placing a diffraction grating over a telescope's objective lens. A diffraction grating produces a spectrum by causing interference of light waves. *What causes the lines in spectra?*

Properties of Stars

The color of a star indicates its temperature. For example, hot stars are a blue-white color. A relatively cool star looks orange or red. Stars that have the same temperature as the Sun have a yellow color.

Astronomers study the composition of stars by observing their spectra. When fitted into a telescope, a spectroscope acts like a prism. It spreads light out in the rainbow band called a spectrum. When light from a star passes through a spectroscope, it breaks into its component colors. Look at the spectrum of a star in **Figure 5.** Notice the dark lines caused by elements in the star's atmosphere. Light radiated from a star passes through the star's atmosphere. As it does, elements in the atmosphere absorb some of this light. The wavelengths of visible light that are absorbed appear as dark lines in the spectrum. Each element absorbs certain wavelengths, producing a certain pattern of dark lines. Every chemical element produces a unique pattern of dark lines. Like a fingerprint, the patterns of lines can be used to identify which elements are in a star's atmosphere.

Section 1 Assessment

1. What is a constellation?

2. How does Earth's revolution affect the viewing of constellations throughout the year?

3. If two stars give off equal amounts of light, why might one look brighter?

4. If the spectrum of a star shows the same absorption lines as the Sun, what can be said about the star's composition?

5. **Think Critically** Several thousand stars have large enough parallaxes that their distances can be studied using parallax. Most of these stars are invisible to the naked eye. What does this indicate about their absolute magnitudes?

Skill Builder Activities

6. **Recognizing Cause and Effect** Suppose you viewed Proxima Centauri through a telescope today. How old were you when the light that you see left Proxima Centauri? Why might Proxima Centauri look dimmer than Betelgeuse, a large star that is 520 light-years away? **For more help, refer to the Science Skill Handbook.**

7. **Using Graphics Software** Use graphics software on a computer to make a star chart of major constellations visible from where you live during the current season. Include several reference points to help others find the charted constellations. **For more help, refer to the Technology Skill Handbook.**

The Sun

The Sun's Layers

Within the universe, the Sun is an ordinary star—not too spectacular. However, to you it's important. The Sun is the center of the solar system, and it makes life possible on Earth. More than 99 percent of all the matter in the solar system is in the Sun.

Notice the different layers of the Sun, shown in **Figure 6,** as you read about them. Like other stars, the Sun is an enormous ball of gas that produces energy by fusing hydrogen into helium in its core. This energy travels outward through the radiation zone and the convection zone. In the convection zone, gases circulate in giant swirls. Finally, energy passes into the Sun's atmosphere.

The Sun's Atmosphere

The lowest layer of the Sun's atmosphere and the layer from which light is given off is the **photosphere.** The photosphere often is called the surface of the Sun, although the surface is not a smooth feature. Temperatures there are about 6,000 K. Above the photosphere is the **chromosphere.** This layer extends upward about 2,000 km above the photosphere. A transition zone occurs between 2,000 km and 10,000 km above the photosphere. Above the transition zone is the **corona.** This is the largest layer of the Sun's atmosphere and extends millions of kilometers into space. Temperatures in the corona are as high as 2 million K. Charged particles continually escape from the corona and move through space as solar wind.

Figure 6
Energy produced by fusion in the Sun's core travels outward by radiation and convection. The Sun's atmosphere—the photosphere, chromosphere, and corona—shines by the energy produced in the core.

As You Read

What You'll Learn
- **Describe** the strucure of the Sun.
- **Explain** how sunspots, prominences, and solar flares are related.
- **Explain** why the Sun is considered an average star and how it differs from stars in binary systems.

Vocabulary
photosphere   corona
chromosphere   sunspot

Why It's Important
The Sun is the source of most energy on Earth.

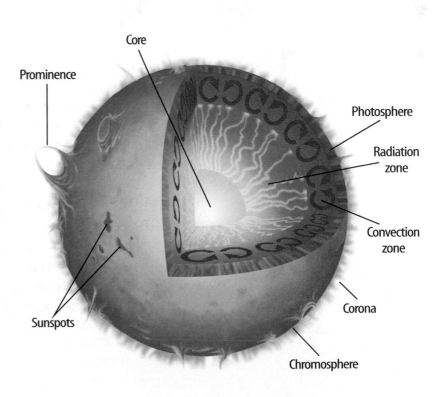

Core

Prominence

Photosphere

Radiation zone

Convection zone

Sunspots

Corona

Chromosphere

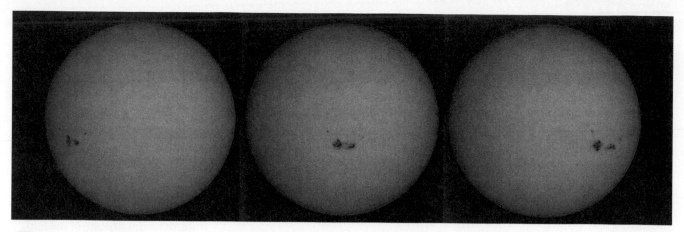

A Notice how these sunspots move as the Sun rotates.

Figure 7
Sunspots are bright, but when viewed against the rest of the photosphere, they appear dark.

B This is a close-up photo of a large sunspot.

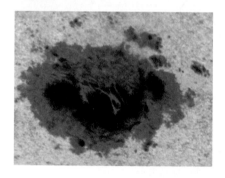

Surface Features

From the viewpoint that you observe the Sun, its surface appears to be a smooth layer. But the Sun's surface has many features, including sunspots, prominences, flares, and CMEs.

Sunspots Areas of the Sun's surface that appear dark because they are cooler than surrounding areas are called **sunspots.** Ever since Galileo Galilei viewed sunspots with a telescope, scientists have been studying them. Because scientists could observe the movement of individual sunspots, shown in **Figure 7,** they concluded that the Sun rotates. However, the Sun doesn't rotate as a solid body, as Earth does. It rotates faster at its equator than at its poles. Sunspots at the equator take about 25 days to complete one rotation. Near the poles, they take about 33 days.

Sunspots aren't permanent features on the Sun. They appear and disappear over a period of several days, weeks, or months. The number of sunspots increases and decreases in a fairly regular pattern called the sunspot, or solar activity, cycle. Times when many large sunspots occur are called sunspot maximums. Sunspot maximums occur about every 10 to 11 years. Periods of sunspot minimum occur in between.

✔ **Reading Check** *What is a sunspot cycle?*

Prominences and Flares Sunspots are related to several features on the Sun's surface. The intense magnetic fields associated with sunspots might cause prominences, which are huge, arching columns of gas. Notice the huge prominence in **Figure 8A.** Some prominences blast material from the Sun into space at speeds ranging from 600 km/s to more than 1,000 km/s.

Gases near a sunspot sometimes brighten suddenly, shooting outward at high speed. These violent eruptions are called solar flares. You can see a solar flare in **Figure 8B.**

CMEs During a sunspot maximum, like the one that occurred in 2000, brilliant coronal mass ejections (CMEs) are emitted from the Sun. When a CME is released in the direction of Earth, it appears as a halo around the Sun.

CMEs present little danger to life on Earth, but the highly charged solar wind material, along with ultraviolet light and X rays from solar flares, can reach Earth and cause disruption of radio signals. High-energy particles contained in CMEs are carried past Earth's magnetic field. This sets up electrical currents that flow toward the poles. The currents of electricity ionize gas in Earth's atmosphere. The ionized gases produce the light of an aurora, shown in **Figure 8C.** Power distribution equipment also can be affected.

SCIENCE *Online*

Research Visit the Glencoe Science Web site at **science.glencoe.com** for more information about sunspots, solar flares, prominences, and CMEs. Communicate to your class what you learned.

Figure 8
Features such as solar prominences and solar flares can reach hundreds of thousands of kilometers into space. CMEs are generated as magnetic fields above sunspot groups rearrange. CMEs can trigger events that produce auroras.

A Solar prominence

B Solar flare

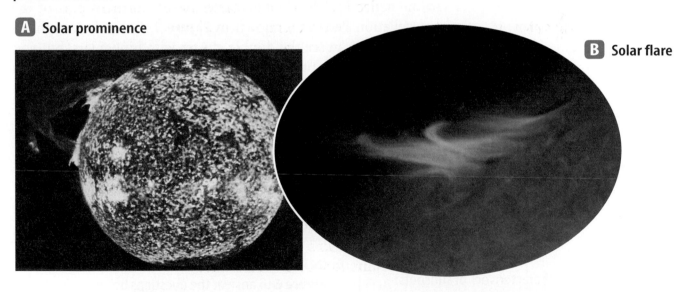

C Aurora

The Sun—An Average Star

The Sun is a middle-aged star. Its absolute magnitude is typical, and it shines with a yellow light. Although the Sun is an average star, it is somewhat unusual in one way. Most stars are part of a system in which two or more stars orbit each other. When two stars orbit each other, they make up a binary system.

In some cases, astronomers can detect binary systems because one star occasionally eclipses the other. Algol, in the constellation Perseus, is an example of this. The total amount of light from the star system becomes dim and then bright again on a regular cycle.

In other cases, three stars orbit around each other, forming a triple star system. The closest star system to the Sun—the Alpha Centauri system, including Proxima Centauri—is a triple star.

Stars also can move through space together as a cluster. In a star cluster, many stars are relatively close to one another, so their gravitational attraction to each other is strong. Most star clusters are far from the solar system, and each appears as a fuzzy patch in the night sky. The double cluster in the northern part of the constellation Perseus is shown in **Figure 9.** On a dark night in autumn, you can see the double cluster with binoculars, but you can't see its individual stars. The Pleiades star cluster can be seen in the constellation of Taurus in the winter sky. On a clear, dark night, you might be able to see seven of the stars in this cluster.

Figure 9
Most stars were formed originally in large clusters containing hundreds, or even thousands, of stars.

Section Assessment

1. What are the different layers that make up the Sun?

2. Describe the characteristics of sunspots.

3. How are sunspots, prominences, solar flares, and CMEs related? How does each affect Earth?

4. What characteristics does the Sun have in common with other stars? What characteristic makes it different from most other stars?

5. **Think Critically** Because most stars are found in multiple-star systems, what might explain why the Sun is a single star?

Skill Builder Activities

6. **Interpreting Scientific Illustrations** Use **Figure 6** to answer the questions below. **For more help, refer to the** Science Skill Handbook.
   a. Which layers make up the Sun's atmosphere?
   b. What process circulates gas in the Sun's convection zone?

7. **Communicating** Explain how the Sun generates energy. In your Science Journal, write a short paragraph hypothesizing what might happen to the Sun when it depletes its supply of hydrogen. **For more help, refer to the** Science Skill Handbook.

Activity

Sunspots

Sunspots can be observed moving across the face of the Sun as it rotates. Measure the movement of sunspots, and use your data to determine the Sun's period of rotation.

What You'll Investigate
Can sunspot motion be used to determine the Sun's period of rotation?

Materials
several books   clipboard
piece of cardboard   small tripod
drawing paper   scissors
refracting telescope

Goals
■ **Observe** sunspots and estimate their size.
■ **Estimate** the rate of apparent motion of sunspots.

Safety Precautions
Handle scissors with care.

Procedure

1. Find a location where the Sun can be viewed at the same time of day for a minimum of five days. **WARNING:** *Do not look directly at the Sun. Do not look through the telescope at the Sun. You could damage your eyes.*

2. If the telescope has a small finder scope attached, remove it or keep it covered.

3. Set up the telescope with the eyepiece facing away from the Sun, as shown. Align the telescope so that the shadow it casts on the ground is the smallest size possible. Cut and attach the cardboard as shown in the photo.

4. Use books to prop the clipboard upright. Point the eyepiece at the drawing paper.

5. Move the clipboard back and forth until you have the largest image of the Sun on the paper. Adjust the telescope to form a clear image. Trace the outline of the Sun on the paper.

6. Trace any sunspots that appear as dark areas on the Sun's image. Repeat this step at the same time each day for a week.

7. Using the Sun's diameter (approximately 1,390,000 km), estimate the size of the largest sunspots that you observed.

8. **Calculate** how many kilometers the sunspots appear to move each day.

9. **Predict** how many days it will take for the same group of sunspots to return to the same position in which they appeared on day 1.

Conclude and Apply

1. What was the estimated size and rate of apparent motion of the largest sunspots?

2. **Infer** how sunspots can be used to determine that the Sun's surface is not solid like Earth's.

*C*ommunicating
Your Data

Compare your conclusions with those of other students in your class. **For more help, refer to the** Science Skill Handbook.

Evolution of Stars

Classifying Stars

When you look at the night sky, all stars might appear to be similar, but they are quite different. Like people, they vary in age and size, but stars also vary in temperature.

In the early 1900s, Ejnar Hertzsprung and Henry Russell made some important observations. They noticed that in general, stars with higher temperatures also have brighter absolute magnitudes.

Hertzsprung and Russell developed a graph, shown in **Figure 10,** to show this relationship. They placed temperatures across the bottom and absolute magnitudes up one side. A graph that shows the relationship of a star's temperature to its absolute magnitude is called a Hertzsprung-Russell (H-R) diagram.

The Main Sequence As you can see, stars seem to fit into specific areas of the graph. Most stars fit into a diagonal band that runs from the upper left to the lower right of the chart. This band, called the main sequence, contains hot, blue, bright stars in the upper left and cool, red, dim stars in the lower right. Yellow, main sequence stars, like the Sun, fall in between.

Figure 10
The relationships among a star's color, temperature, and brightness are shown in this Hertzsprung-Russell diagram. Main sequence stars run from the upper-left corner to the lower-right corner. Stars in the upper left are hot, bright stars, and stars in the lower right are cool, faint stars. *What type of star shown in the diagram is the coolest, brightest star?*

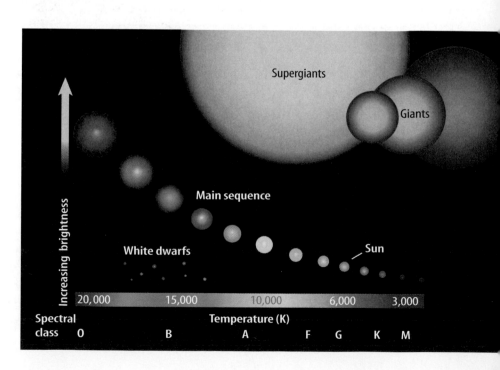

Dwarfs and Giants About 90 percent of all stars are main sequence stars. Most of these are small, red stars found in the lower right of the H-R diagram. Among main sequence stars, the hottest stars generate the most light and the coolest ones generate the least. What about the ten percent of stars that are not part of the main sequence? Some of these stars are hot but not bright. These small stars are located on the lower left of the H-R diagram and are called white dwarfs. Other stars are extremely bright but not hot. These large stars on the upper right of the H-R diagram are called giants, or red giants because they are usually red in color. The largest giants are called supergiants. **Figure 11** shows the supergiant, Antares—a star 300 times the Sun's diameter—in the constellation Scorpius. It is 5,600 times as bright as the Sun.

 **Reading Check** *What kinds of stars are on the main sequence?*

Figure 11
Antares is a bright, supergiant located 400 light-years from Earth. Although its temperature is only about 3,500 K, it is the 16th brightest star in the sky.

How do stars shine?

When the H-R diagram was developed, scientists didn't know what caused stars to shine. Hertzsprung and Russell developed their diagram without knowing what produced the light and heat of stars.

For centuries, people were puzzled by the questions of what stars were made of and how they produced light. Many people had estimated that Earth was only a few thousand years old. The Sun could have been made of coal and shined for that long. However, when people realized that Earth was much older, they wondered what material possibly could burn for so many years. Early in the twentieth century, scientists began to understand the process that keeps stars shining for billions of years.

Generating Energy In the 1930s, scientists discovered reactions between the nuclei of atoms. They hypothesized that temperatures in the center of the Sun must be high enough to cause hydrogen to fuse to make helium. That reaction would release tremendous amounts of energy. In this reaction, four hydrogen nuclei combine to create one helium nucleus. The mass of one helium nucleus is less than the mass of four hydrogen nuclei, so some mass is lost in the reaction.

Years earlier, in 1905, Albert Einstein had proposed a theory stating that mass can be converted into energy. This was stated as the famous equation $E = mc^2$. In this equation, E is the energy produced, m is the mass, and c is the speed of light. The small amount of mass "lost" when hydrogen atoms fuse to form a helium atom is converted to a large amount of energy.

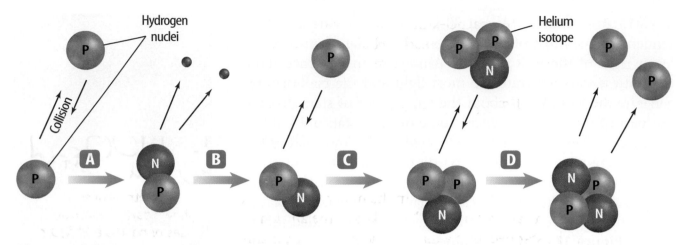

A One proton decays to a neutron, releasing subatomic particles and some energy.

B Another proton fuses with a proton and neutron to form an isotope of helium. Energy is given off again.

C Two helium isotopes fuse.

D A helium nucleus (two protons and two neutrons) forms as two protons break away. In the process, still more energy is released.

Figure 12
Fusion begins in a star's core as protons (hydrogen nuclei) collide.
What happens to the "lost" mass during this process?

Fusion Shown in **Figure 12,** fusion occurs in the cores of stars. Only in the core are temperatures high enough to cause atoms to fuse. Normally, they would repel each other, but in the core of a star where temperatures can exceed 15,000,000 K, atoms can move so fast that some of them fuse upon colliding.

Evolution of Stars

The H-R diagram explained a lot about stars. However, it also led to more questions. Many wondered why some stars didn't fit in the main sequence group and what happened when a star depleted its supply of hydrogen fuel. Today, scientists have theories of how stars evolve, what makes them different from one another, and what happens when they die. **Figure 13** illustrates the lives of different types of stars.

When hydrogen fuel is depleted, a star loses its main sequence status. This can take less than 1 million years for the brightest stars to many billions of years for the faintest stars. The Sun has a main sequence life span of about 10 billion years. Half of its life span is still in the future.

Nebula Stars begin as a large cloud of gas and dust called a **nebula.** As the particles of gas and dust exert a gravitational force on each other, the nebula begins to contract. Gravitational forces cause instability within the nebula. The nebula can break apart into smaller pieces. Each piece eventually will collapse to form a star.

A Star Is Born As the particles in the smaller clouds move closer together, the temperatures in each nebula increase. When the temperature inside the core of a nebula reaches 10 million K, fusion begins. The energy released radiates outward through the condensing ball of gas. As the energy radiates into space, stars are born.

✔ **Reading Check** *How are stars born?*

Main Sequence to Giant Stars In the newly formed star, the heat from fusion causes pressure that balances the attraction due to gravity. The star becomes a main sequence star. It continues to use up its hydrogen fuel.

When hydrogen in the core of the star is depleted, a balance no longer exists between pressure and gravity. The core contracts, and temperatures inside the star increase. This causes the outer layers of the star to expand and cool. In this late stage of its life cycle, a star is called a **giant.**

After the core temperature reaches 100 million K, helium nuclei fuse to form carbon in the giant's core. By this time, the star has expanded to an enormous size, and its outer layers are much cooler than they were when it was a main sequence star. In about 5 billion years, the Sun will become a giant.

White Dwarfs After the star's core uses up its helium, it contracts even more and its outer layers escape into space. This leaves behind the hot, dense core. The core contracts under the force of gravity. At this stage in a star's evolution, it becomes a **white dwarf.** A white dwarf is about the size of Earth.

Chemistry INTEGRATION

The spectrum of a star shows dark absorption lines of helium and hydrogen and is bright in the blue end. Describe as much as you can about the star's composition and surface temperature.

Figure 13
The life of a star depends greatly on its mass. Massive stars eventually become neutron stars or possibly black holes. *What happens to stars that are the size of the Sun?*

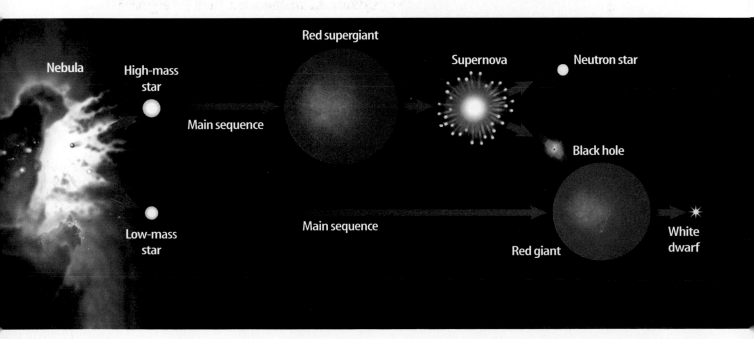

Nebula — High-mass star — Main sequence — Red supergiant — Supernova — Neutron star — Black hole

Low-mass star — Main sequence — Red giant — White dwarf

About forty years ago, radio waves were detected coming from some small regions of space. These radio sources were called quasi-stellar radio sources, which was shortened to quasars. Today, quasars are known to be distant galaxies with supermassive, rotating black holes in their centers. Radio waves and other types of radiation are produced as matter falls into the black holes. Research to learn how scientists solved the mystery of quasars.

Figure 14
The black hole at the center of galaxy M87 pulls matter into it at extremely high velocities. Some matter is ejected to produce a jet of gas that streams away from the center of the galaxy at nearly light speed.

Supergiants and Supernovas In stars that are more than ten times more massive than the Sun, the stages of evolution occur more quickly and more violently. Look back at **Figure 13.** In massive stars, the core heats up to much higher temperatures. Heavier and heavier elements form by fusion, and the star expands into a **supergiant.** Eventually, iron forms in the core. Much of the star's energy is no longer used to produce light and heat, and the core collapses violently, sending a shock wave outward through the star. The outer portion of the star explodes, producing a supernova. A supernova can be millions of times brighter than the original star was.

Neutron Stars If the collapsed core of a supernova is about twice as massive as the Sun, it may shrink to approximately 20 km in diameter. Only neutrons can exist in the dense core, and it becomes a **neutron star.** Neutron stars are so dense that a teaspoonful would weigh about 100 million metric tons in Earth's gravity. As dense as neutron stars are, they can contract only so far because the neutrons resist the inward pull of gravity.

Black Holes If the remaining dense core from a supernova is more than three times more massive than the Sun, probably nothing can stop the core's collapse. Under these conditions, all of the core's mass collapses to a point that has no volume. The gravity from this mass is so strong that nothing can escape from it, not even light. Because light cannot escape, the region is called a **black hole.** If you could shine a flashlight on a black hole, the light simply would disappear into it.

✔ **Reading Check** *What is a black hole?*

Black holes, however, are not like giant vacuum cleaners, sucking in distant objects. A black hole has an event horizon, which is a region inside of which nothing can escape. If something—including light—crosses the event horizon, it will be pulled into the black hole. Beyond the event horizon, the black hole's gravity pulls on objects just as it would if the mass had not collapsed. Stars and planets can orbit around a black hole.

The photograph in **Figure 14** was taken by the *Hubble Space Telescope.* It shows a jet of gas streaming out of the center of galaxy M87. This jet of gas formed as matter flowed toward a black hole, and some of the gas was ejected along the polar axis without falling in.

Recycling Matter A star begins its life as a nebula, such as the one shown in **Figure 15.** Where does the matter in a nebula come from? Nebulas form partly from the matter that was once in other stars. A star ejects enormous amounts of matter during its lifetime. Some of this matter is incorporated into nebulas, which can evolve to form new stars. The matter in stars is recycled many times.

What about the matter created in the cores of stars? Are elements such as carbon and iron also recycled? These elements can become parts of new stars. In fact, spectrographs have shown that the Sun contains some carbon, iron, and other such elements. Because the Sun is an average, main sequence star, it is too young and its mass is too small to have formed these elements itself. The Sun condensed from material that was created in stars that died many billions of years ago.

Some elements condense to form planets and other bodies rather than stars. In fact, your body contains many atoms that were fused in the cores of ancient stars. Evidence suggests that the first stars formed from hydrogen and helium and that all the other elements have formed in the cores of stars or as stars explode.

Figure 15
Stars are forming in the Orion Nebula and other similar nebulae.

Section Assessment

1. Explain why giants are not in the main sequence on the H-R diagram. How do their temperatures and absolute magnitudes compare with those of main sequence stars?

2. What can be said about the absolute magnitudes of two equal-sized stars whose colors are blue and yellow?

3. How do stars produce energy?

4. Outline the history and probable future of the Sun.

5. **Think Critically** Why doesn't the helium currently in the Sun's core undergo fusion?

Skill Builder Activities

6. **Sequencing** Sequence the following in order of most evolved to least evolved: *main sequence star, supergiant, neutron star,* and *nebula.* **For more help, refer to the Science Skill Handbook.**

7. **Solving One-Step Equations** Assume that a star's core has shrunk to a diameter of 12 km. What would be the circumference of the shrunken stellar core? Use the equation $C = \pi d$. How does this compare with the circumference of Earth with a diameter of 12,756 km? **For more help, refer to the Math Skill Handbook.**

Galaxies and the Universe

As You Read

What **You'll Learn**
- **Identify** the three main types of galaxies.
- **List** several characteristics of the Milky Way Galaxy.
- **Describe** evidence that supports the Big Bang theory.

Vocabulary
galaxy
Big Bang theory

Why **It's Important**
Studying the universe could help scientists determine whether life is possible elsewhere.

Galaxies

Long ago, people believed that Earth was the center of the universe. Today you know that the Sun is the center of the solar system. But where is the solar system in relation to the galaxy? Where is the galaxy located in the universe?

You are on Earth, and Earth orbits the Sun. Does the Sun orbit anything? How does it interact with other objects in the universe? The Sun is one star among many in a **galaxy**—a large group of stars, gas, and dust held together by gravity. The galaxy in which Earth is found is called the Milky Way. It might contain as many as one trillion stars, including the Sun. Galaxies are separated by huge distances—often millions of light-years.

In the same way that stars are grouped together within galaxies, galaxies are grouped into clusters. The cluster that the Milky Way belongs to is called the Local Group. It contains more than 30 galaxies of various sizes and types. The three major types of galaxies are spiral, elliptical, and irregular.

Spiral Galaxies The Milky Way is a spiral galaxy, as shown in **Figure 16.** Notice that spiral galaxies have spiral arms that wind outward from inner regions. These arms are made up of bright stars and dust. The fuzzy patch seen in the constellation of Andromeda is a spiral galaxy. It's so far away that you can't see its individual stars. Instead, its combined light appears as a hazy spot in the sky. The Andromeda Galaxy is about 2 million light-years away and is a member of the Local Group.

Arms in a normal spiral start close to the center of the galaxy. Barred spirals have spiral arms extending from a large bar of stars and gas that passes through the center of the galaxy.

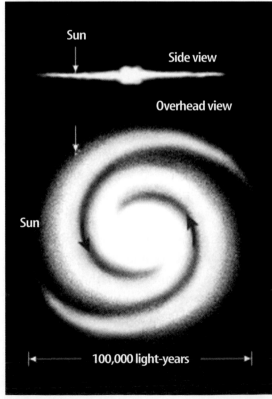

Figure 16
This illustration shows a side view and an overhead view of the Milky Way. *What group of galaxies is the Milky Way part of?*

Elliptical Galaxies A common type of galaxy is the elliptical galaxy. **Figure 17** shows an elliptical galaxy in the constellation Andromeda. These galaxies are shaped like large, three-dimensional ellipses. Many are football shaped, but others are round. Some elliptical galaxies are small, while others are so large that several galaxies the size of the Milky Way would fit inside one of them.

Irregular Galaxies The third type—an irregular galaxy—includes most of those galaxies that don't fit into the other classifications. Irregular galaxies have many different shapes. They are smaller than the other types of galaxies. Two irregular galaxies called the Clouds of Magellan orbit the Milky Way. The Large Magellanic Cloud is shown in **Figure 18.**

✔ **Reading Check** *How do the three different types of galaxies differ?*

The Milky Way Galaxy

The Milky Way might contain one trillion stars. The visible disk of stars shown in **Figure 16** is about 100,000 light-years across. Find the location of the Sun. Notice that it is located about 30,000 light-years from the galaxy's center in one of the spiral arms. In the galaxy, all stars orbit around a central region, or core. Based on a distance of 30,000 light-years and a speed of 235 km/s, the Sun orbits the center of the Milky Way once every 240 million years.

The Milky Way usually is classified as a normal spiral galaxy. However, some evidence suggests that it might be a barred spiral. It is difficult to know for sure because astronomers have limited data about how the galaxy looks from the outside.

You can't see the normal spiral or barred shape of the Milky Way because you are located within one of its spiral arms. You can, however, see the Milky Way stretching across the sky as a misty band of faint light. You can see the brightest part of the Milky Way if you look low in the southern sky on a moonless summer night. All the stars you can see in the night sky belong to the Milky Way.

Figure 17
This photo shows an example of an elliptical galaxy. *What are the two other types of galaxies?*

Figure 18
The Large Magellanic Cloud is an irregular galaxy. It's a member of the Local Group, and it orbits the Milky Way.

Origin of the Universe

People have long wondered how the universe formed. Several models of its origin have been proposed. One model was the steady state theory. It proposed that the universe always has been the same as it is now. The universe always has existed and always will. As matter in the universe expands outward, new matter is created to keep the overall density of the universe the same or in a steady state. However, evidence indicates that the universe was much different in the past from what it is today.

A second idea is called the oscillating model. In this model, the universe began with expansion occurring in all areas of the universe. Over time, the expansion slowed and the matter in the universe contracted. Then the process began again—repeating over and over, oscillating back and forth.

Neither of these theories can be proven or disproven, but evidence suggests that a third idea is more likely to be correct. The universe started with a big bang and has been expanding ever since. This theory will be described later.

Expansion of the Universe

What does it sound like when a train is blowing its whistle while it travels past you? The whistle has a higher pitch as the train approaches you. Then the whistle seems to drop in pitch as the train moves away. This effect is called the Doppler shift. The Doppler shift occurs with light as well as with sound. **Figure 19** shows how the Doppler shift causes changes in the light coming from distant stars and galaxies. If a star is moving toward Earth, its wavelengths of light are compressed. If a star is moving away from Earth, its wavelengths of light are stretched.

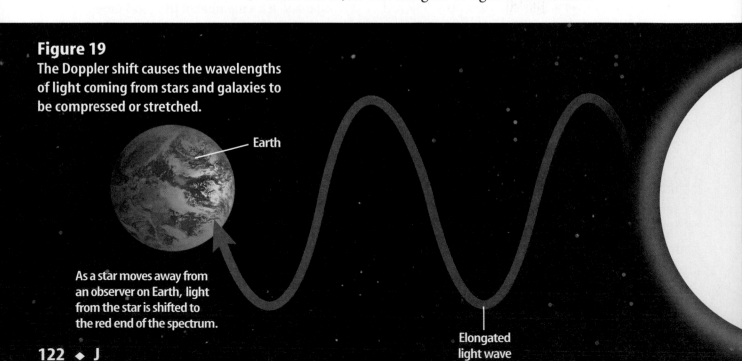

Figure 19
The Doppler shift causes the wavelengths of light coming from stars and galaxies to be compressed or stretched.

Earth

As a star moves away from an observer on Earth, light from the star is shifted to the red end of the spectrum.

Elongated light wave

The Doppler Shift Look at the spectrum of a star in **Figure 20A.** Note the position of the dark lines. How do they compare with the lines in **Figures 20B** and **20C?** They have shifted in position. What caused this shift? As you just read, when a star is moving toward Earth, its wavelengths of light are compressed, just as the sound waves from the train's whistle are. This causes the dark lines in the spectrum to shift toward the blue-violet end of the spectrum. A red shift in the spectrum occurs when a star is moving away from Earth. In a red shift, the dark lines shift toward the red end of the spectrum.

Figure 20
A This spectrum shows dark absorption lines. **B** The dark lines shift toward the blue-violet end for a star moving toward Earth. **C** The lines shift toward the red end for a star moving away from Earth.

Red Shift In 1929, Edwin Hubble published an interesting fact about the light coming from most galaxies. When a spectrograph is used to study light from galaxies beyond the Local Group, a red shift occurs in the light. What does this red shift tell you about the universe?

Because all galaxies beyond the Local Group show a red shift in their spectra, they must be moving away from Earth. If all galaxies outside the Local Group are moving away from Earth, then the entire universe must be expanding. Remember the Explore Activity at the beginning of the chapter? The dots on the balloon moved apart as the model universe expanded. Regardless of which dot you picked, all the other dots moved away from it. In a similar way, galaxies beyond the Local Group are moving away from Earth.

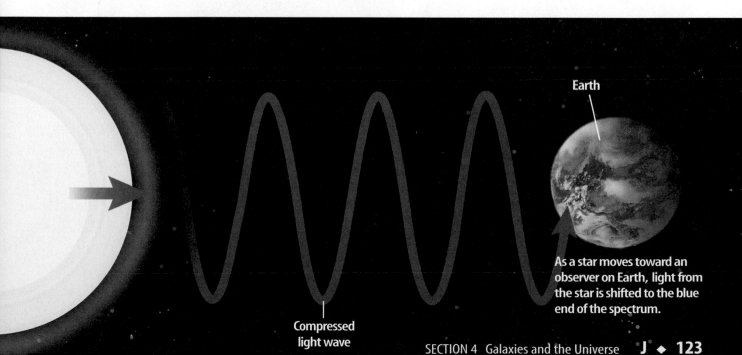

Earth

As a star moves toward an observer on Earth, light from the star is shifted to the blue end of the spectrum.

Compressed
light wave

VISUALIZING THE BIG BANG THEORY

Figure 21

The Big Bang theory states that the universe probably began 12 billion to 15 billion years ago with an enormous explosion. Even today, galaxies are rushing apart from this explosion.

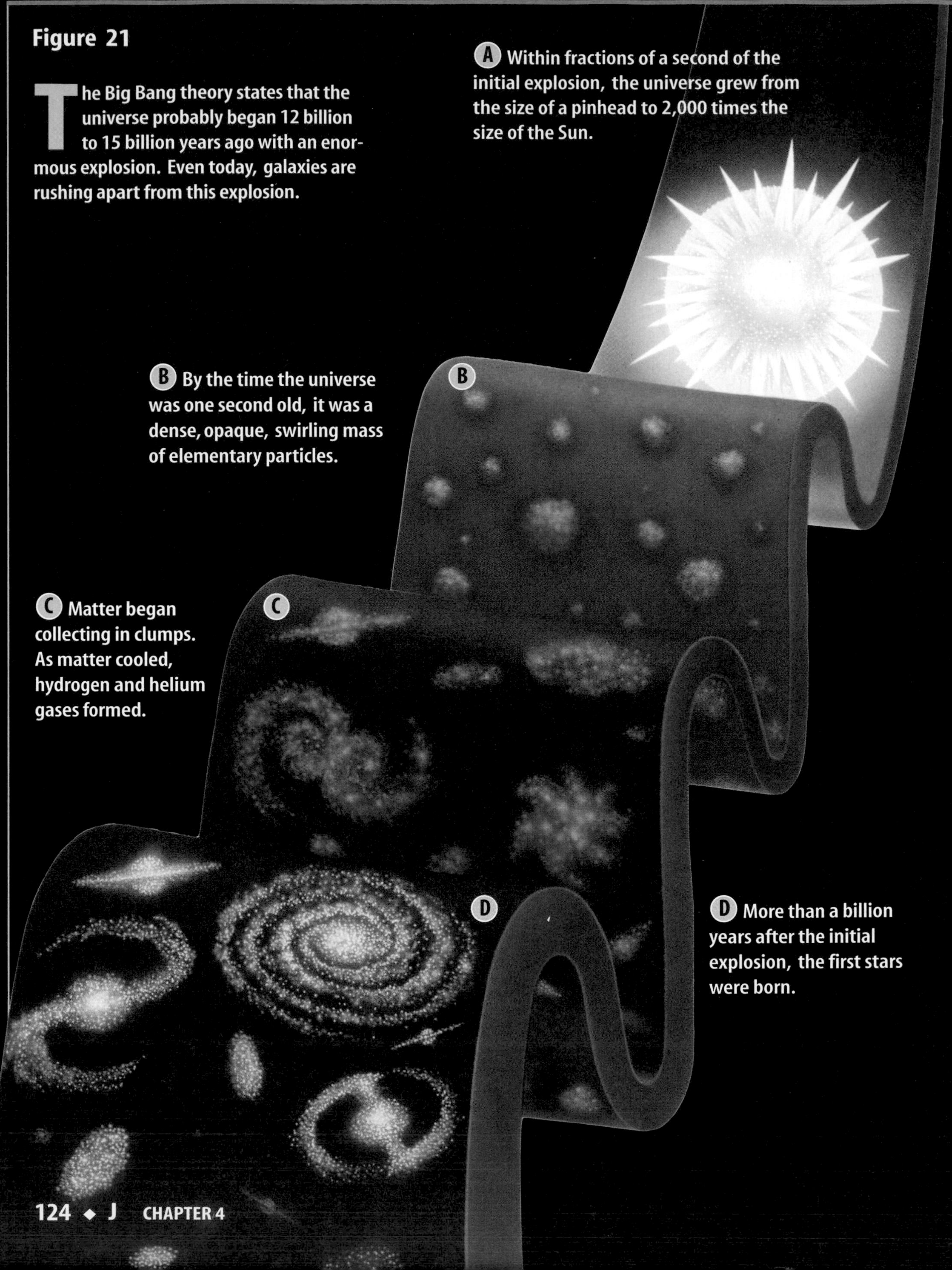

A Within fractions of a second of the initial explosion, the universe grew from the size of a pinhead to 2,000 times the size of the Sun.

B By the time the universe was one second old, it was a dense, opaque, swirling mass of elementary particles.

C Matter began collecting in clumps. As matter cooled, hydrogen and helium gases formed.

D More than a billion years after the initial explosion, the first stars were born.

The Big Bang Theory

When scientists determined that the universe was expanding, they realized that galaxy clusters must have been closer together in the past. The leading theory about the formation of the universe, called the **Big Bang theory,** is based on this explanation. **Figure 21** illustrates the Big Bang theory. According to this theory, approximately 12 billion to 15 billion years ago, the universe began with an enormous explosion. The entire universe began to expand everywhere at the same time.

Looking Back in Time The time-exposure photograph shown in **Figure 22** was taken by the *Hubble Space Telescope.* It shows more than 1,500 galaxies at distances of more than 10 billion light-years. These galaxies could date back to when the universe was no more than 1 billion years old and are in various stages of development. One astronomer says humans might be looking back to a time when the Milky Way was forming. Studies like this eventually will allow astronomers to determine the approximate age of the universe.

Whether the universe will expand forever or stop expanding is still unknown. If enough matter exists, gravity might halt the expansion, and the universe will contract until everything comes to a single point. However, recent studies of distant supernovas indicate that some energy might be causing the universe to expand faster. If this is correct, the universe might expand forever.

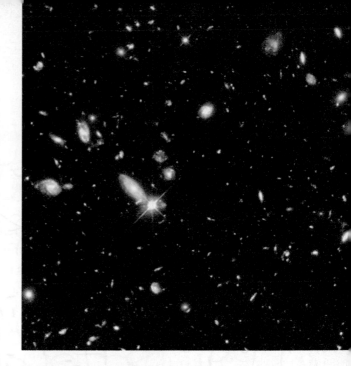

Figure 22
The light from the galaxies in this photo mosaic took billions of years to reach Earth.

Section 4 Assessment

1. List the three major types of galaxies. What do they have in common?

2. What is the name of the galaxy that you live in? What motion do its stars exhibit?

3. What is the Doppler shift?

4. How far away are the most distant galaxies?

5. **Think Critically** All galaxies outside the Local Group show a red shift. Within the Local Group, some galaxies show a red shift and some show a blue shift. What does this tell you about the galaxies in the Local Group?

Skill Builder Activities

6. **Comparing and Contrasting** Compare and contrast the three models of the origin of the universe. **For more help, refer to the Science Skill Handbook.**

7. **Communicating** Research and write a report in your Science Journal about the most recent evidence supporting or disputing the Big Bang theory. Describe how the Big Bang theory explains observations of galaxies made with spectrometers. **For more help, refer to the Science Skill Handbook.**

Activity

Measuring Parallax

Parallax is the apparent shift in the position of an object when viewed from two locations. The nearer an object is to the observer, the greater its parallax is. Do this activity to design a model and use it in an experiment that will show how distance affects the amount of observed parallax.

Recognizing the Problem

How can you build a model to show the relationship between distance and parallax?

Form a Hypothesis

State a hypothesis about how a model must be built in order for it to be used to show how distance affects the amount of observed parallax.

Possible Materials

meterstick   masking tape
metric ruler   pencil

Goals

- **Design** a model to show how the distance from an observer to an object affects the object's parallax shift.
- **Design** an experiment that shows how distance affects the amount of observed parallax.

Safety Precautions

WARNING: *Be sure to wear goggles to protect your eyes.*

Test Your Hypothesis

Plan

1. As a group, agree upon and write your hypothesis statement.

2. **List** the steps you need to take to build your model. Be specific, describing exactly what you will do at each step.

3. Devise a method to test how distance from an observer to an object, such as a pencil, affects the relative position of the object.

4. **List** the steps you will take to test your hypothesis. Be specific, describing exactly what you will do at each step.

5. Read over your plan for the model to be used in this experiment.

6. How will you determine changes in observed parallax? Remember, these changes should occur when the distance from the observer to the object is changed.

7. You should measure shifts in parallax from several different positions. How will these positions differ?

8. How will you measure distances accurately and compare relative position shift?

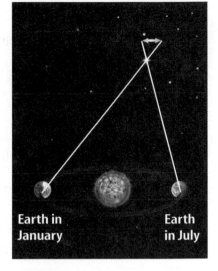

Earth in January   Earth in July

Do

1. Make sure your teacher approves your plan before you start.

2. **Construct** the model your team has planned.

3. Carry out the experiment as planned.

4. While conducting the experiment, record any observations that you or other members of your group make in your Science Journal.

Analyze Your Data

1. **Compare** what happened to the object when it was viewed with one eye closed, then the other.

2. At what distance from the observer did the object appear to shift the most?

Draw Conclusions

1. **Infer** what happened to the apparent shift of the object's location as the distance from the observer was increased or decreased.

2. **Describe** how astronomers might use parallax to study stars.

*C*ommunicating
Your Data

Prepare a chart showing the results of your experiment. **Share** the chart with members of your class. **For more help, refer to the Science Skill Handbook.**

Science Stats

Stars and Galaxies

Did you know...

...The 11,000-kg Hubble Space Telescope orbits Earth every 95 minutes—that's a speed of about 27,250 km/h. The heavy telescope moves more than 750 times faster than the fastest human does on Earth.

...A star in Earth's galaxy explodes as a supernova about once a century. The most famous supernova of this galaxy occurred in 1054 and was recorded by the ancient Chinese and Koreans. The explosion was so powerful that it could be seen during the day, and its brightness lasted for weeks. Other major supernovas in the Milky Way that were observed from Earth occurred in 185, 393, 1006, 1181, 1572, and 1604.

...The large loops of material called solar prominences can extend more than 320,000 km above the Sun's surface. This is so high that two Jupiters and three Earths could fit under the arch.

. . . Some of the most famous stars on Earth can be found on the Hollywood Walk of Fame. The walk contains more than 2,000 stars in honor of various Hollywood film actors and actresses and is located in Hollywood, California.

. . . The red giant star Betelgeuse has a diameter larger than that of Earth's Sun. This gigantic star measures 450,520,000 km in diameter, while the Sun's diameter is a mere 1,390,176 km.

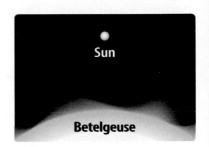

Distance (light-years) from Earth to the Brightest Stars Visible from the Northern Hemisphere in January

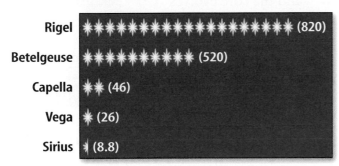

Rigel ✳✳✳✳✳✳✳✳✳✳✳✳✳✳✳✳✳✳✳✳✳ (820)
Betelgeuse ✳✳✳✳✳✳✳✳✳ (520)
Capella ✳✳ (46)
Vega ✳ (26)
Sirius ✳ (8.8)

. . . Just as Earth goes around the Sun, the whole solar system is going around the center of the Milky Way. It takes Earth one year to go around the Sun, but it takes the solar system about 240 million years to go around the center of the Milky Way.

Do the Math

1. Compare the diameter of Betelgeuse to that of the Sun.
2. The Sun orbits the Milky Way once every 240 million years. About how many revolutions of the galaxy has it made since its formation?
3. How many kilometers does the *Hubble Space Telescope* travel in one minute? About how long would it take the fastest human to travel that distance?

Go Further

Is it possible for Earth astronauts to travel to the nearest stars? For more information go to the Glencoe Science Web site at **science.glencoe.com.** How long would such a trip take? What problems would have to be overcome? Write a brief report on what you find.

Chapter 4 Study Guide

Reviewing Main Ideas

Section 1 Stars

1. Constellations are groups of stars that change positions throughout the year because Earth moves. The constellations seem to move because Earth rotates on its axis and revolves around the Sun.

2. The magnitude of a star is a measure of the star's brightness. Absolute magnitude is a measure of the light actually given off by a star. Apparent magnitude is a measure of the amount of light received on Earth.

3. Parallax is the apparent shift in the position of an object when viewed from two different positions. The closer to Earth a star is, the greater its shift in parallax is.

4. A star's composition can be determined from the star's spectrum.

Section 2 The Sun

1. The Sun produces energy by fusing hydrogen into helium in its core. Light is given off from the photosphere, which is the lowest layer of the Sun's atmosphere.

2. Sunspots are areas of the Sun that are cooler and less bright than surrounding areas.

3. Sunspots, prominences, flares, and CMEs are caused by the intense magnetic field of the Sun, which is a main sequence star. *Why is the Sun, shown here, considered an average star?*

Section 3 Evolution of Stars

1. Stars are classified by their positions on the H-R diagram. Most stars are main sequence stars.

2. When hydrogen is depleted in a main sequence star, the star's core collapses and its temperature increases. The star becomes a giant or a supergiant. As the star evolves, it might become a white dwarf.

3. Stars with large masses can explode to form a supernova. The outer layers are blown away and the core evolves into a neutron star or black hole. *At what temperature does fusion begin inside a nebula like the one shown here?*

Section 4 Galaxies and the Universe

1. A galaxy is a large group of stars, gas, and dust held together by gravity. Galaxies can be spiral, elliptical, or irregular in shape.

2. The Milky Way is a spiral galaxy containing about 200 billion stars.

3. The most accepted theory about the origin of the universe is the Big Bang theory.

FOLDABLES
Reading & Study Skills

After You Read

To help you review what you have read in this chapter, use your Foldable to explain the relationship among stars, galaxies, and the universe.

Visualizing Main Ideas

Complete the following concept map that shows the evolution of a main sequence star with a mass similar to that of the Sun.

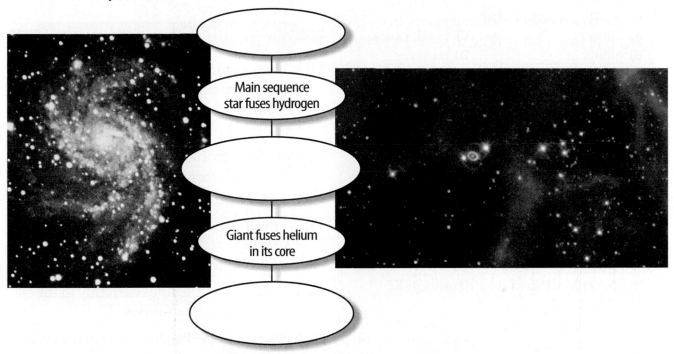

Main sequence star fuses hydrogen

Giant fuses helium in its core

Vocabulary Review

Vocabulary Review

a. absolute magnitude
b. apparent magnitude
c. Big Bang theory
d. black hole
e. chromosphere
f. constellation
g. corona
h. galaxy
i. giant
j. light-year
k. nebula
l. neutron star
m. photosphere
n. sunspot
o. supergiant
p. white dwarf

Study Tip

As you read, look up the definition of any prefixes you do not recognize. Once you know the meaning of a prefix, you'll be able to figure out the definitions of many new words.

Using Vocabulary

Explain the difference between the terms in each of the following sets.

1. absolute magnitude, apparent magnitude

2. black hole, neutron star

3. chromosphere, photosphere

4. galaxy, constellation

5. light-year, galaxy

6. giant, white dwarf

7. corona, sunspot

8. giant, supergiant

9. apparent magnitude, light-year

10. galaxy, Big Bang theory

Chapter ④ Assessment

Checking Concepts

Choose the word or phrase that best answers the question.

1. What are constellations?
   - **A)** clusters
   - **B)** giants
   - **C)** black holes
   - **D)** patterns

2. What is a measure of the amount of a star's light received on Earth?
   - **A)** absolute magnitude
   - **B)** apparent magnitude
   - **C)** fusion
   - **D)** parallax

3. What increases as an object comes closer to an observer?
   - **A)** absolute magnitude
   - **B)** red shift
   - **C)** parallax
   - **D)** blue shift

4. What happens after a nebula contracts and temperatures increase to 10 million K?
   - **A)** a black hole forms
   - **B)** a supernova forms
   - **C)** fusion begins
   - **D)** white dwarfs form

5. What is about 20 km in size?
   - **A)** giant
   - **B)** white dwarf
   - **C)** black hole
   - **D)** neutron star

6. What does the Sun fuse hydrogen into?
   - **A)** carbon
   - **B)** oxygen
   - **C)** iron
   - **D)** helium

7. What are loops of matter flowing from the Sun called?
   - **A)** sunspots
   - **B)** auroras
   - **C)** coronas
   - **D)** prominences

8. What are groups of galaxies called?
   - **A)** clusters
   - **B)** supergiants
   - **C)** giants
   - **D)** binary systems

9. Which galaxies are sometimes shaped like footballs?
   - **A)** spiral
   - **B)** elliptical
   - **C)** barred
   - **D)** irregular

10. What do scientists study to determine shifts in wavelengths of light?
    - **A)** spectrum
    - **B)** surface
    - **C)** corona
    - **D)** chromosphere

Thinking Critically

11. What is significant about the 1995 discovery by the *Hubble Space Telescope* of more than 1,500 galaxies, some at distances of more than 10 billion light-years?

12. How do scientists know that black holes exist if these objects don't emit any visible light?

13. Why can parallax be used only to measure distances to stars that are relatively close to the solar system?

14. Why doesn't the helium currently in the Sun's core undergo fusion?

15. Betelgeuse is the brightest star in the constellation Orion. However, Betelgeuse is a cool, red star that is 520 light-years from Earth. How can Betelgeuse look so bright if it is far away and has a cool surface?

Developing Skills

16. **Concept Mapping** Make a concept map that shows the relationship of temperature, color, and brightness of stars and their positions on the H-R diagram.

17. **Comparing and Contrasting** Compare and contrast the Sun with other stars on the H-R diagram.

18. **Measuring in SI** The Milky Way is 100,000 light-years in diameter. What scale would you use if you were to construct a model of the Milky Way with a diameter of 20 cm? What scale would you use to construct a model with a diameter of 5 m?

19. Interpreting Data Use the chart below to answer the following questions.

Magnitude and Distance of Stars			
Star	Apparent Magnitude	Absolute Magnitude	Distance in Light-Years
A	-26	4.8	0.000,02
B	-1.5	1.4	8.7
C	0.1	4.4	4.3
D	0.1	-7.0	815
E	0.4	-5.9	520
F	1.0	-0.6	45

a. Which star appears brightest from Earth? Which star appears dimmest from Earth?

b. Which star would appear brightest from a distance of 10 light-years? Which star would appear dimmest from this distance?

20. Making a Model Design and construct scale models of a spiral and a barred spiral Milky Way. Show the approximate position of the Sun in each.

Performance Assessment

21. Story Write a short science-fiction story about an astronaut traveling through the universe. In your story, tell what the astronaut observes. Use as many of the vocabulary terms from this chapter as you can.

TECHNOLOGY

Go to the Glencoe Science Web site at **science.glencoe.com** or use the **Glencoe Science CD-ROM** for additional chapter assessment.

Test Practice

The diagram below shows the distance from Earth to Proxima Centauri.

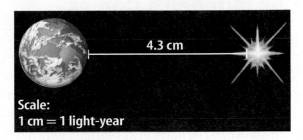

Scale:
1 cm = 1 light-year

Study the picture and answer the following questions.

1. Which of these instruments should you use to view Proxima Centauri?
 A) binoculars
 B) magnifying glass
 C) telescope
 D) microscope

2. What is the approximate distance of Proxima Centauri from Earth?
 F) 3.2 light-years
 G) 4.3 light-years
 H) 5.2 light-years
 J) 6.2 light-years

3. If astronomers shined a beam of laser light from Earth, how long would it take to reach Proxima Centauri?
 A) 3.2 years
 B) 4.3 years
 C) 5.2 years
 D) 6.2 years

4. At this scale, how far from Earth would you draw a star that is 100 light-years away?
 F) 50 cm **H)** 100 cm
 G) 75 cm **J)** 200 cm

Reading Comprehension

Read the passage. Then read each question following the passage. Determine the best answer.

Miss Mitchell's Comet

Maria Mitchell, born in 1818, grew up on the island of Nantucket, off the coast of Massachusetts. Maria Mitchell's father believed girls should aspire to high academic goals. An astronomer himself, he encouraged his daughter's interest in the stars and planets. Mr. Mitchell built a small observatory including a telescope on the roof of the family home.

One night in 1847, Maria spotted a star that she had never noticed before. It was five degrees above the North Star. The next night, Maria looked for the star, and it had moved. Maria realized that what she saw was not a star but a comet. Maria told her father the news. Mr. Mitchell wrote a letter to Professor William Bond of the Harvard University Observatory. Professor Bond sent Maria's name to the King of Denmark, who had offered a prize to the first person who discovered a comet using a telescope instead of binoculars or the unaided eye. Maria became acknowledged as a scholar, and in 1848 she became the first woman admitted to the American Academy of Arts and Sciences. After studying, Maria traveled the world. She lectured about astronomy and encouraged girls to get involved in science. She was Professor of Astronomy at Vassar College in Poughkeepsie, New York from 1865 until a year before her death in 1889.

Today, the Maria Mitchell Association continues her work. Every year, it awards a prize to a group or person who encourages the advancement of females in science. The association is at Maria's house on Nantucket where there is a large observatory.

Test-Taking Tip When asked the order of events in a story, find each answer choice in the passage and number them 1 to 4, from first to last.

1. Which of these happened first in Maria Mitchell's life?
   A) Maria joined the American Academy of Arts and Sciences.
   B) Maria began teaching at Vassar College.
   C) Maria discovered a comet while looking through a telescope.
   D) Maria traveled the world, lecturing about astronomy.

2. The main idea of this passage is that Maria _____.
   F) was not sure if she saw a star or a comet
   G) used her success to encourage others
   H) grew up on Nantucket Island
   J) received credit for her comet because of her father's help

Reasoning and Skills

Read each question and choose the best answer.

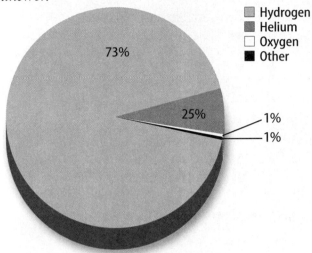

- Hydrogen
- Helium
- Oxygen
- Other

73%

25%

1%
1%

1. The circle graph shows the percentages of elements found in the Sun. What element is most abundant in the Sun?
A) Helium
C) Hydrogen
B) Other
D) Oxygen

Test-Taking Tip The key next to the graph is shaded to represent the elements found in the Sun.

2. The Sun produces energy by a process called fusion. During fusion, hydrogen nuclei combine to form helium. How would the circle graph shown above change as the Sun ages?
F) The helium slice would get larger.
G) The hydrogen slice would get larger.
H) The helium slice would get smaller.
J) The circle graph would not change.

Test-Taking Tip Think about what happens during fusion. Then examine the circle graph and select the best answer.

Consider this question carefully before writing your answer on a separate sheet of paper.

3. Astronomers indicate the brightness of a star in two ways—absolute magnitude and apparent magnitude. What do these terms mean, and why is it helpful to talk about the stars in two different ways?

Test-Taking Tip After defining each term on a separate sheet of paper, decide what the major difference between the two is. Then decide why this difference is important and carefully write out your answer.

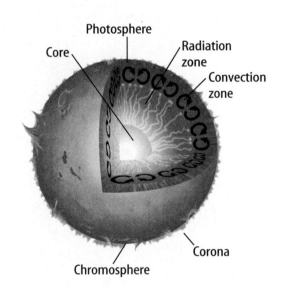

Photosphere
Core
Radiation zone
Convection zone
Corona
Chromosphere

4. The figure above represents a cross-section of ____.
A) Earth
C) the Sun
B) the Moon
D) Saturn

Test-Taking Tip Use key words from the graphic, such as Photosphere, to identify the correct answer.

Student Resources

Student Resources

Field GUIDE

For thousands of years, people have looked at the night sky and wondered about what they saw. To early Greek and Roman astronomers, groups of stars seemed to form pictures of animals, heroes, and other characters in myths. These star groups are called **constellations.** Constellations have guided travelers and have been an important part of some religions for a long time.

The Stars of the Zodiac

Are you a Leo, a Libra, a Capricorn, or a Virgo? The sign you were born under represents the constellation that the Sun was in at the moment of your first breath. What are the Zodiac signs, and why are they represented as constellations in the sky?

The Ancient Greeks noticed that the planets moved along a path in the sky. They also noticed star groups behind the revolving planets. They divided this path in the sky into 12 equal sectors, or divisions, and named them according to the star group that is found there. For example, Leo is a constellation resembling a lion; Aries is a ram. Ancient people referred to these star groups as the *Zodiac,* which means "carved figure" in Greek.

Backyard Astronomy

Big Dipper

Ursa Major

You've probably heard of the Big Dipper and even found it in the night sky. The Big Dipper is not a constellation. It's one part of a large constellation named Ursa Major, which is Latin for "Great Bear." The next time you look at the night sky, find the Big Dipper. Then try to find the rest of the stars that form the Great Bear.

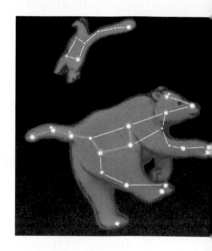

The Great Bear is just one of 88 identified constellations. You can't see all 88 constellations from the northern hemisphere, which is where you live. Some constellations are visible only in the northern hemisphere, and others are visible only in the southern hemisphere.

Field Activity

Observe the sky each night at the same time for a week. Use the appropriate star map and the instructions on the third page of this Field Guide to find the Big Dipper, Little Dipper, and Polaris. Then find at least three constellations. Draw the constellations in your Science Journal and label them with their names.

Constellations

The constellations always are in the same part of the sky, but they appear to move over time. As Earth rotates on its polar axis, the constellations appear to move from east to west across the sky each night. As Earth revolves around the Sun and the seasons change, some constellations come into view and others move out of view. For example, in the northern hemisphere, you can see Orion in winter and spring but not during summer and autumn. Pegasus is visible in autumn and winter but not in spring and summer. Other constellations, including Cassiopeia (ka see uh PEE uh) and the Great Bear, are visible to you all year.

In the northern hemisphere, all of the constellations rotate in a big circle around a bright star called Polaris, the North Star, which lies at the tail end of a group of stars called the Little Dipper. The Little Dipper is part of a constellation called Ursa Minor, which is Latin for "Little Bear." Ancient sailors used the North Star to navigate the oceans and find their way home.

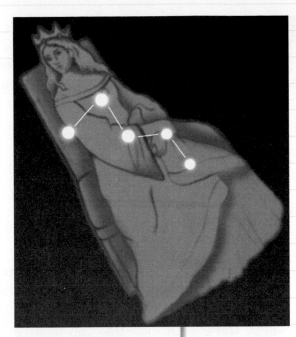

To find Cassiopeia, look for five bright stars that form a large *W* or a large *M*.

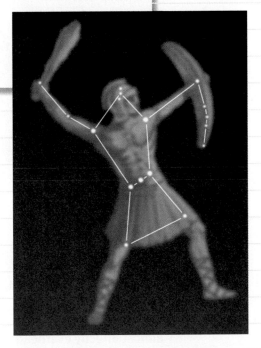

To find Orion, look for three bright stars close together in a straight line. These stars form Orion's belt.

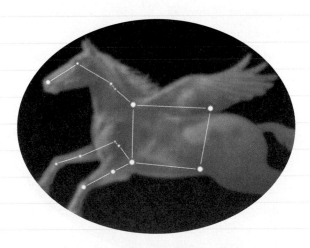

To find Pegasus, look for four bright stars that form a large square.

How to Find Constellations

Use these instructions to find constellations in the sky. The only time you'll be able to see the stars well is on a clear night without bright moonlight or light from buildings.

1. Choose the star map that shows the night sky for the season it is now. Take this book and a compass outside with you.

2. Use the compass to determine which direction is north, and stand facing that way. Turn the star map so the word *North* is right-side up. Compare the star patterns on the map with the stars you see in the northern sky. Find the Big Dipper. Use the picture on the first page of the field guide to help you.

3. Find the two stars that form the outer side of the Big Dipper's bowl. Imagine a line that connects those two stars and extends straight up from the dipper's bowl. Follow that line until you find a bright star. That star is Polaris, the North Star.

4. Starting from Polaris, find the stars that form the Little Bear. Find the stars that form the Great Bear.

5. Use the star map to find other constellations in the northern sky.

6. Turn around to face south. Turn the star map so the word *South* is right-side up. Use the map to find constellations in the southern sky.

7. Repeat step 6 facing west, then east.

8. As you search, try to find Cassiopeia. Look for Orion and/or Pegasus, depending on the season. Use the star map and the pictures on the second page of the field guide to help you.

Cygnus (SIHG nus), the "northern cross," is almost directly overhead in the autumn night sky.

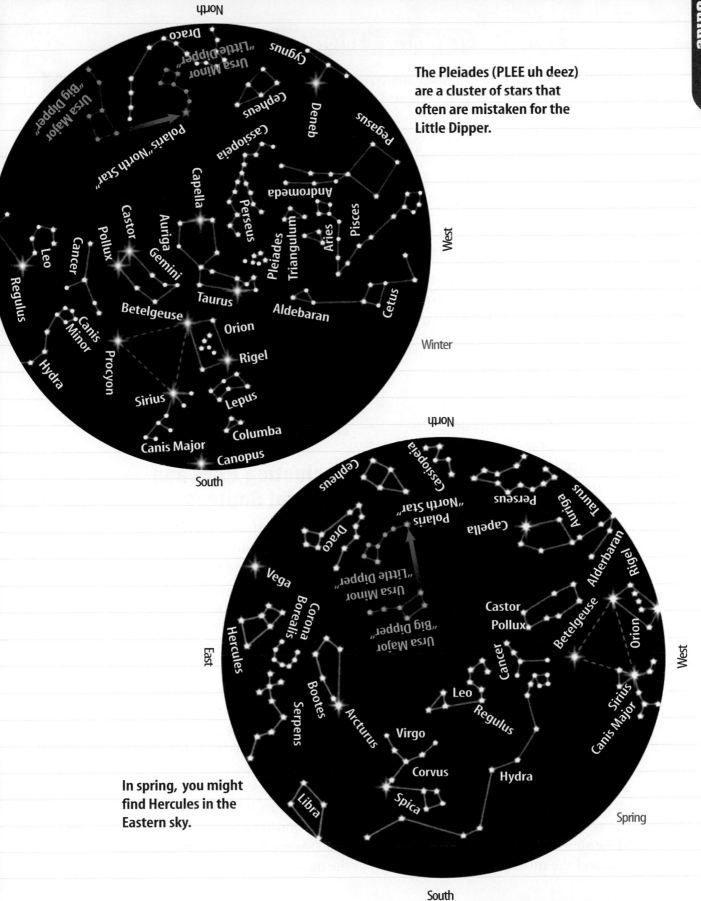

The Pleiades (PLEE uh deez) are a cluster of stars that often are mistaken for the Little Dipper.

In spring, you might find Hercules in the Eastern sky.

Organizing Information

As you study science, you will make many observations and conduct investigations and experiments. You will also research information that is available from many sources. These activities will involve organizing and recording data. The quality of the data you collect and the way you organize it will determine how well others can understand and use it. In **Figure 1,** the student is obtaining and recording information using a thermometer.

Putting your observations in writing is an important way of communicating to others the information you have found and the results of your investigations and experiments.

Researching Information

Scientists work to build on and add to human knowledge of the world. Before moving in a new direction, it is important to gather the information that already is known about a subject. You will look for such information in various reference sources. Follow these steps to research information on a scientific subject:

Step 1 Determine exactly what you need to know about the subject. For instance, you might want to find out what happened when Mount St. Helens erupted in 1980.

Step 2 Make a list of questions, such as: When did the eruption begin? How long did it last? What kind of material was expelled and how much?

Step 3 Use multiple sources such as textbooks, encyclopedias, government documents, professional journals, science magazines, and the Internet.

Step 4 List where you found the sources. Make sure the sources you use are reliable and the most current available.

Figure 1
Collecting data is one way to gather information directly.

Evaluating Print and Nonprint Sources

Not all sources of information are reliable. Evaluate the sources you use for information, and use only those you know to be dependable. For example, suppose you live in an area where earthquakes are common and you want to know what to do to keep safe. You might find two Web sites on earthquake safety. One Web site contains "Earthquake Tips" written by a company that sells metal scrapings to help secure your hot-water tank to the wall. The other is a Web page on "Earthquake Safety" written by the U.S. Geological Survey. You would choose the second Web site as the more reliable source of information.

In science, information can change rapidly. Always consult the most current sources. A 1985 source about the Moon would not reflect the most recent research and findings.

Interpreting Scientific Illustrations

As you research a science topic, you will see drawings, diagrams, and photographs. Illustrations help you understand what you read. Some illustrations are included to help you understand an idea that you can't see easily by yourself. For instance, you can't see the layers of Earth, but you can look at a diagram of Earth's layers, as labeled in **Figure 2,** that helps you understand what the layers are and where they are located. Visualizing a drawing helps many people remember details more easily. Illustrations also provide examples that clarify difficult concepts or give additional information about the topic you are studying.

Most illustrations have a label or caption. A label or caption identifies the illustration or provides additional information to better explain it. Can you find the caption or labels in **Figure 2?**

Venn Diagram

Although it is not a concept map, a Venn diagram illustrates how two subjects compare and contrast. In other words, you can see the characteristics that the subjects have in common and those that they do not.

The Venn diagram in **Figure 3** shows the relationship between two types of rocks made from the same basic chemical. Both rocks share the chemical calcium carbonate. However, due to the way they are formed, one rock is the sedimentary rock limestone, and the other is the metamorphic rock marble.

Concept Mapping

If you were taking a car trip, you might take some sort of road map. By using a map, you begin to learn where you are in relation to other places on the map.

A concept map is similar to a road map, but a concept map shows relationships among ideas (or concepts) rather than places. It is a diagram that visually shows how concepts are related. Because a concept map shows relationships among ideas, it can make the meanings of ideas and terms clear and help you understand what you are studying.

Overall, concept maps are useful for breaking large concepts down into smaller parts, making learning easier.

Figure 2
This cross section shows a slice through Earth's interior and the positions of its layers.

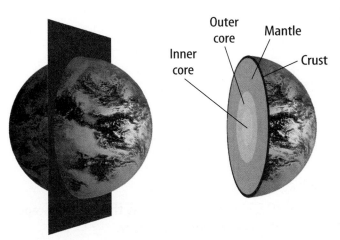

Figure 3
A Venn diagram shows how objects or concepts are alike and how they are different.

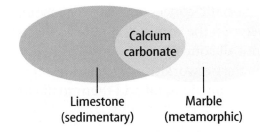

Science Skill Handbook

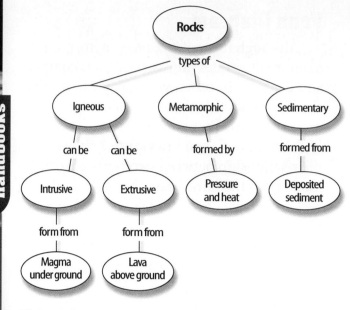

Figure 4
A network tree shows how concepts or objects are related.

Network Tree Look at the network tree in **Figure 4,** that shows the three main types of rock. A network tree is a type of concept map. Notice how some words are in ovals while others are written across connecting lines. The words inside the ovals are science terms or concepts. The words written on the connecting lines describe the relationships between the concepts.

When constructing a network tree, write the topic on a note card or piece of paper. Write the major concepts related to that topic on separate note cards or pieces of paper. Then arrange them in order from general to specific. Branch the related concepts from the major concept and describe the relationships on the connecting lines. Continue branching to more specific concepts. Write the relationships between the concepts on the connecting lines until all concepts are mapped. Then examine the network tree for relationships that cross branches, and add them to the network tree.

Events Chain An events chain is another type of concept map. It models the order of items or their sequence. In science, an events chain can be used to describe a sequence of events, the steps in a procedure, or the stages of a process.

When making an events chain, first find the one event that starts the chain. This event is called the *initiating event*. Then, find the next event in the chain and continue until you reach an outcome. Suppose you are asked to describe why and how a sound might make an echo. You might draw an events chain such as the one in **Figure 5.** Notice that connecting words are not necessary in an events chain.

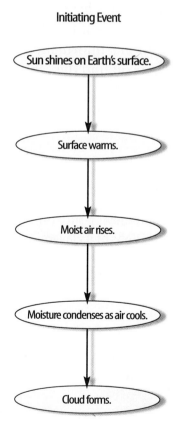

Figure 5
Events chains show the order of steps in a process or event.

Cycle Map A cycle concept map is a specific type of events chain map. In a cycle concept map, the series of events does not produce a final outcome. Instead, the last event in the chain relates back to the beginning event.

You first decide what event will be used as the beginning event. Once that is decided, you list events in order that occur after it. Words are written between events that describe what happens from one event to the next. The last event in a cycle concept map relates back to the beginning event. The number of events in a cycle concept varies but is usually three or more. Look at the cycle map shown in **Figure 6.**

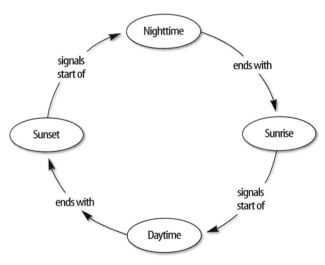

Figure 6
A cycle map shows events that occur in a cycle.

Spider Map A type of concept map that you can use for brainstorming is the spider map. When you have a central idea, you might find you have a jumble of ideas that relate to it but are not necessarily clearly related to each other. The spider map on mining in **Figure 7** shows that if you write these ideas outside the main concept, then you can begin to separate and group unrelated terms so they become more useful.

Figure 7
A spider map allows you to list ideas that relate to a central topic but not necessarily to one another.

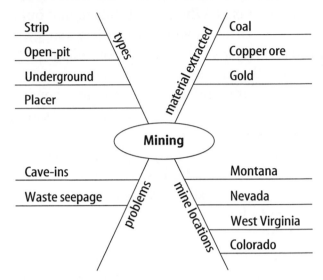

Writing a Paper

You will write papers often when researching science topics or reporting the results of investigations or experiments. Scientists frequently write papers to share their data and conclusions with other scientists and the public. When writing a paper, use these steps.

Step 1 Assemble your data by using graphs, tables, or a concept map. Create an outline.

Step 2 Start with an introduction that contains a clear statement of purpose and what you intend to discuss or prove.

Step 3 Organize the body into paragraphs. Each paragraph should start with a topic sentence, and the remaining sentences in that paragraph should support your point.

Step 4 Position data to help support your points.

Step 5 Summarize the main points and finish with a conclusion statement.

Step 6 Use tables, graphs, charts, and illustrations whenever possible.

Science Skill Handbook

You might say the work of a scientist is to solve problems. When you decide to find out why one corner of your yard is always soggy, you are problem solving, too. You might observe that the corner is lower than the surrounding area and has less vegetation growing in it. You might decide to see whether planting some grass will keep the corner drier.

Scientists use orderly approaches to solve problems. The methods scientists use include identifying a question, making observations, forming a hypothesis, testing a hypothesis, analyzing results, and drawing conclusions.

Scientific investigations involve careful observation under controlled conditions. Such observation of an object or a process can suggest new and interesting questions about it. These questions sometimes lead to the formation of a hypothesis. Scientific investigations are designed to test a hypothesis.

Identifying a Question

The first step in a scientific investigation or experiment is to identify a question to be answered or a problem to be solved. You might be interested in knowing why a rock like the one in **Figure 8** looks the way it does.

Figure 8
When you find a rock, you might ask yourself, "How did this rock form?"

Forming Hypotheses

Hypotheses are based on observations that have been made. A hypothesis is a possible explanation based on previous knowledge and observations.

Perhaps a scientist has observed that thunderstorms happen more often on hot days than on cooler days. Based on these observations, the scientist can make a statement that he or she can test. The statement is a hypothesis. The hypothesis could be: *Warm temperatures cause thunderstorms*. A hypothesis has to be something you can test by using an investigation. A testable hypothesis is a valid hypothesis.

Predicting

When you apply a hypothesis, or general explanation, to a specific situation, you predict something about that situation. First, you must identify which hypothesis fits the situation you are considering. People use predictions to make everyday decisions. Based on previous observations and experiences, you might form a prediction that if warm temperatures cause thunderstorms, then more thunderstorms will occur in summer months than in spring months. Someone could use these predictions to plan when to take a camping trip or when to schedule an outdoor activity.

Testing a Hypothesis

To test a hypothesis, you need a procedure. A procedure is the plan you follow in your experiment. A procedure tells you what materials to use, as well as how and in what order to use them. When you follow a procedure, data are generated that support or do not support the original hypothesis statement.

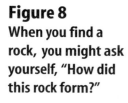

For example, premium gasoline costs more than regular gasoline. Does premium gasoline increase the efficiency or fuel mileage of your family car? You decide to test the hypothesis: "If premium gasoline is more efficient, then it should increase the fuel mileage of my family's car." Then you write the procedure shown in **Figure 9** for your experiment and generate the data presented in the table below.

Figure 9
A procedure tells you what to do step by step.

Procedure
1. Use regular gasoline for two weeks.
2. Record the number of kilometers between fill-ups and the amount of gasoline used.
3. Switch to premium gasoline for two weeks.
4. Record the number of kilometers between fill-ups and the amount of gasoline used.

Gasoline Data			
Type of Gasoline	Kilometers Traveled	Liters Used	Liters per Kilometer
Regular	762	45.34	0.059
Premium	661	42.30	0.064

These data show that premium gasoline is less efficient than regular gasoline in one particular car. It took more gasoline to travel 1 km (0.064) using premium gasoline than it did to travel 1 km using regular gasoline (0.059). This conclusion does not support the hypothesis.

Are all investigations alike? Keep in mind as you perform investigations in science that a hypothesis can be tested in many ways. Not every investigation makes use of all the ways that are described on these pages, and not all hypotheses are tested by investigations. Scientists encounter many variations in the methods that are used when they perform experiments. The skills in this handbook are here for you to use and practice.

Identifying and Manipulating Variables and Controls

In any experiment, it is important to keep everything the same except for the item you are testing. The one factor you change is called the independent variable. The factor that changes as a result of the independent variable is called the dependent variable. Always make sure you have only one independent variable. If you allow more than one, you will not know what causes the changes you observe in the dependent variable. Many experiments also have controls—individual instances or experimental subjects for which the independent variable is not changed. You can then compare the test results to the control results.

For example, in the fuel-mileage experiment, you made everything the same except the type of gasoline that was used. The driver, the type of automobile, and the type of driving were the same throughout. In this way, you could be sure that any mileage differences were caused by the type of fuel—the independent variable. The fuel mileage was the dependent variable.

If you could repeat the experiment using several automobiles of the same type on a standard driving track with the same driver, you could make one automobile a control by using regular gasoline over the four-week period.

Collecting Data

Whether you are carrying out an investigation or a short observational experiment, you will collect data, or information. Scientists collect data accurately as numbers and descriptions and organize it in specific ways.

Observing Scientists observe items and events, then record what they see. When they use only words to describe an observation, it is called qualitative data. For example, a scientist might describe the color, texture, or odor of a substance produced in a chemical reaction. Scientists' observations also can describe how much there is of something. These observations use numbers, as well as words, in the description and are called quantitative data. For example, if a sample of the element gold is described as being "shiny and very dense," the data are clearly qualitative. Quantitative data on this sample of gold might include "a mass of 30 g and a density of 19.3 g/cm^3." Quantitative data often are organized into tables. Then, from information in the table, a graph can be drawn. Graphs can reveal relationships that exist in experimental data.

When you make observations in science, you should examine the entire object or situation first, then look carefully for details. If you're looking at a rock sample, for instance, check the general color and pattern of the rock before using a hand lens to examine the small mineral grains that make up its underlying structure. Remember to record accurately everything you see.

Scientists try to make careful and accurate observations. When possible, they use instruments such as microscopes, metric rulers, graduated cylinders, thermometers, and balances. Measurements provide numerical data that can be repeated and checked.

Sampling When working with large numbers of objects or a large population, scientists usually cannot observe or study every one of them. Instead, they use a sample or a portion of the total number. To *sample* is to take a small, representative portion of the objects or organisms of a population for research. By making careful observations or manipulating variables within a portion of a group, information is discovered and conclusions are drawn that might apply to the whole population.

Estimating Scientific work also involves estimating. To *estimate* is to make a judgment about the amount or the number of something without measuring every part of an object or counting every member of a population. Scientists first measure or count the amount or number in a small sample. A chemist, for example, might remove a 10-g piece of a large rock that is rich in copper ore. Then the chemist can determine the percentage of copper by mass and multiply that percentage by the mass of the rock to get an estimate of the total mass of copper in the rock. See **Figure 10** for another example.

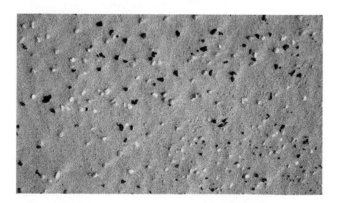

Figure 10
In a 1 m^2 frame positioned on a beach, count all the pebbles that you can see on the surface that are longer than 2.5 cm. Multiply this number by the area of the beach. This will give you an estimate for the total number of pebbles on the beach.

Measuring in SI

The metric system of measurement was developed in 1795. A modern form of the metric system, called the International System, or SI, was adopted in 1960. SI provides standard measurements that all scientists around the world can understand.

The metric system is convenient because unit sizes vary by multiples of 10. When changing from smaller units to larger units, divide by a multiple of 10. When changing from larger units to smaller, multiply by a multiple of 10. To convert millimeters to centimeters, divide the millimeters by 10. To convert 30 mm to centimeters, divide 30 by 10 (30 mm equal 3 cm).

Prefixes are used to name units. Look at the table below for some common metric prefixes and their meanings. Do you see how the prefix *kilo-* attached to the unit *gram* is *kilogram*, or 1,000 g?

Metric Prefixes			
Prefix	**Symbol**	**Meaning**	
kilo-	k	1,000	thousand
hecto-	h	100	hundred
deka-	da	10	ten
deci-	d	0.1	tenth
centi-	c	0.01	hundredth
milli-	m	0.001	thousandth

Now look at the metric ruler shown in **Figure 11.** The centimeter lines are the long, numbered lines, and the shorter lines are millimeter lines.

When using a metric ruler, line up the 0-cm mark with the end of the object being measured, and read the number of the unit where the object ends. In this instance, it would be 4.5 cm.

Figure 11
This metric ruler shows centimeter and millimeter divisions.

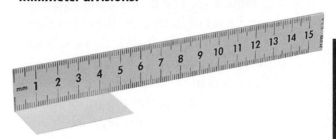

Liquid Volume In some science activities, you will measure liquids. The unit that is used to measure liquids is the liter. A liter has the volume of 1,000 cm³. The prefix *milli-* means "thousandth (0.001)." A milliliter is one thousandth of 1 L, and 1 L has the volume of 1,000 mL. One milliliter of liquid completely fills a cube measuring 1 cm on each side. Therefore, 1 mL equals 1 cm³.

You will use beakers and graduated cylinders to measure liquid volume. A graduated cylinder, as illustrated in **Figure 12,** is marked from bottom to top in milliliters. This one contains 79 mL of a liquid.

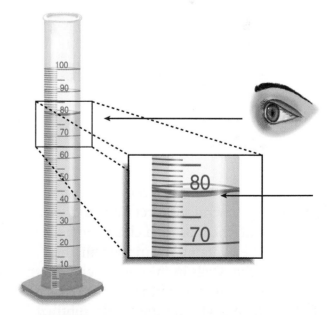

Figure 12
Graduated cylinders measure liquid volume.

Mass Scientists measure mass in grams. You might use a beam balance similar to the one shown in **Figure 13.** The balance has a pan on one side and a set of beams on the other side. Each beam has a rider that slides on the beam.

Before you find the mass of an object, slide all the riders back to the zero point. Check the pointer on the right to make sure it swings an equal distance above and below the zero point. If the swing is unequal, find and turn the adjusting screw until you have an equal swing.

Place an object on the pan. Slide the largest rider along its beam until the pointer drops below zero. Then move it back one notch. Repeat the process on each beam until the pointer swings an equal distance above and below the zero point. Sum the masses on each beam to find the mass of the object. Move all riders back to zero when finished.

Figure 13
A triple beam balance is used to determine the mass of an object.

You should never place a hot object on the pan or pour chemicals directly onto the pan. Instead, find the mass of a clean container. Remove the container from the pan, then place the chemicals in the container. Find the mass of the container with the chemicals in it. To find the mass of the chemicals, subtract the mass of the empty container from the mass of the filled container.

Making and Using Tables

Browse through your textbook and you will see tables in the text and in the activities. In a table, data, or information, are arranged so that they are easier to understand. Activity tables help organize the data you collect during an activity so results can be interpreted.

Making Tables To make a table, list the items to be compared in the first column and the characteristics to be compared in the first row. The title should clearly indicate the content of the table, and the column or row heads should tell the reader what information is found in there. The table below lists materials collected for recycling on three weekly pick-up days. The inclusion of kilograms in parentheses also identifies for the reader that the figures are mass units.

Recyclable Materials Collected During Week			
Day of Week	Paper (kg)	Aluminum (kg)	Glass (kg)
Monday	5.0	4.0	12.0
Wednesday	4.0	1.0	10.0
Friday	2.5	2.0	10.0

Using Tables How much paper, in kilograms, is being recycled on Wednesday? Locate the column labeled "Paper (kg)" and the row "Wednesday." The information in the box where the column and row intersect is the answer. Did you answer "4.0"? How much aluminum, in kilograms, is being recycled on Friday? If you answered "2.0," you understand how to read the table. How much glass is collected for recycling each week? Locate the column labeled "Glass (kg)" and add the figures for all three rows. If you answered "32.0," then you know how to locate and use the data provided in the table.

Recording Data

To be useful, the data you collect must be recorded carefully. Accuracy is key. A well-thought-out experiment includes a way to record procedures, observations, and results accurately. Data tables are one way to organize and record results. Set up the tables you will need ahead of time so you can record the data right away.

Record information properly and neatly. Never put unidentified data on scraps of paper. Instead, data should be written in a notebook like the one in **Figure 14.** Write in pencil so information isn't lost if your data gets wet. At each point in the experiment, record your data and label it. That way, your information will be accurate and you will not have to determine what the figures mean when you look at your notes later.

Figure 14
Record data neatly and clearly so it is easy to understand.

Recording Observations

It is important to record observations accurately and completely. That is why you always should record observations in your notes immediately as you make them. It is easy to miss details or make mistakes when recording results from memory. Do not include your personal thoughts when you record your data. Record only what you observe to eliminate bias. For example, when you record the time required for five students to climb the same set of stairs, you would note which student took the longest time. However, you would not refer to that student's time as "the worst time of all the students in the group."

Making Models

You can organize the observations and other data you collect and record in many ways. Making models is one way to help you better understand the parts of a structure you have been observing or the way a process for which you have been taking various measurements works.

Models often show things that are too large or too small for normal viewing. For example, you normally won't see the inside of an atom. However, you can understand the structure of the atom better by making a three-dimensional model of an atom. The relative sizes, the positions, and the movements of protons, neutrons, and electrons can be explained in words. An atomic model made of a plastic-ball nucleus and pipe-cleaner electron shells can help you visualize how the parts of the atom relate to each other.

Other models can be devised on a computer. Some models, such as those that illustrate the chemical combinations of different elements, are mathematical and are represented by equations.

Making and Using Graphs

After scientists organize data in tables, they might display the data in a graph that shows the relationship of one variable to another. A graph makes interpretation and analysis of data easier. Three types of graphs are the line graph, the bar graph, and the circle graph.

Line Graphs A line graph like in **Figure 15** is used to show the relationship between two variables. The variables being compared go on two axes of the graph. For data from an experiment, the independent variable always goes on the horizontal axis, called the *x*-axis. The dependent variable always goes on the vertical axis, called the *y*-axis. After drawing your axes, label each with a scale. Next, plot the data points.

A data point is the intersection of the recorded value of the dependent variable for each tested value of the independent variable. After all the points are plotted, connect them.

Bar Graphs Bar graphs compare data that do not change continuously. Vertical bars show the relationships among data.

To make a bar graph, set up the *y*-axis as you did for the line graph. Draw vertical bars of equal size from the *x*-axis up to the point on the *y*-axis that represents the value of *x*.

Figure 16
The amount of aluminum collected for recycling during one week can be shown as a bar graph or circle graph.

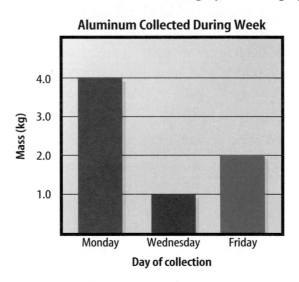

Circle Graphs A circle graph uses a circle divided into sections to display data as parts (fractions or percentages) of a whole. The size of each section corresponds to the fraction or percentage of the data that the section represents. So, the entire circle represents 100 percent, one-half represents 50 percent, one-fifth represents 20 percent, and so on.

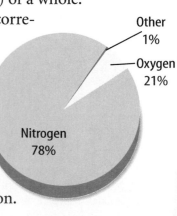

Figure 15
This line graph shows the relationship between degree of slope and the loss of soil in grams from a container during an experiment.

Analyzing Results

To determine the meaning of your observations and investigation results, you will need to look for patterns in the data. You can organize your information in several of the ways that are discussed in this handbook. Then you must think critically to determine what the data mean. Scientists use several approaches when they analyze the data they have collected and recorded. Each approach is useful for identifying specific patterns in the data.

Forming Operational Definitions

An operational definition defines an object by showing how it functions, works, or behaves. Such definitions are written in terms of how an object works or how it can be used; that is, they describe its job or purpose.

For example, a ruler can be defined as a tool that measures the length of an object (how it can be used). A ruler also can be defined as something that contains a series of marks that can be used as a standard when measuring (how it works).

Classifying

Classifying is the process of sorting objects or events into groups based on common features. When classifying, first observe the objects or events to be classified. Then select one feature that is shared by some members in the group but not by all. Place those members that share that feature into a subgroup. You can classify members into smaller and smaller subgroups based on characteristics.

How might you classify a group of rocks? You might first classify them by color, putting all of the black, white, and red rocks into separate groups. Within each group, you could then look for another common feature to classify further, such as size or whether the rocks have sharp or smooth edges.

Remember that when you classify, you are grouping objects or events for a purpose. For example, classifying rocks can be the first step in identifying them. You might know that obsidian is a black, shiny rock with sharp edges. To find it in a large group of rocks, you might start with the classification scheme mentioned. You'll locate obsidian within the group of black, sharp-edged rocks that you separate from the rest. Pumice could be located by its white color and by the fact that it contains many small holes called vesicles. Keep your purpose in mind as you select the features to form groups and subgroups.

Figure 17
Color is one of many characteristics that are used to classify rocks.

Science Skill Handbook

Comparing and Contrasting

Observations can be analyzed by noting the similarities and differences between two or more objects or events that you observe. When you look at objects or events to see how they are similar, you are comparing them. Contrasting is looking for differences in objects or events. The table below compares and contrasts the characteristics of two minerals.

Mineral Characteristics		
Mineral	Graphite	Gold
Color	black	bright yellow
Hardness	1–2	2.5–3
Luster	metallic	metallic
Uses	pencil "lead"	jewelry, electronics

Recognizing Cause and Effect

Have you ever heard a loud pop right before the power went out and then suggested that an electric transformer probably blew out? If so, you have observed an effect and inferred a cause. The event is the effect, and the reason for the event is the cause.

When scientists are unsure of the cause of a certain event, they design controlled experiments to determine what caused it.

Interpreting Data

The word *interpret* means "to explain the meaning of something." Look at the problem originally being explored in an experiment and figure out what the data show. Identify the control group and the test group so you can see whether or not changes in the independent variable have had an effect. Look for differences in the dependent variable between the control and test groups.

These differences you observe can be qualitative or quantitative. You would be able to describe a qualitative difference using only words, whereas you would measure a quantitative difference and describe it using numbers. If there are differences, the independent variable that is being tested could have had an effect. If no differences are found between the control and test groups, the variable that is being tested apparently had no effect.

For example, suppose that three beakers each contain 100 mL of water. The beakers are placed on hot plates, and two of the hot plates are turned on, but the third is left off for a period of 5 min. Suppose you are then asked to describe any differences in the water in the three beakers. A qualitative difference might be the appearance of bubbles rising to the top in the water that is being heated but no rising bubbles in the unheated water. A quantitative difference might be a difference in the amount of water that is present in the beakers.

Inferring Scientists often make inferences based on their observations. An inference is an attempt to explain, or interpret, observations or to indicate what caused what you observed. An inference is a type of conclusion.

When making an inference, be certain to use accurate data and accurately described observations. Analyze all of the data that you've collected. Then, based on everything you know, explain or interpret what you've observed.

Drawing Conclusions

When scientists have analyzed the data they collected, they proceed to draw conclusions about what the data mean. These conclusions are sometimes stated using words similar to those found in the hypothesis formed earlier in the process.

Conclusions To analyze your data, you must review all of the observations and measurements that you made and recorded. Recheck all data for accuracy. After your data are rechecked and organized, you are almost ready to draw a conclusion such as "salt water boils at a higher temperature than freshwater."

Before you can draw a conclusion, however, you must determine whether the data allow you to come to a conclusion that supports a hypothesis. Sometimes that will be the case; other times it will not.

If your data do not support a hypothesis, it does not mean that the hypothesis is wrong. It means only that the results of the investigation did not support the hypothesis. Maybe the experiment needs to be redesigned, but very likely, some of the initial observations on which the hypothesis was based were incomplete or biased. Perhaps more observation or research is needed to refine the hypothesis.

Avoiding Bias Sometimes drawing a conclusion involves making judgments. When you make a judgment, you form an opinion about what your data mean. It is important to be honest and to avoid reaching a conclusion if there is no supporting evidence for it or if it is based on a small sample. It also is important not to allow any expectations of results to bias your judgments. If possible, it is a good idea to collect additional data. Scientists do this all the time.

For example, the *Hubble Space Telescope* was sent into space in April, 1990, to provide scientists with clearer views of the universe. *Hubble* is the size of a school bus and has a 2.4-m-diameter mirror. *Hubble* helped scientists answer questions about the planet Pluto.

For many years, scientists had only been able to hypothesize about the surface of the planet Pluto. *Hubble* has now provided pictures of Pluto's surface that show a rough texture with light and dark regions on it. This might be the best information about Pluto scientists will have until they are able to send a space probe to it.

Evaluating Others' Data and Conclusions

Sometimes scientists have to use data that they did not collect themselves, or they have to rely on observations and conclusions drawn by other researchers. In cases such as these, the data must be evaluated carefully.

How were the data obtained? How was the investigation done? Was it carried out properly? Has it been duplicated by other researchers? Were they able to follow the exact procedure? Did they come up with the same results? Look at the conclusion, as well. Would you reach the same conclusion from these results? Only when you have confidence in the data of others can you believe it is true and feel comfortable using it.

Communicating

The communication of ideas is an important part of the work of scientists. A discovery that is not reported will not advance the scientific community's understanding or knowledge. Communication among scientists also is important as a way of improving their investigations.

Scientists communicate in many ways, from writing articles in journals and magazines that explain their investigations and experiments, to announcing important discoveries on television and radio, to sharing ideas with colleagues on the Internet or presenting them as lectures.

People who study science rely on computers to record and store data and to analyze results from investigations. Whether you work in a laboratory or just need to write a lab report with tables, good computer skills are a necessity.

Using a Word Processor

Suppose your teacher has assigned a written report. After you've completed your research and decided how you want to write the information, you need to put all that information on paper. The easiest way to do this is with a word processing application on a computer.

A computer application that allows you to type your information, change it as many times as you need to, and then print it out so that it looks neat and clean is called a word processing application. You also can use this type of application to create tables and columns, add bullets or cartoon art to your page, include page numbers, and check your spelling.

Helpful Hints

- If you aren't sure how to do something using your word processing program, look in the help menu. You will find a list of topics there to click on for help. After you locate the help topic you need, just follow the step-by-step instructions you see on your screen.
- Just because you've spell checked your report doesn't mean that the spelling is perfect. The spell check feature can't catch misspelled words that look like other words. If you've accidentally typed *mind* instead of *mine*, the spell checker won't know the difference. Always reread your report to make sure you didn't miss any mistakes.

Figure 18
You can use computer programs to make graphs and tables.

Using a Database

Imagine you're in the middle of a research project, busily gathering facts and information. You soon realize that it's becoming more difficult to organize and keep track of all the information. The tool to use to solve information overload is a database. Just as a file cabinet organizes paper records, a database organizes computer records. However, a database is more powerful than a simple file cabinet because at the click of a mouse, the contents can be reshuffled and reorganized. At computer-quick speeds, databases can sort information by any characteristics and filter data into multiple categories.

Helpful Hints

- Before setting up a database, take some time to learn the features of your database software by practicing with established database software.
- Periodically save your database as you enter data. That way, if something happens such as your computer malfunctions or the power goes off, you won't lose all of your work.

Doing a Database Search

When searching for information in a database, use the following search strategies to get the best results. These are the same search methods used for searching internet databases.

- Place the word *and* between two words in your search if you want the database to look for any entries that have both the words. For example, "Earth *and* Mars" would give you information that mentions both Earth and Mars.

- Place the word *or* between two words if you want the database to show entries that have at least one of the words. For example "Earth *or* Mars" would show you information that mentions either Earth or Mars.

- Place the word *not* between two words if you want the database to look for entries that have the first word but do not have the second word. For example, "Moon *not* phases" would show you information that mentions the Moon but does not mention its phases.

In summary, databases can be used to store large amounts of information about a particular subject. Databases allow biologists, Earth scientists, and physical scientists to search for information quickly and accurately.

Using an Electronic Spreadsheet

Your science fair experiment has produced lots of numbers. How do you keep track of all the data, and how can you easily work out all the calculations needed? You can use a computer program called a spreadsheet to record data that involve numbers. A spreadsheet is an electronic mathematical worksheet.

Type your data in rows and columns, just as they would look in a data table on a sheet of paper. A spreadsheet uses simple math to do data calculations. For example, you could add, subtract, divide, or multiply any of the values in the spreadsheet by another number. You also could set up a series of math steps you want to apply to the data. If you want to add 12 to all the numbers and then multiply all the numbers by 10, the computer does all the calculations for you in the spreadsheet. Below is an example of a spreadsheet that records weather data.

Helpful Hints

- Before you set up the spreadsheet, identify how you want to organize the data. Include any formulas you will need to use.
- Make sure you have entered the correct data into the correct rows and columns.
- You also can display your results in a graph. Pick the style of graph that best represents the data with which you are working.

Figure 19

A spreadsheet allows you to display large amounts of data and do calculations automatically.

	A	B	C	D	E
1	Readings	Temperature	Wind speed	Precipitation	
2	10:00 A.M.	21°C	24 km/h	–	
3	12:00 noon	23°C	26 km/h	–	
4	2:00 P.M.	25°C	24 km/h	light drizzle (.5cm)	
5					
6					
7					
8					
9					
10					
11					
12					
13					
14					
15					
16					
17					
18					

Using a Computerized Card Catalog

When you have a report or paper to research, you probably go to the library. To find the information you need in the library, you might have to use a computerized card catalog. This type of card catalog allows you to search for information by subject, by title, or by author. The computer then will display all the holdings the library has on the subject, title, or author requested.

A library's holdings can include books, magazines, databases, videos, and audio materials. When you have chosen something from this list, the computer will show whether an item is available and where in the library to find it.

Helpful Hints

- Remember that you can use the computer to search by subject, author, or title. If you know a book's author but not the title, you can search for all the books the library has by that author.

- When searching by subject, it's often most helpful to narrow your search by using specific search terms, such as *and, or,* and *not.* If you don't find enough sources, you can broaden your search.

- Pay attention to the type of materials found in your search. If you need a book, you can eliminate any videos or other resources that come up in your search.

- Knowing how your library is arranged can save you a lot of time. If you need help, the librarian will show you where certain types of materials are kept and how to find specific items.

Using Graphics Software

Are you having trouble finding that exact piece of art you're looking for? Do you have a picture in your mind of what you want but can't seem to find the right graphic to represent your ideas? To solve these problems, you can use graphics software. Graphics software allows you to create and change images and diagrams in almost unlimited ways. Typical uses for graphics software include arranging clip art, changing scanned images, and constructing pictures from scratch. Most graphics software applications work in similar ways. They use the same basic tools and functions. Once you master one graphics application, you can use other graphics applications.

Figure 20
Graphics software can use your data to draw bar graphs.

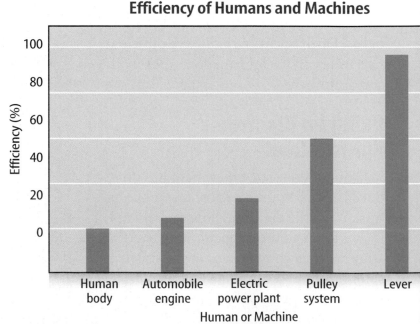

Efficiency of Humans and Machines

Figure 21

You can use this circle graph to find the names of the major gases that make up Earth's atmosphere.

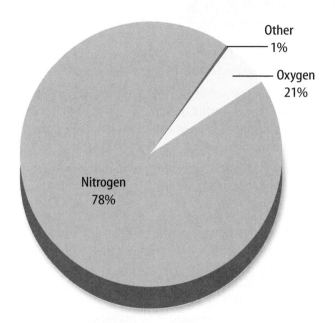

Other
1%

Oxygen
21%

Nitrogen
78%

Helpful Hints

- As with any method of drawing, the more you practice using the graphics software, the better your results will be.
- Start by using the software to manipulate existing drawings. Once you master this, making your own illustrations will be easier.
- Clip art is available on CD-ROMs and the Internet. With these resources, finding a piece of clip art to suit your purposes is simple.
- As you work on a drawing, save it often.

Developing Multimedia Presentations

It's your turn—you have to present your science report to the entire class. How do you do it? You can use many different sources of information to get the class excited about your presentation. Posters, videos, photographs, sound, computers, and the Internet can help show your ideas.

First, determine what important points you want to make in your presentation. Then, write an outline of what materials and types of media would best illustrate those points. Maybe you could start with an outline on an overhead projector, then show a video, followed by something from the Internet or a slide show accompanied by music or recorded voices. You might choose to use a presentation builder computer application that can combine all these elements into one presentation. Make sure the presentation is well constructed to make the most impact on the audience.

Figure 22

Multimedia presentations use many types of print and electronic materials.

Helpful Hints

- Carefully consider what media will best communicate the point you are trying to make.
- Make sure you know how to use any equipment you will be using in your presentation.
- Practice the presentation several times.
- If possible, set up all of the equipment ahead of time. Make sure everything is working correctly.

Math Skill Handbook

Use this Math Skill Handbook to help solve problems you are given in this text. You might find it useful to review topics in this Math Skill Handbook first.

Converting Units

In science, quantities such as length, mass, and time sometimes are measured using different units. Suppose you want to know how many miles are in 12.7 km.

Conversion factors are used to change from one unit of measure to another. A conversion factor is a ratio that is equal to one. For example, there are 1,000 mL in 1 L, so 1,000 mL equals 1 L, or:

$$1,000 \text{ mL} = 1 \text{ L}$$

If both sides are divided by 1 L, this equation becomes:

$$\frac{1,000 \text{ mL}}{1 \text{ L}} = 1$$

The **ratio** on the left side of this equation is equal to 1 and is a conversion factor. You can make another conversion factor by dividing both sides of the top equation by 1,000 mL:

$$1 = \frac{1 \text{ L}}{1,000 \text{ mL}}$$

To **convert units,** you multiply by the appropriate conversion factor. For example, how many milliliters are in 1.255 L? To convert 1.255 L to milliliters, multiply 1.255 L by a conversion factor.

Use the **conversion factor** with new units (mL) in the numerator and the old units (L) in the denominator.

$$1.255 \text{ L} \times \frac{1,000 \text{ mL}}{1 \text{ L}} = 1,255 \text{ mL}$$

The unit L divides in this equation, just as if it were a number.

Example 1 There are 2.54 cm in 1 inch. If a meterstick has a length of 100 cm, how long is the meterstick in inches?

Step 1 Decide which conversion factor to use. You know the length of the meterstick in centimeters, so centimeters are the old units. You want to find the length in inches, so inch is the new unit.

Step 2 Form the conversion factor. Start with the relationship between the old and new units.

$$2.54 \text{ cm} = 1 \text{ inch}$$

Step 3 Form the conversion factor with the old unit (centimeter) on the bottom by dividing both sides by 2.54 cm.

$$1 = \frac{2.54 \text{ cm}}{2.54 \text{ cm}} = \frac{1 \text{ inch}}{2.54 \text{ cm}}$$

Step 4 Multiply the old measurement by the conversion factor.

$$100 \text{ cm} \times \frac{1 \text{ inch}}{2.54 \text{ cm}} = 39.37 \text{ inches}$$

The meterstick is 39.37 inches long.

Example 2 There are 365 days in one year. If a person is 14 years old, what is his or her age in days? (Ignore leap years).

Step 1 Decide which conversion factor to use. You want to convert years to days.

Step 2 Form the conversion factor. Start with the relation between the old and new units.

$$1 \text{ year} = 365 \text{ days}$$

Step 3 Form the conversion factor with the old unit (year) on the bottom by dividing both sides by 1 year.

$$1 = \frac{1 \text{ year}}{1 \text{ year}} = \frac{365 \text{ days}}{1 \text{ year}}$$

Step 4 Multiply the old measurement by the conversion factor:

$$14 \text{ years} \times \frac{365 \text{ days}}{1 \text{ year}} = 5,110 \text{ days}$$

The person's age is 5,110 days.

Practice Problem A book has a mass of 2.31 kg. If there are 1,000 g in 1 kg, what is the mass of the book in grams?

Using Fractions

A **fraction** is a number that compares a part to the whole. For example, in the fraction $\frac{2}{3}$, the 2 represents the part and the 3 represents the whole. In the fraction $\frac{2}{3}$, the top number, 2, is called the numerator. The bottom number, 3, is called the denominator.

Sometimes fractions are not written in their simplest form. To determine a fraction's **simplest form,** you must find the greatest common factor (GCF) of the numerator and denominator. The greatest common factor is the largest common factor of all the factors the two numbers have in common.

For example, because the number 3 divides into 12 and 30 evenly, it is a common factor of 12 and 30. However, because the number 6 is the largest number that evenly divides into 12 and 30, it is the **greatest common factor.**

After you find the greatest common factor, you can write a fraction in its simplest form. Divide both the numerator and the denominator by the greatest common factor. The number that results is the fraction in its **simplest form.**

Example Twelve of the 20 peaks in a mountain range have elevations over 10,000 m. What fraction of the peaks in the mountain range are over 10,000 m? Write the fraction in simplest form.

Step 1 Write the fraction.

$$\frac{\text{part}}{\text{whole}} = \frac{12}{20}$$

Step 2 To find the GCF of the numerator and denominator, list all of the factors of each number.

Factors of 12: 1, 2, 3, 4, 6, 12 (the numbers that divide evenly into 12)

Factors of 20: 1, 2, 4, 5, 10, 20 (the numbers that divide evenly into 20)

Step 3 List the common factors.

1, 2, 4.

Step 4 Choose the greatest factor in the list of common factors.

The GCF of 12 and 20 is 4.

Step 5 Divide the numerator and denominator by the GCF.

$$\frac{12 \div 4}{20 \div 4} = \frac{3}{5}$$

In the mountain range, $\frac{3}{5}$ of the peaks are over 10,000 m.

Practice Problem There are 90 rides at an amusement park. Of those rides, 66 have a height restriction. What fraction of the rides has a height restriction? Write the fraction in simplest form.

Math Skill Handbook

Calculating Ratios

A **ratio** is a comparison of two numbers by division.

Ratios can be written 3 to 5 or 3:5. Ratios also can be written as fractions, such as $\frac{3}{5}$. Ratios, like fractions, can be written in simplest form. Recall that a fraction is in **simplest form** when the greatest common factor (GCF) of the numerator and denominator is 1.

Example A particular geologic sample contains 40 kg of shale and 64 kg of granite. What is the ratio of shale to granite as a fraction in simplest form?

Step 1 Write the ratio as a fraction. $\dfrac{\text{shale}}{\text{granite}} = \dfrac{40}{64}$

Step 2 Express the fraction in simplest form. The GCF of 40 and 64 is 8.

$$\frac{40}{64} = \frac{40 \div 8}{64 \div 8} = \frac{5}{8}$$

The ratio of shale to granite in the sample is $\frac{5}{8}$.

Practice Problem Two metal rods measure 100 cm and 144 cm in length. What is the ratio of their lengths in simplest fraction form?

Using Decimals

A **decimal** is a fraction with a denominator of 10, 100, 1,000, or another power of 10. For example, 0.854 is the same as the fraction $\frac{854}{1,000}$.

In a decimal, the decimal point separates the ones place and the tenths place. For example, 0.27 means twenty-seven hundredths, or $\frac{27}{100}$, where 27 is the **number of units** out of 100 units. Any fraction can be written as a decimal using division.

Example Write $\frac{5}{8}$ as a decimal.

Step 1 Write a division problem with the numerator, 5, as the dividend and the denominator, 8, as the divisor. Write 5 as 5.000.

Step 2 Solve the problem.

```
      0.625
 8)5.000
    4 8
      20
      16
      40
      40
       0
```

Therefore, $\frac{5}{8} = 0.625$.

Practice Problem Write $\frac{19}{25}$ as a decimal.

Using Percentages

The word *percent* means "out of one hundred." A **percent** is a ratio that compares a number to 100. Suppose you read that 77 percent of Earth's surface is covered by water. That is the same as reading that the fraction of Earth's surface covered by water is $\frac{77}{100}$. To express a fraction as a percent, first find an equivalent decimal for the fraction. Then, multiply the decimal by 100 and add the percent symbol. For example, $\frac{1}{2} = 1 \div 2 = 0.5$. Then $0.5 \cdot 100 = 50 = 50\%$.

Example Express $\frac{13}{20}$ as a percent.

Step 1 Find the equivalent decimal for the fraction.

$$
\begin{array}{r}
0.65 \\
20)\overline{13.00} \\
\underline{12\,0} \\
100 \\
\underline{100} \\
0
\end{array}
$$

Step 2 Rewrite the fraction $\frac{13}{20}$ as 0.65.

Step 3 Multiply 0.65 by 100 and add the % sign.

$0.65 \cdot 100 = 65 = 65\%$

So, $\frac{13}{20} = 65\%$.

Practice Problem In one year, 73 of 365 days were rainy in one city. What percent of the days in that city were rainy?

Using Precision and Significant Digits

When you make a **measurement,** the value you record depends on the precision of the measuring instrument. When adding or subtracting numbers with different precision, the answer is rounded to the smallest number of decimal places of any number in the sum or difference. When multiplying or dividing, the answer is rounded to the smallest number of significant figures of any number being multiplied or divided. When counting the number of **significant figures,** all digits are counted except zeros at the end of a number with no decimal such as 2,500, and zeros at the beginning of a decimal such as 0.03020.

Example The lengths 5.28 and 5.2 are measured in meters. Find the sum of these lengths and report the sum using the least precise measurement.

Step 1 Find the sum.

5.28 m	2 digits after the decimal
+ 5.2 m	1 digit after the decimal
10.48 m	

Step 2 Round to one digit after the decimal because the least number of digits after the decimal of the numbers being added is 1.

The sum is 10.5 m.

Practice Problem Multiply the numbers in the example using the rule for multiplying and dividing. Report the answer with the correct number of significant figures.

Math Skill Handbook

Solving One-Step Equations

An **equation** is a statement that two things are equal. For example, $A = B$ is an equation that states that A is equal to B.

Sometimes one side of the equation will contain a **variable** whose value is not known. In the equation $3x = 12$, the variable is x.

The equation is solved when the variable is replaced with a value that makes both sides of the equation equal to each other. For example, the solution of the equation $3x = 12$ is $x = 4$. If the x is replaced with 4, then the equation becomes $3 \cdot 4 = 12$, or $12 = 12$.

To solve an equation such as $8x = 40$, divide both sides of the equation by the number that multiplies the variable.

$$8x = 40$$
$$\frac{8x}{8} = \frac{40}{8}$$
$$x = 5$$

You can check your answer by replacing the variable with your solution and seeing if both sides of the equation are the same.

$$8x = 8 \cdot 5 = 40$$

The left and right sides of the equation are the same, so $x = 5$ is the solution.

Sometimes an equation is written in this way: $a = bc$. This also is called a **formula.** The letters can be replaced by numbers, but the numbers must still make both sides of the equation the same.

Example 1 Solve the equation $10x = 35$.

Step 1 Find the solution by dividing each side of the equation by 10.

$$10x = 35 \qquad \frac{10x}{10} = \frac{35}{10} \qquad x = 3.5$$

Step 2 Check the solution.

$$10x = 35 \qquad 10 \times 3.5 = 35 \qquad 35 = 35$$

Both sides of the equation are equal, so $x = 3.5$ is the solution to the equation.

Example 2 In the formula $a = bc$, find the value of c if $a = 20$ and $b = 2$.

Step 1 Rearrange the formula so the unknown value is by itself on one side of the equation by dividing both sides by b.

$$a = bc$$
$$\frac{a}{b} = \frac{bc}{b}$$
$$\frac{a}{b} = c$$

Step 2 Replace the variables a and b with the values that are given.

$$\frac{a}{b} = c$$
$$\frac{20}{2} = c$$
$$10 = c$$

Step 3 Check the solution.

$$a = bc$$
$$20 = 2 \times 10$$
$$20 = 20$$

Both sides of the equation are equal, so $c = 10$ is the solution when $a = 20$ and $b = 2$.

Practice Problem In the formula $h = gd$, find the value of d if $g = 12.3$ and $h = 17.4$.

Using Proportions

A **proportion** is an equation that shows that two ratios are equivalent. The ratios $\frac{2}{4}$ and $\frac{5}{10}$ are equivalent, so they can be written as $\frac{2}{4} = \frac{5}{10}$. This equation is an example of a proportion.

When two ratios form a proportion, the **cross products** are equal. To find the cross products in the proportion $\frac{2}{4} = \frac{5}{10}$, multiply the 2 and the 10, and the 4 and the 5. Therefore $2 \cdot 10 = 4 \cdot 5$, or $20 = 20$.

Because you know that both proportions are equal, you can use cross products to find a missing term in a proportion. This is known as **solving the proportion.** Solving a proportion is similar to solving an equation.

Example The heights of a tree and a pole are proportional to the lengths of their shadows. The tree casts a shadow of 24 m at the same time that a 6-m pole casts a shadow of 4 m. What is the height of the tree?

Step 1 Write a proportion.

$$\frac{\text{height of tree}}{\text{height of pole}} = \frac{\text{length of tree's shadow}}{\text{length of pole's shadow}}$$

Step 2 Substitute the known values into the proportion. Let h represent the unknown value, the height of the tree.

$$\frac{h}{6} = \frac{24}{4}$$

Step 3 Find the cross products.

$$h \cdot 4 = 6 \cdot 24$$

Step 4 Simplify the equation.

$$4h = 144$$

Step 5 Divide each side by 4.

$$\frac{4h}{4} = \frac{144}{4}$$

$$h = 36$$

The height of the tree is 36 m.

Practice Problem The ratios of the weights of two objects on the Moon and on Earth are in proportion. A rock weighing 3 N on the Moon weighs 18 N on Earth. How much would a rock that weighs 5 N on the Moon weigh on Earth?

Using Statistics

Statistics is the branch of mathematics that deals with collecting, analyzing, and presenting data. In statistics, there are three common ways to summarize the data with a single number—the mean, the median, and the mode.

The **mean** of a set of data is the arithmetic average. It is found by adding the numbers in the data set and dividing by the number of items in the set.

The **median** is the middle number in a set of data when the data are arranged in numerical order. If there were an even number of data points, the median would be the mean of the two middle numbers.

The **mode** of a set of data is the number or item that appears most often.

Another number that often is used to describe a set of data is the range. The **range** is the difference between the largest number and the smallest number in a set of data.

A **frequency table** shows how many times each piece of data occurs, usually in a survey. The frequency table below shows the results of a student survey on favorite color.

Color	Tally	Frequency
red	IIII	4
blue	IIII	5
black	II	2
green	III	3
purple	IIII II	7
yellow	IIII I	6

Based on the frequency table data, which color is the favorite?

Example The high temperatures (in °C) on five consecutive days at a desert observation station are 39°, 37°, 44°, 36°, and 44°. Find the mean, median, mode, and range of this set.

To find the mean:
Step 1 Find the sum of the numbers.

$$39 + 37 + 44 + 36 + 44 = 200$$

Step 2 Divide the sum by the number of items, which is 5.

$$200 \div 5 = 40$$

The mean high temperature is 40°C.

To find the median:
Step 1 Arrange the temperatures from least to greatest.

$$36, \ 37, \ \underline{39}, \ 44, \ 44$$

Step 2 Determine the middle temperature.

The median high temperature is 39°C.

To find the mode:
Step 1 Group the numbers that are the same together.

$$44, 44, 36, 37, 39$$

Step 2 Determine the number that occurs most in the set.

$$\underline{44, 44}, 36, 37, 39$$

The mode measure is 44°C.

To find the range:
Step 1 Arrange the temperatures from largest to smallest.

$$44, 44, 39, 37, 36$$

Step 2 Determine the largest and smallest temperature in the set.

$$\underline{44}, 44, 39, 37, \underline{36}$$

Step 3 Find the difference between the largest and smallest temperatures.

$$44 - 36 = 8$$

The range is 8°C.

Practice Problem Find the mean, median, mode, and range for the data set 8, 4, 12, 8, 11, 14, 16.

Safety in the Science Classroom

1. Always obtain your teacher's permission to begin an investigation.

2. Study the procedure. If you have questions, ask your teacher. Be sure you understand any safety symbols shown on the page.

3. Use the safety equipment provided for you. Goggles and a safety apron should be worn during most investigations.

4. Always slant test tubes away from yourself and others when heating them or adding substances to them.

5. Never eat or drink in the lab, and never use lab glassware as food or drink containers. Never inhale chemicals. Do not taste any substances or draw any material into a tube with your mouth.

6. Report any spill, accident, or injury, no matter how small, immediately to your teacher; then follow his or her instructions.

7. Know the location and proper use of the fire extinguisher, safety shower, fire blanket, first aid kit, and fire alarm.

8. Keep all materials away from open flames. Tie back long hair and tie down loose clothing.

9. If your clothing should catch fire, smother it with the fire blanket, or get under a safety shower. NEVER RUN.

10. If a fire should occur, turn off the gas; then leave the room according to established procedures.

Follow these procedures as you clean up your work area

1. Turn off the water and gas. Disconnect electrical devices.

2. Clean all pieces of equipment and return all materials to their proper places.

3. Dispose of chemicals and other materials as directed by your teacher. Place broken glass and solid substances in the proper containers. Make sure never to discard materials in the sink.

4. Clean your work area. Wash your hands thoroughly after working in the laboratory.

First Aid	
Injury	**Safe Response ALWAYS NOTIFY YOUR TEACHER IMMEDIATELY**
Burns	Apply cold water.
Cuts and Bruises	Stop any bleeding by applying direct pressure. Cover cuts with a clean dressing. Apply ice packs or cold compresses to bruises.
Fainting	Leave the person lying down. Loosen any tight clothing and keep crowds away.
Foreign Matter in Eye	Flush with plenty of water. Use eyewash bottle or fountain.
Poisoning	Note the suspected poisoning agent.
Any Spills on Skin	Flush with large amounts of water or use safety shower.

REFERENCE HANDBOOK B

SI—Metric/English, English/Metric Conversions

	When you want to convert:	To:	Multiply by:
Length	inches	centimeters	2.54
	centimeters	inches	0.39
	yards	meters	0.91
	meters	yards	1.09
	miles	kilometers	1.61
	kilometers	miles	0.62
Mass and Weight*	ounces	grams	28.35
	grams	ounces	0.04
	pounds	kilograms	0.45
	kilograms	pounds	2.2
	tons (short)	tonnes (metric tons)	0.91
	tonnes (metric tons)	tons (short)	1.10
	pounds	newtons	4.45
	newtons	pounds	0.22
Volume	cubic inches	cubic centimeters	16.39
	cubic centimeters	cubic inches	0.06
	liters	quarts	1.06
	quarts	liters	0.95
	gallons	liters	3.78
Area	square inches	square centimeters	6.45
	square centimeters	square inches	0.16
	square yards	square meters	0.83
	square meters	square yards	1.19
	square miles	square kilometers	2.59
	square kilometers	square miles	0.39
	hectares	acres	2.47
	acres	hectares	0.40
Temperature	To convert °Celsius to °Fahrenheit		$°C \times 9/5 + 32$
	To convert °Fahrenheit to °Celsius		$5/9 \ (°F - 32)$

*Weight is measured in standard Earth gravity.

REFERENCE HANDBOOK C

Rocks		
Rock Type	**Rock Name**	**Characteristics**
Igneous (intrusive)	Granite	Large mineral grains of quartz, feldspar, hornblende, and mica. Usually light in color.
	Diorite	Large mineral grains of feldspar, hornblende, and mica. Less quartz than granite. Intermediate in color.
	Gabbro	Large mineral grains of feldspar, augite, and olivine. No quartz. Dark in color.
Igneous (extrusive)	Rhyolite	Small mineral grains of quartz, feldspar, hornblende, and mica, or no visible grains. Light in color.
	Andesite	Small mineral grains of feldspar, hornblende, and mica or no visible grains. Intermediate in color.
	Basalt	Small mineral grains of feldspar, augite, and olivine or no visible grains. No quartz. Dark in color.
	Obsidian	Glassy texture. No visible grains. Volcanic glass. Fracture looks like broken glass.
	Pumice	Frothy texture. Floats in water. Usually light in color.
Sedimentary (detrital)	Conglomerate	Coarse grained. Gravel or pebble size grains.
	Sandstone	Sand-sized grains 1/16 to 2 mm.
	Siltstone	Grains are smaller than sand but larger than clay.
	Shale	Smallest grains. Often dark in color. Usually platy.
Sedimentary (chemical or organic)	Limestone	Major mineral is calcite. Usually forms in oceans, lakes, and caves. Often contains fossils.
	Coal	Occurs in swampy areas. Compacted layers of organic material, mainly plant remains.
Sedimentary (chemical)	Rock Salt	Commonly forms by the evaporation of seawater.
Metamorphic (foliated)	Gneiss	Banding due to alternate layers of different minerals, of different colors. Parent rock often is granite.
	Schist	Parallel arrangement of sheetlike minerals, mainly micas. Forms from different parent rocks.
	Phyllite	Shiny or silky appearance. May look wrinkled. Common parent rocks are shale and slate.
	Slate	Harder, denser, and shinier than shale. Common parent rock is shale.
Metamorphic (non-foliated)	Marble	Calcite or dolomite. Common parent rock is limestone.
	Soapstone	Mainly of talc. Soft with greasy feel.
	Quartzite	Hard with interlocking quartz crystals. Common parent rock is sandstone.

REFERENCE HANDBOOK D

Minerals

Mineral (formula)	Color	Streak	Hardness	Breakage Pattern	Uses and Other Properties
Graphite (C)	black to gray	black to gray	1–1.5	basal cleavage (scales)	pencil lead, lubricants for locks, rods to control some small nuclear reactions, battery poles
Galena (PbS)	gray	gray to black	2.5	cubic cleavage perfect	source of lead, used for pipes, shields for X rays, fishing equipment sinkers
Hematite (Fe_2O_3)	black or reddish-brown	reddish-brown	5.5–6.5	irregular fracture	source of iron; converted to pig iron, made into steel
Magnetite (Fe_3O_4)	black	black	6	conchoidal fracture	source of iron, attracts a magnet
Pyrite (FeS_2)	light, brassy, yellow	greenish-black	6–6.5	uneven fracture	fool's gold
Talc ($Mg_3 Si_4O_{10} (OH)_2$)	white, greenish	white	1	cleavage in one direction	used for talcum powder, sculptures, paper, and tabletops
Gypsum ($CaSO_4 \cdot 2H_2O$)	colorless, gray, white, brown	white	2	basal cleavage	used in plaster of paris and dry wall for building construction
Sphalerite (ZnS)	brown, reddish-brown, greenish	light to dark brown	3.5–4	cleavage in six directions	main ore of zinc; used in paints, dyes, and medicine
Muscovite ($KAl_3Si_3 O_{10}(OH)_2$)	white, light gray, yellow, rose, green	colorless	2–2.5	basal cleavage	occurs in large, flexible plates; used as an insulator in electrical equipment, lubricant
Biotite ($K(Mg,Fe)_3 (AlSi_3O_{10}) (OH)_2$)	black to dark brown	colorless	2.5–3	basal cleavage	occurs in large, flexible plates
Halite (NaCl)	colorless, red, white, blue	colorless	2.5	cubic cleavage	salt; soluble in water; a preservative

Minerals

Mineral (formula)	Color	Streak	Hardness	Breakage Pattern	Uses and Other Properties
Calcite ($CaCO_3$)	colorless, white, pale blue	colorless, white	3	cleavage in three directions	fizzes when HCl is added; used in cements and other building materials
Dolomite ($CaMg(CO_3)_2$)	colorless, white, pink, green, gray, black	white	3.5–4	cleavage in three directions	concrete and cement; used as an ornamental building stone
Fluorite (CaF_2)	colorless, white, blue, green, red, yellow, purple	colorless	4	cleavage in four directions	used in the manufacture of optical equipment; glows under ultraviolet light
Hornblende ($(CaNa)_{2-3}$ $(Mg,Al,$ $Fe)_5-(Al,Si)_2$ Si_6O_{22} $(OH)_2$)	green to black	gray to white	5–6	cleavage in two directions	will transmit light on thin edges; 6-sided cross section
Feldspar ($KAlSi_3O_8$) ($NaAl$ Si_3O_8), ($CaAl_2Si_2$ O_8)	colorless, white to gray, green	colorless	6	two cleavage planes meet at 90° angle	used in the manufacture of ceramics
Augite ((Ca,Na) (Mg,Fe,Al) $(Al,Si)_2 O_6$)	black	colorless	6	cleavage in two directions	square or 8-sided cross section
Olivine ($(Mg,Fe)_2$ SiO_4)	olive, green	none	6.5–7	conchoidal fracture	gemstones, refractory sand
Quartz (SiO_2)	colorless, various colors	none	7	conchoidal fracture	used in glass manufacture, electronic equipment, radios, computers, watches, gemstones

PERIODIC TABLE OF THE ELEMENTS

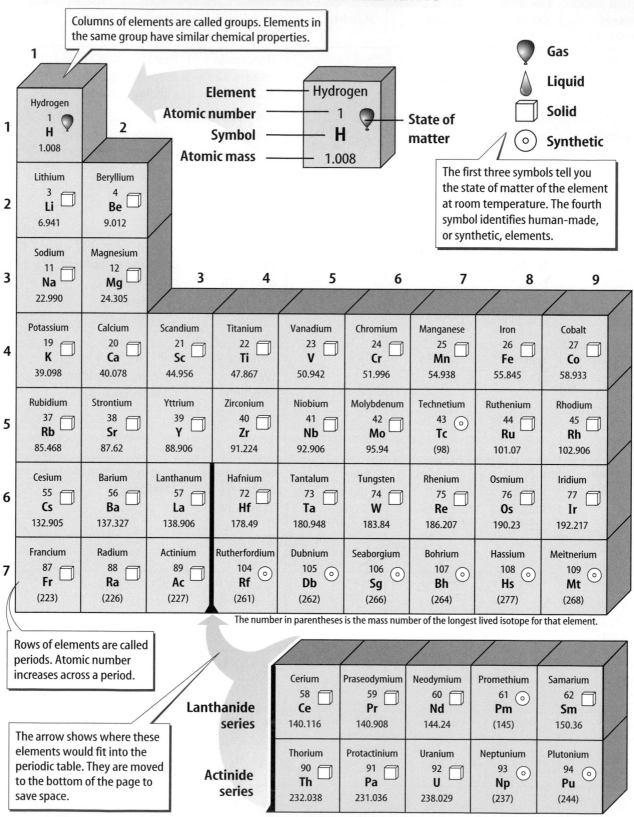

Columns of elements are called groups. Elements in the same group have similar chemical properties.

Element — Hydrogen
Atomic number — 1
Symbol — H
Atomic mass — 1.008
State of matter

Gas
Liquid
Solid
Synthetic

The first three symbols tell you the state of matter of the element at room temperature. The fourth symbol identifies human-made, or synthetic, elements.

1

1 Hydrogen 1 H 1.008

2 Lithium 3 Li 6.941 — Beryllium 4 Be 9.012

3 Sodium 11 Na 22.990 — Magnesium 12 Mg 24.305

	1	**2**	**3**	**4**	**5**	**6**	**7**	**8**	**9**
4	Potassium 19 K 39.098	Calcium 20 Ca 40.078	Scandium 21 Sc 44.956	Titanium 22 Ti 47.867	Vanadium 23 V 50.942	Chromium 24 Cr 51.996	Manganese 25 Mn 54.938	Iron 26 Fe 55.845	Cobalt 27 Co 58.933
5	Rubidium 37 Rb 85.468	Strontium 38 Sr 87.62	Yttrium 39 Y 88.906	Zirconium 40 Zr 91.224	Niobium 41 Nb 92.906	Molybdenum 42 Mo 95.94	Technetium 43 Tc (98)	Ruthenium 44 Ru 101.07	Rhodium 45 Rh 102.906
6	Cesium 55 Cs 132.905	Barium 56 Ba 137.327	Lanthanum 57 La 138.906	Hafnium 72 Hf 178.49	Tantalum 73 Ta 180.948	Tungsten 74 W 183.84	Rhenium 75 Re 186.207	Osmium 76 Os 190.23	Iridium 77 Ir 192.217
7	Francium 87 Fr (223)	Radium 88 Ra (226)	Actinium 89 Ac (227)	Rutherfordium 104 Rf (261)	Dubnium 105 Db (262)	Seaborgium 106 Sg (266)	Bohrium 107 Bh (264)	Hassium 108 Hs (277)	Meitnerium 109 Mt (268)

The number in parentheses is the mass number of the longest lived isotope for that element.

Rows of elements are called periods. Atomic number increases across a period.

The arrow shows where these elements would fit into the periodic table. They are moved to the bottom of the page to save space.

Lanthanide series

Cerium 58 Ce 140.116	Praseodymium 59 Pr 140.908	Neodymium 60 Nd 144.24	Promethium 61 Pm (145)	Samarium 62 Sm 150.36

Actinide series

Thorium 90 Th 232.038	Protactinium 91 Pa 231.036	Uranium 92 U 238.029	Neptunium 93 Np (237)	Plutonium 94 Pu (244)

Reference Handbook

REFERENCE HANDBOOK E

Metal

Metalloid

Nonmetal

Recently discovered

The color of an element's block tells you if the element is a metal, nonmetal, metalloid, or has been discovered so recently that more study is needed.

SCIENCE Online
Visit the Glencoe Science Web site at **science.glencoe.com** for updates to the periodic table.

18
Helium 2 He 4.003

13	14	15	16	17
Boron 5 B 10.811	Carbon 6 C 12.011	Nitrogen 7 N 14.007	Oxygen 8 O 15.999	Fluorine 9 F 18.998	Neon 10 Ne 20.180
Aluminum 13 Al 26.982	Silicon 14 Si 28.086	Phosphorus 15 P 30.974	Sulfur 16 S 32.065	Chlorine 17 Cl 35.453	Argon 18 Ar 39.948

10	11	12						
Nickel 28 Ni 58.693	Copper 29 Cu 63.546	Zinc 30 Zn 65.39	Gallium 31 Ga 69.723	Germanium 32 Ge 72.64	Arsenic 33 As 74.922	Selenium 34 Se 78.96	Bromine 35 Br 79.904	Krypton 36 Kr 83.80
Palladium 46 Pd 106.42	Silver 47 Ag 107.868	Cadmium 48 Cd 112.411	Indium 49 In 114.818	Tin 50 Sn 118.710	Antimony 51 Sb 121.760	Tellurium 52 Te 127.60	Iodine 53 I 126.904	Xenon 54 Xe 131.293
Platinum 78 Pt 195.078	Gold 79 Au 196.967	Mercury 80 Hg 200.59	Thallium 81 Tl 204.383	Lead 82 Pb 207.2	Bismuth 83 Bi 208.980	Polonium 84 Po (209)	Astatine 85 At (210)	Radon 86 Rn (222)
Ununnilium * 110 Uun (281)	Unununium * 111 Uuu (272)	Ununbium * 112 Uub (285)		Ununquadium * 114 Uuq (289)		Ununhexium * 116 Uuh (289)		Ununoctium * 118 Uuo (293)

* Names not officially assigned. Discovery of elements 114, 116, and 118 recently reported. Further information not yet available.

Europium 63 Eu 151.964	Gadolinium 64 Gd 157.25	Terbium 65 Tb 158.925	Dysprosium 66 Dy 162.50	Holmium 67 Ho 164.930	Erbium 68 Er 167.259	Thulium 69 Tm 168.934	Ytterbium 70 Yb 173.04	Lutetium 71 Lu 174.967
Americium 95 Am (243)	Curium 96 Cm (247)	Berkelium 97 Bk (247)	Californium 98 Cf (251)	Einsteinium 99 Es (252)	Fermium 100 Fm (257)	Mendelevium 101 Md (258)	Nobelium 102 No (259)	Lawrencium 103 Lr (262)

English Glossary

This glossary defines each key term that appears in bold type in the text. It also shows the chapter, section, and page number where you can find the word used.

A

absolute magnitude: a measure of the amount of light that a star actually emits. (Chap. 4, Sec. 1, p. 106)

apparent magnitude: a measure of the amount of light from a star that is received on Earth. (Chap. 4, Sec. 1, p. 106)

asteroid: a piece of rock similar to the material that formed into planets; usually found in the asteroid belt. (Chap. 3, Sec. 4, p. 92)

axis: imaginary vertical line that cuts through the center of Earth and around which Earth spins. (Chap. 2, Sec. 1, p. 41)

B

big bang theory: states that approximately 12 to 15 billion years ago, the formation of the universe began with a fiery explosion. (Chap. 4, Sec. 4, p. 125)

black hole: remnant of a star that is so dense that nothing, not even light, can escape its gravity field. (Chap. 4, Sec. 3, p. 118)

C

chromosphere: layer of the Sun's atmosphere found above the photosphere and below the transition zone and corona. (Chap. 4, Sec. 2, p. 109)

comet: a mass that travels through space and is composed of rock particles and dust mixed with frozen water, methane, and ammonia; tends to vaporize and break up after passing close to the Sun many times. (Chap. 3, Sec. 4, p. 90)

onstellation: a group of stars that forms a pattern resembling a familiar object, character, or animal, and that changes position throughout the year because Earth moves. (Chap. 4, Sec. 1, p. 104)

corona: largest layer of the Sun's atmosphere from which charged particles continually escape into space. (Chap. 4, Sec. 2, p. 109)

E

Earth: third planet from the Sun; its atmosphere protects life and its surface temperatures allow water to exist as a solid, liquid, and gas. (Chap. 3, Sec. 2, p. 78)

electromagnetic spectrum: arrangement of electromagnetic radiation—including radio waves, visible light from the Sun, gamma rays, X rays, ultraviolet waves, infrared waves, and microwaves—according to their wavelengths. (Chap. 1, Sec. 1, p. 9)

ellipse (eeLIHPS): elongated, closed curve that describes Earth's yearlong orbit around the Sun. (Chap. 2, Sec. 1, p. 45)

equinox (EE kwuh nahks): twice-yearly time, each spring and fall, when the Sun is directly over the equator and the number of daylight and nighttime hours are equal worldwide. (Chap. 2, Sec. 1, p. 45)

F

full moon: phase that occurs when all of the Moon's surface facing Earth reflects light. (Chap. 2, Sec. 2, p. 47)

G

galaxy: a large group of stars, dust, and gas that is held together by gravity and can be elliptical, spiral, or irregular. (Chap. 4, Sec. 4, p. 120)

giant: late stage in a star's life cycle where its hydrogen is used up, its core contracts, and its outer layers expand and cool. (Chap. 4, Sec. 3, p. 117)

Great Red Spot: a giant, high-pressure continuous storm on Jupiter. (Chap. 3, Sec. 3, p. 82)

I

impact basin: a hollow left on the surface of the Moon caused by an object striking its surface. (Chap. 2, Sec. 3, p. 57)

J

Jupiter: largest planet and fifth planet from the Sun; has faint rings, seventeen moons, an atmosphere formed mostly of hydrogen and helium, and its surface has continuous storms. (Chap. 3, Sec. 3, p. 82)

L

light-year: distance light travels in one year; the unit of measure used by astronomers to determine distances in space. (Chap. 4, Sec. 1, p. 107)

lunar eclipse: occurs when Earth's shadow falls on the Moon. (Chap. 2, Sec. 2, p. 50)

M

maria: dark-colored, relatively flat regions of the Moon formed when ancient lava reached the surface and filled craters on the Moon's surface. (Chap. 2, Sec. 2, p. 51)

Mars: fourth planet from the Sun; appears reddish because of iron oxide in weathered rocks; has polar ice caps, a thin atmosphere, and two moons. (Chap. 3, Sec. 2, p. 78)

Mercury: planet closest to the Sun; has a thin atmosphere with temperature extremes, an iron core, and many craters and high cliffs. (Chap. 3, Sec. 2, p. 76)

meteor: a meteoroid that burns up in Earth's atmosphere. (Chap. 3, Sec. 4, p. 91)

meteorite: a meteoroid that does not completely burn up in the atmosphere and strikes the surface of a moon or planet. (Chap. 3, Sec. 4, p. 92)

moon phase: change in appearance of the Moon as viewed from the Earth, due to the relative positions of the Moon, Earth, and Sun. (Chap. 2, Sec. 2, p. 47)

N

nebula: a large cloud of dust and gas that can break apart into smaller pieces and form stars. (Chap. 4, Sec. 3, p. 116)

Neptune: large, gaseous planet with rings, dark-colored storms, and eight moons; has a distinctive blue-green color. (Chap. 3, Sec. 3, p. 86)

neutron star: collapsed core of a supernova that shrinks to about 20 km in diameter and whose dense core has only neutrons. (Chap. 4, Sec. 3, p. 118)

new moon: moon phase that occurs when the Moon is between Earth and the Sun, at which point the Moon cannot be seen because its lighted half is facing the Sun and its dark side faces Earth. (Chap. 2, Sec. 2, p. 47)

O

observatory: a building used to house an optical telescope; often has a dome-shaped roof that can be opened for viewing. (Chap. 1, Sec. 1, p. 10)

orbit: curved path of a satellite that results from a combination of the satellite's forward movement and the gravitational pull of Earth. (Chap. 1, Sec. 2, p. 17)

P

photosphere: lowest layer of the Sun's atmosphere and the layer that gives off light. (Chap. 4, Sec. 2, p. 109)

Pluto: smallest planet and usually considered to be the ninth planet from the Sun; has a thin atmosphere and a solid, icy-rock surface. (Chap. 3, Sec. 3, p. 87)

Project Apollo: final stage of the U.S. space program to reach the Moon, with *Apollo II* landing on the Moon's surface on July 20, 1969. (Chap. 1, Sec. 2, p. 22)

Project Gemini: early U.S. space program where one *Gemini* astronaut team connected with another spacecraft in orbit; also studied the effects of space travel on the human body. (Chap. 1, Sec. 2, p. 21)

Project Mercury: first U.S. space program that orbited a piloted spacecraft around Earth and brought it back safely. (Chap. 1, Sec. 2, p. 21)

R

radio telescope: an instrument that collects and records radio waves traveling through space and can be used day or night under most weather conditions; provides information to map the universe and look for life on other planets. (Chap. 1, Sec. 1, p. 13)

reflecting telescope: an optical magnifying instrument that uses a concave mirror in the base of the telescope to focus light from an object and form an image at the focal point. (Chap. 1, Sec. 1, p. 10)

refracting telescope: an optical magnifying instrument in which light from an object passes through a double convex lens and is bent to form an image at the focal point. (Chap. 1, Sec. 1, p. 10)

revolution: Earth's yearlong elliptical orbit around the Sun. (Chap. 2, Sec. 1, p. 43)

rocket: a motor that does not require air to burn either liquid or solid propellant and can carry objects into space. (Chap. 1, Sec. 2, p. 15)

rotation: spinning of Earth on its imaginary axis, which takes about 24 hours to complete, and causes day and night to occur. (Chap 2, Sec. 1, p. 41)

S

satellite: any natural or artificial object that revolves around another object in space. (Chap. 1, Sec. 2, p. 17)

Saturn: second-largest planet and sixth planet from the Sun; has a thick atmosphere, a complex ring system, and at least eighteen moons. (Chap. 3, Sec. 3, p. 84)

solar eclipse: occurs when the Moon passes directly between the Sun and Earth and casts a shadow over part of Earth. (Chap. 2, Sec. 2, p.49)

solar system: system made up of the nine unique planets, including Earth, and many smaller objects, that orbit the Sun. (Chap. 3, Sec. 1, p. 71)

solstice: twice-yearly point at which the Sun reaches its greatest distance north or south of the equator (Chap. 2, Sec. 1, p. 44)

space probe: an instrument that carries data-gathering equipment deep into space and sends information back to Earth. (Chap. 1, Sec. 2, p. 18)

space shuttle: a reusable spacecraft designed to make many trips and that carries astronauts, satellites, and other cargo to and from space. (Chap. 1, Sec. 3, p. 23)

space station: a large structure with living quarters, work and exercise areas, and equipment and support systems for humans to live and work in space; can provide the opportunity to conduct research not possible on Earth. (Chap. 1, Sec. 3, p. 24)

sphere (SFIHR): a round, three-dimensional object whose surface is the same distance from its center at all points; Earth is a sphere that bulges somewhat at the equator and is slightly flattened at the poles. (Chap. 2, Sec. 1, p. 40)

sunspot: an area of the Sun that is cooler and not as bright as surrounding areas and that is caused by the Sun's intense magnetic field. (Chap. 4, Sec. 2, p. 110)

supergiant: life cycle stage of a massive star where the core reaches extremely high temperatures, heavy elements form by fusion, and the star expands. (Chap. 4, Sec. 3, p. 118)

U

Uranus: seventh planet from the Sun; is large and gaseous with thin, dark rings and rotates tilted on its side. (Chap. 3, Sec. 3, p. 85)

V

Venus: second planet from the Sun; has a dense atmosphere with high temperatures, a surface with craters, faultlike cracks, and volcanoes; sometimes called Earth's twin. (Chap. 3, Sec. 2, p. 77)

W

waning: describes phases that occur after a full moon, as the visible lighted side of the Moon grows smaller. (Chap. 2, Sec. 2, p. 47)

waxing: describes phases following a new moon, as more of the Moon's lighted side becomes visible. (Chap. 2, Sec. 2, p. 47)

white dwarf: stage in which a star has used up its helium and its outer layers escape into space, leaving behind a hot, dense core that contracts. (Chap. 4, Sec. 3, p. 117)

English Glossary

Spanish Glossary

Este glossario define cada término clave que aparece en negrillas en el texto. También muestra, el capítulo, la sección y el número de página donde se usa dicho término.

A

absolute magnitude/magnitud absoluta: Medida de la cantidad de luz que realmente emite una estrella. (Cap. 4, Sec. 1, pág. 106)

apparent magnitude/magnitud aparente: Medida de la cantidad de luz emitida por una estrella que recibe la Tierra. (Cap. 4, Sec. 1, pág. 106)

asteroid/asteroide: Fragmento rocoso de material similar al que originó los planetas, el que generalmente se encuentra en el cinturón de asteroides. (Cap. 3, Sec. 4, pág. 92)

axis/eje: Línea vertical imaginaria que pasa a través del centro de la Tierra y alrededor de la cual gira nuestro planeta. (Cap. 2, Sec. 1, pág. 41)

B

big bang theory/teoría de la gran explosión: Establece que aproximadamente hace 12 a 15 billones de años el universo empezó a formarse a partir de una intensa explosión. (Cap. 4, Sec. 4, pág. 125)

black hole/agujero negro: Remanente que queda de una estrella y que es tan denso que nada, ni siquiera la luz, puede escapar de su campo de gravedad. (Cap. 4, Sec. 3, pág. 118)

C

chromosphere/cromosfera: Capa de la atmósfera solar ubicada sobre la fotosfera y debajo de la zona de transición y de la corona. (Cap. 4, Sec. 2, pág. 109)

comet/cometa: Masa que viaja por el espacio y que consta de partículas rocosas y polvo mezclados con agua congelada, metano y amoniaco. Los cometas tienden a evaporarse y fragmentarse después de pasar varias veces cerca del Sol. (Cap. 3, Sec. 4, pág. 90)

constellation/constelación: Un grupo de estrellas que forma un patrón parecido a un objeto, personaje o animal, el cual cambia de posición a lo largo del año debido al movimiento de la Tierra. (Cap. 4, Sec. 1, pág. 104)

corona/corona: La capa más grande de la atmósfera solar de la cual las partículas cargadas se escapan continuamente. (Cap. 4, Sec. 2, pág. 109)

E

Earth/Tierra: Tercer planeta más cercano al Sol. Su atmósfera protege las formas de vida y la temperatura en su superficie permite que el agua exista en forma sólida, líquida y gaseosa. (Cap. 3, Sec. 2, pág. 78)

electromagnetic spectrum/espectro electromagnético: Arreglo de la radiación electromagnética de acuerdo con sus longitudes de onda. Incluye las ondas radiales, la luz visible proveniente del Sol, los rayos gama, los rayos X, las ondas ultravioleta, las ondas infrarrojas y las microondas. (Cap. 1, Sec. 1, pág. 9)

ellipse/elipse: Trayectoria curva cerrada y elongada que describe la órbita anual alrededor del Sol que efectúa la Tierra. (Cap. 2, Sec. 1, pág. 45)

equinox/equinoccio: Ocurre dos veces al año, en la primavera y en el verano, cuando el Sol está directamente sobre el ecuador, ocasionando que la noche y el día tengan la misma duración en todo el mundo. (Cap. 2, Sec. 1, pág. 45)

F

full moon/luna llena: Fase lunar que ocurre cuando toda la superficie lunar que da la cara a la Tierra refleja luz. (Cap. 2, Sec. 2, pág. 47)

G

galaxy/galaxia: Grupo enorme de estrellas, polvo y gases que se mantiene unido por la gravedad y el cual puede ser elíptico, espiral o irregular. (Cap. 4, Sec. 4, pág. 120)

giant/gigante: Etapa tardía en el ciclo de vida de una estrella en que la estrella ha agotado su hidrógeno, causando la contracción de su núcleo y la expansión y enfriamiento de sus capas externas. (Cap. 4, Sec. 3, pág. 117)

Great Red Spot/Gran Mancha Roja: Tormenta gigantesca, continua y de altas presiones en Júpiter. (Cap. 3, Sec. 3, pág. 82)

I

impact basin/cuenca de impacto: Cavidad formada sobre la superficie de la Luna por el impacto de un objeto. (Cap. 2, Sec. 3, pág. 57)

J

Jupiter/Júpiter: Quinto planeta desde el Sol. Es el más grande de los planetas, con anillos indistintos, diecisiete lunas, una atmósfera formada principalmente de hidrógeno y helio y su superficie presenta tormentas continuas. (Cap. 3, Sec. 3, pág. 82)

L

light-year/año luz: Distancia que la luz viaja en un año; los astrónomos usan esta unidad de medida para determinar distancias en el espacio. (Cap. 4, Sec. 1, pág. 107)

lunar eclipse/eclipse lunar: Ocurre cuando la sombra de la Tierra cubre la Luna. (Cap. 2, Sec. 2, pág. 50)

M

maria/mares: Regiones de la Luna relativamente planas y de color oscuro que se formaron cuando la lava alcanzó la superficie y llenó los cráteres en la superficie lunar. (Cap. 2, Sec. 2, pág. 51)

Mars/Marte: Cuarto planeta a partir del Sol. Es de color rojizo debido al óxido de fierro de las rocas erosionadas, posee casquetes polares, una atmósfera tenue y dos lunas. (Cap. 3, Sec. 2, pág. 78)

Mercury/Mercurio: Planeta más cercano al Sol. Tiene una atmósfera muy tenue con temperaturas extremas, un núcleo de hierro, muchos cráteres y grandes despeñaderos. (Cap. 3, Sec. 2, pág. 76)

meteor/meteoro: Meteoroide que se quema al entrar a la atmósfera de la Tierra. (Cap. 3, Sec. 4, pág. 91)

meteorite/meteorito: Meteoroide que no se quema completamente al entrar a la atmósfera de un cuerpo celeste y que choca contra la superficie de una luna o un planeta. (Cap. 3, Sec. 4, pág. 92)

moon phase/fase lunar: Cambio en la apariencia de la Luna, vista desde la Tierra, debido a las posiciones relativas de la Luna, la Tierra y el Sol. (Cap. 2, Sec. 2, pág. 47)

N

nebula/nebulosa: Nube extensa de gas y polvo que puede separarse en fragmentos más pequeños y formar estrellas. (Cap. 4, Sec. 3, pág. 116)

Neptune/Neptuno: Planeta grande y gaseoso, con anillos, tormentas de color oscuro, ocho lunas y de un color verde azulado que lo distingue del resto de los planetas. (Cap. 3, Sec. 3, pág. 86)

Spanish Glossary

neutron star/estrella de neutrones: Centro colapsado de una supernova que se encoge a unos 20 km de diámetro y cuyo núcleo denso solo contiene neutrones. (Cap. 4, Sec. 3, pág. 118)

new moon/luna nueva: Fase lunar que ocurra cuando la Luna está entre el Sol y la Tierra. En esta fase no se puede ver la Luna porque su mitad iluminada mira hacia el Sol mientras que su mitad oscura mira hacia la Tierra. (Cap. 2, Sec. 2, pág. 47)

O

observatory/observatorio: Edificio cuyo techo a menudo tiene forma de domo y que se puede abrir para hacer observaciones con un telescopio óptico. (Cap. 1, Sec. 1, pág. 10)

orbit/órbita: Trayectoria curva de un satélite que resulta de la combinación entre el movimiento hacia adelante del satélite y la atracción gravitatoria de la Tierra. (Cap. 1, Sec. 2, pág. 17).

P

photosphere/fotosfera: La capa más baja de la atmósfera del Sol, la cual despide la luz solar. (Cap. 4, Sec. 2, pág. 109)

Pluto/Plutón: Es el planeta más pequeño del sistema solar y a menudo se le considera como el noveno planeta a partir del Sol. Posee una atmósfera muy delgada y una superficie rocosa sólida y helada. (Cap. 3, Sec. 3, pág. 87)

Project Apollo/Proyecto Apolo: Etapa final del programa espacial de EE.UU. que permitió que el Apolo 11 alunizara en la superficie de la Luna el 20 de julio de 1969. (Cap. 1, Sec. 2, pág. 22)

Project Gemini/Proyecto Géminis: Etapa inicial del programa espacial de EE.UU. durante la cual un equipo de astronautas del Géminis hizo conexión con otra nave espacial en órbita y se realizaron estudios acerca del efecto de los viajes espaciales en el cuerpo humano. (Cap. 1, Sec. 2, pág. 21)

Project Mercury/Proyecto Mercurio: Primer programa espacial de EE.UU. que permitió que una nave espacial girara en órbitas alrededor de la Tierra y retornara a salvo. (Cap. 1, Sec. 2, pág. 21)

R

radio telescope/radiotelescopio: Instrumento que capta y registra ondas radiales del espacio, durante el día y la noche y bajo casi cualquier condición atmosférica, proporcionando información que sirve para elaborar un mapa del universo y para la búsqueda de vida en otros planetas. (Cap. 1, Sec. 1, pág. 13)

reflecting telescope/telescopio reflector: Instrumento óptico de aumento que usa un espejo cóncavo en la base del microscopio, para enfocar la luz proveniente de un objeto y formar una imagen en el punto focal. (Cap. 1, Sec. 1, pág. 10)

refracting telescope/telescopio refractor: Instrumento óptico que aumenta el tamaño de las imágenes al hacer pasar la luz, proveniente del objeto, a través de una lente convexa doble y desviándola para formar una imagen en el punto focal. (Cap. 1, Sec. 1, pág. 10)

revolution/traslación: Órbita elíptica de la Tierra alrededor del Sol y que dura todo un año. (Cap. 2, Sec. 1, pág. 43)

rocket/cohete: Motor que no requiere aire para quemar el combustible propulsor sólido o líquido y que sirve para transportar objetos hacia el espacio. (Cap. 1, Sec. 2, pág. 15)

rotation/rotación: Giro de la Tierra, alrededor de su eje imaginario, que dura 24 horas y que ocasiona el día y la noche. (Cap. 2, Sec. 1, pág. 41)

S

satellite/satélite: Cualquier objeto natural o artificial que gira alrededor de otro objeto en el espacio. (Cap. 1, Sec. 2, pág. 17)

Saturn/Saturno: Es el segundo planeta más grande y el sexto planeta a partir del Sol. Tiene una atmósfera muy densa, un complejo sistema de anillos y, por lo menos, dieciocho lunas. (Cap. 3, Sec. 3, pág. 84)

solar eclipse/eclipse solar: Ocurre cuando la Luna se atraviesa entre el Sol y la Tierra y proyecta su sombra sobre una parte de la Tierra. (Cap. 2, Sec. 2, pág. 49)

solar system/sistema solar: Sistema formado por nueve planetas diferentes, incluyendo la Tierra, y muchos otros astros más pequeños que giran alrededor del Sol. (Cap. 3, Sec. 1, pág. 71)

solstice/solsticio: Ocurre dos veces al año y es el punto en que el Sol se aleja más del ecuador, hacia el norte o hacia el sur. (Cap. 2, Sec. 1, pág. 44)

space probe/sonda espacial: Instrumento dotado con equipo que recoge diferentes tipos de información en el espacio exterior, los que después transmite hacia la Tierra. (Cap. 1, Sec. 2, pág. 18)

space shuttle/transbordador espacial: Nave espacial reutilizable diseñada para realizar múltiples viajes con astronautas y satélites, u otros tipos de carga, hacia el espacio o para traerlos de vuelta hacia la Tierra.(Cap. 1, Sec. 3, pág. 23)

space station/estación espacial: Estructura de gran tamaño con habitaciones, áreas de trabajo y ejercicio; con equipo y diferentes sistemas para que los humanos puedan vivir en el espacio. Sirve también para hacer investigaciones imposibles de realizar en la Tierra. (Cap. 1, Sec. 3, pág. 24)

sphere/esfera: Objeto tridimensional redondo en que cualquier punto sobre su superficie está equidistante del centro. La Tierra es una esfera un poco alargada en el ecuador y ligeramente achatada en los polos. (Cap. 2, Sec. 1, pág. 40)

sunspot/mancha solar: Área del Sol que es menos caliente y no tan brillante como las áreas circundantes y que se debe al intenso campo magnético del Sol. (Cap. 4, Sec. 2, pág. 110)

supergiant/supergigante: Etapa del ciclo de vida de una estrella masiva cuando su núcleo alcanza temperaturas extremadamente elevadas, se forman elementos pesados mediante fusión y la estrella se expande. (Cap. 4, Sec. 3, pág. 118)

U

Uranus/Urano: Séptimo planeta a partir del Sol. Es grande y gaseoso, tiene anillos oscuros y delgados y rota inclinado hacia uno de sus lados. (Cap. 3, Sec. 3, pág. 85)

V

Venus/Venus: Segundo planeta más cercano al Sol. Tiene una atmósfera muy densa y con temperaturas elevadas, su superficie está cubierta de cráteres, fallas y volcanes. A veces llamado el planeta gemelo de la Tierra. (Cap. 3, Sec. 2, pág. 77)

W

waning/octante menguante: Describe la fase que ocurre después de la luna nueva, cuando el lado visible de la Luna que vemos desde la Tierra empieza a decrecer. (Cap. 2, Sec. 2, pág. 47)

waxing/octante creciente: Describe la fase después de la luna nueva, cuando la parte iluminada de la Luna que vemos desde la Tierra empieza a ser más visible. (Cap. 2, Sec. 2, pág. 47)

white dwarf/enana blanca: Etapa en que la estrella agota el helio y sus capas externas se escapan al espacio, dejando atrás un núcleo caliente y denso que se contrae. (Cap. 4, Sec. 3, pág. 117)

Index

The index for *Astronomy* will help you locate major topics in the book quickly and easily. Each entry in the index is followed by the number of the pages on which the entry is discussed. A page number given in **boldfaced type** indicates the page on which that entry is defined. A page number given in *italic type* indicates a page on which the entry is used in an illustration or photograph. The abbreviation *act.* indicates a page on which the entry is used in an activity.

Index

Index

Index

Index

Credits

Credits

PERIODIC TABLE OF THE ELEMENTS

Columns of elements are called groups. Elements in the same group have similar chemical properties.

Gas
Liquid
Solid
Synthetic

Element — Hydrogen
Atomic number — 1
Symbol — H
Atomic mass — 1.008
State of matter

The first three symbols tell you the state of matter of the element at room temperature. The fourth symbol identifies human-made, or synthetic, elements.

1	2	3	4	5	6	7	8	9
1 Hydrogen 1 H 1.008	**2**							
2 Lithium 3 Li 6.941	Beryllium 4 Be 9.012							
3 Sodium 11 Na 22.990	Magnesium 12 Mg 24.305	**3**	**4**	**5**	**6**	**7**	**8**	**9**
4 Potassium 19 K 39.098	Calcium 20 Ca 40.078	Scandium 21 Sc 44.956	Titanium 22 Ti 47.867	Vanadium 23 V 50.942	Chromium 24 Cr 51.996	Manganese 25 Mn 54.938	Iron 26 Fe 55.845	Cobalt 27 Co 58.933
5 Rubidium 37 Rb 85.468	Strontium 38 Sr 87.62	Yttrium 39 Y 88.906	Zirconium 40 Zr 91.224	Niobium 41 Nb 92.906	Molybdenum 42 Mo 95.94	Technetium 43 Tc (98)	Ruthenium 44 Ru 101.07	Rhodium 45 Rh 102.906
6 Cesium 55 Cs 132.905	Barium 56 Ba 137.327	Lanthanum 57 La 138.906	Hafnium 72 Hf 178.49	Tantalum 73 Ta 180.948	Tungsten 74 W 183.84	Rhenium 75 Re 186.207	Osmium 76 Os 190.23	Iridium 77 Ir 192.217
7 Francium 87 Fr (223)	Radium 88 Ra (226)	Actinium 89 Ac (227)	Rutherfordium 104 Rf (261)	Dubnium 105 Db (262)	Seaborgium 106 Sg (266)	Bohrium 107 Bh (264)	Hassium 108 Hs (277)	Meitnerium 109 Mt (268)

The number in parentheses is the mass number of the longest lived isotope for that element.

Rows of elements are called periods. Atomic number increases across a period.

The arrow shows where these elements would fit into the periodic table. They are moved to the bottom of the page to save space.

Lanthanide series

Cerium 58 Ce 140.116	Praseodymium 59 Pr 140.908	Neodymium 60 Nd 144.24	Promethium 61 Pm (145)	Samarium 62 Sm 150.36

Actinide series

Thorium 90 Th 232.038	Protactinium 91 Pa 231.036	Uranium 92 U 238.029	Neptunium 93 Np (237)	Plutonium 94 Pu (244)